Diary of the 1914–1918 War

Work published with the support of the
Centre d'Histoire des Sociétés
of the Université de Picardie-Jules-Verne
and of the Conseil Général des Ardennes.

The photographs, old documents and postcards
were provided by the Société d'Histoire et d'Archéologie du Sedanais,
the Dominican Archives and private collections.
We thank them all for their support.

Yves Congar

Diary of the 1914–1918 War

Notes and Commentary by

Stéphane Audoin-Rouzeau

and Dominique Congar

Translated from the French by

Mary John Ronayne OP

Helen T Frank

2015

ATF Press acknowledges the financial support given by the Australian and New Zealand Congregations of Dominican Sisters towards the translation and production costs associated with this volume.

ISBN: 9781925309041 (paperback)
ISBN: 9781925309058 (hardback)
ISBN: 9781925309065 (epub)
ISBN: 9781925309072 (pdf)

Lay-out by Astrid Sengkey
Text Minion Pro Size 11

An imprint of the ATF Ltd.
PO Box 504
Hindmarsh, SA 5007
ABN 90 116 359 963

Making a lasting impact
www.atfpress.com

LIST OF CONTENTS

Sedan, Town Hall

TRANSLATORS' NOTE

The editors of the French original of young Yves Congar's Diary of the 1914-1918 War explain that they had respected the original French text as far as possible in transcribing it for publication. This created a number of problems for the translators, faced with a text written by a child aged ten in 1914 and fourteen when the war came to an end in 1918; a text, moreover, which not only reproduced the spelling and grammatical errors found in the original, but also the vocabulary of the dialect of the Ardennes where the Congar family lived. In order to convey both the meaning and the mood of the original as simply and faithfully as possible, a number of the footnotes in the French text clarifying mis-spellings or other anomalies in the French have been omitted in the English text, while at the same time additional footnotes have been inserted where deemed necessary.

Ten-year old Yves' spelling was poor, and he was very sparing in the use of full stops and capital letters. Where necessary, words or punctuation not actually in the original have been inserted in square brackets in the translation, while at the same time all question marks and other oddities contained in the French text as printed have been faithfully reproduced.

It seems important to note that the diary as we have it is the result of careful editing on the part of its youthful author. He seems to have made brief notes of events more or less as they happened, and to have written them up (and illustrated them) at some later date. This is clear from the entry for 9th March 1918 which begins as follows:

'There were bombs at one o'clock in the morning; I do not remember having heard them (I am writing this on 13th April, my birthday, on which there was a real bombardment)'.

This procedure probably explains the confusion about dates that is apparent from time to time and perhaps also the fact that he never actually finished the diary. The last entry was written on 8th November 1918, three days before the Armistice, and it was not until July 1923 that he finally rounded off his diary, so to speak, largely on the basis of his brother Robert's own diary entries about the last days of the war.

Mary John RONAYNE OP
Helen T FRANK
24 October 2014

INTRODUCTORY COMMENTS BY JEAN-PIERRE JOSSUA OP

YVES CONGAR was born in Sedan in 1904. A primary reason for publishing his diary of the 1914-1918 war is the fact that he was deeply rooted in his environment, his hometown, his country, with the patriotism and that love for the army characteristic of a frontier area, even though all these things are expressed here in a child's way. He was rooted also in his Christian family, in his Catholic Church, with its strong tradition of faith and liturgy. And the fact that this theologian-to-be was to become a pioneer of Christian unity is also linked with his having witnessed in Sedan the friendly way in which Catholics, Protestants and Jews lived together.

This brings us to a second reason for publishing such a diary. Congar was destined to occupy an important place in the history of the Christian Churches during the 20th Century. In order to show how this was so, it is first necessary to summarise his career. In 1921, he entered the University seminary in Paris, which he left in 1925 in order to join the Dominican novitiate. There followed the years he spent in the Saulchoir House of Studies, then located in Kain near Tournai in Belgium, followed by specialised studies. He then became a member of the new team of professors, first at Kain, then at Étiolles near Corbeil, under the leadership of Frère Marie-Dominique Chenu. From 1932 until the Second World War, he taught, contributed to a number of Parisian magazines, created a collection, 'Unam Sanctam' in the recently founded Éditions du Cerf, and published an important work, *Chrétiens désunis* [Divided Christendom] (1937).

After the 'phoney war' and his own imprisonment, he returned to Saulchoir d'Étiolles for some very fruitful years of publication in the stimulating environment which was the Catholic Church after the Liberation. *Vraie et fausse réforme dans l'Église* [True and False Reform in the Church] (1950); *Jalons pour une théologie du laïcat* [Lay People in the Church] (1953), among many others, proved very popular. Disapproved of because of his ecumenical gestures, his involvement in the priest-worker movement, and to a greater extent in the reformist climate that was being reined in during the latter years of the papacy of Pius XII, he experienced enforced silence and exile. Brought to Strasbourg by Mgr Wéber in 1956, he resumed his work in better conditions until the preparations for Vatican II and then the implementation of the Council itself, which represented for him an astonishing rehabilitation, enabling him to collaborate decisively in the composition of the Council documents and to become increasingly influential up to the time of his death in 1995. His death was preceded by a long and painful illness which he lived out as a patient in the Hôpital des Invalides, and he took little notice of his nomination as a cardinal. Between 1960 and 1982, a further wide-ranging series of publications enriched his work. These included *La Tradition et les traditions* [Tradition and Traditions] (1963); *Chrétiens en dialogue* [Dialogue between Christians] (1964); *L'Église: de saint Augustin à l'époque moderne* (1970); *Diversité et communion dans les Églises* [Diversity and Communion] (1982/4).

If one wishes to list in order of importance the reasons for Yves Congar's influence on the Churches in our century, one must begin with the fact of his being a historian and the importance, in his eyes, of history, both of these factors being the fruit of his formation at the Saulchoir, thanks to Frère Chenu. His historical works review many questions, and his recourse to history in order to clarify many of the matters being debated in the Catholic Church and between the Churches was to prove decisive. After his death, it was said that his work in this area had been on the same level as that of a Braudel or a Duby [1].

In the second place, from the early 1930's onwards, Yves Congar was convinced that he was being called to serve the unity of Christians. And he responded to this call with a work, a dedication, an ability to listen and a love for the 'separated brethren' that were truly extraordinary. Personal contacts, meetings, publications, created a considerable stir from 1936 onwards and continued to do so until he was forced to quit this field. Even though, after the Council, he did not become a specialised and official 'ecumenist', his considerable influence nevertheless continued.

Finally, at the time when work for unity, from the Catholic side, was halted – round about 1950 – in order to move things forward on a long-term basis thanks to his Church having progressed, and also with a view to renewing the Church itself (this had always been his particular passion), Frère Congar embarked on the study of a number of problems. These included the Reformation, tradition, the laity, priesthood and other ministries, the missions, all of which were to become the questions and problems which, thanks to the impetus given to them by Pope John XXIII, were to form the agenda of the Council in an attempt to bring the Church up to date. He devoted himself to this work with exceptional competence, loyalty and freedom. Hence, the immense and enduring effect of his work.

Jean-Pierre JOSSUA OP
30 June 1997

1 Both Fernand Braudel and Georges Duby were outstanding French historians (Trans).

FOREWORD

Frère Congar entered the Novitiate of the Province of France of the Order of Preachers in 1925. He died at the Institution des Invalides in Paris on 22nd June, 1995. Hence, this indefatigable preacher and theologian lived among his Dominican brethren for seventy years; in particular he was one of the principal *periti* at the Second Vatican Council, which ended on 7th December, 1965.

One of the things Yves Congar was passionately concerned about was the Church and its unity, as well as its presence in the world of the 20th century.

But, before all that, Yves Congar was a small boy. He was ten years of age when the First World War broke out in 1914. He felt his vocation come to birth in him as far back as 1917, as he hints in his boyhood diary.

His Dominican brethren were particularly touched and moved when the five school exercise books in which he had written throughout the five war years in such a very personal and positive way were discovered after his death.

During those five difficult years, other precocious passions were expressed: France and freedom, which he was to continue to defend in later life, in particular during his years of captivity during the Second World War. And already we see his love of describing in detail what he sees, what he feels and what he thinks.

Thus, once again, but in a very original way, the face and personality of our famous elder brother are presented to us.

Frère Éric T de CLERMONT-TONNERRE OP
Prior Provincial, Province of France, 1992–2001

PREFACE

Monday 3rd January, 1994. Paris, metro line n° 8.

I am on the way to 'Salle Turenne' in the Hôpital des Invalides to visit my uncle. Uncle Vonet – the Dominican Yves Congar – is very ill. He is now almost unable to write or to move without propelling his electric wheelchair as quickly as possible. His memory and his mind have remained intact. That gives me great pleasure whenever I go to see him; we very often have animated conversations.

This visit is one of the first in the year and his thoughts turn to the 1914-1918 war. Yes, it was eighty years ago this year ... Then he talks to me about his boyhood diary which he wrote in Sedan during the five years of that war. From memory, he quotes for me the famous comment he made on 25th August, 1914: 'This is the beginning of a tragic story ...'. There will be several references to it in the course of this book. As happens every time he recalls those terrible events, he is deeply moved and refuses to say any more.

During subsequent visits, Uncle Vonet again mentioned his diary. During the long summer holidays of 1914, my grandmother, Tere, asked her four children to keep a holiday diary that they would write up more or less each day, as they chose. She never thought that her suggestion would reach an ultimate conclusion 80 years later.

There were four Congar children. Pierre, Robert, Marie-Louise and Yves. The close-knit family lived in a large family property situated in the Fond de Givonne, one of the suburbs of Sedan, Ardennes, on the road leading to Belgium, the road to the North, the road of Invasions.

I was intrigued by this wartime diary of which my uncle seemed so very fond. He had undoubtedly included many details, details analysed by a very lively ten-year-old boy, who admired his two older brothers, 'the Big/Older Ones'[1], and was also very close to Mimi, his beloved sister (Mimi was born in 1902, Yves in 1904). Whenever we spoke of the Ardennes, of the trees, the rivers, the mists, the snow, of the house at '85 Fond de Givonne', my uncle became animated and reverted to the sensitivity of his adolescence. He emerged from his surly wild boar shell. Every day he studied the silhouette of this animal, emblem of the Ardennes, in the photograph placed in a prominent position on his desk full of books and magazines in his room at the Invalides, the window of which looked out onto the golden dome where lay the Emperor he so admired.

I was equally moved by all he told me as I, too, had often played with my brothers and sisters and my cousins in the very same places, among the same trees, and we had played the same silly tricks.

But although the year 1994 caused my uncle to recall the year 1914, it also represented an important date for him as he would turn 90 on 13th April, 1994. Every time I visited him, he mentioned what was, for him, this mythical date in order to ensure that we, too, thought about it and took the necessary steps.

We decided to prepare a celebration. The devoted staff of the Invalides helped me considerably. There were to be two stages. First, a drink with his loyal companions in captivity (Colditz – 1939-40 war); then a reception in the room of his beloved Père Tournier[2]. My son Bruno undertook to cut and distribute the birthday cake and to help in pouring the champagne. His Dominican Brethren were there. Yves Congar was deeply moved. The Provincial, Frère Éric de Clermont-Tonnerre, read to him a letter from Pope John Paul II and a great number of greetings from both France and abroad. He also received a lovely letter,

1. 'les grands'
2. Unidentifiable.

Monsieur & Madame G Congar
ont le plaisir de vous faire part de la
Naissance d'un Fils, Georges-Yves
(13 Avril)

Sedan, le 16 Avril 1904

Yves Congar with his wet-nurse.

Monsieur and Madame G Congar have pleasure in informing you of the birth of a son Georges-Yves (13th April).

Sedan, 16th April 1904.

Left: Marie-Louise, Lucie (née Desoye) and Yves, on his mother's lap.
Right: Robert, Georges (the father) and Pierre Congar.

warm and personal, from the Master of the Order, Fr Timothy Radcliffe. The old wild boar from the Ardennes was more than overcome.

Sunday, 30th October, 1994. I learnt, from France-Inter, that my uncle had been nominated Cardinal. He was very pleased. But it had come too late; he was too old, too ill.

Monday, 31st October, 1994. I went to the Salle Turenne at the Invalides to congratulate him. He managed to smile in spite of the intense pain. He asked me to get a cardinal's skull cap for him as soon as possible.

Tuesday, 6th December, 1994. I went to see my uncle. He was no longer in his room but in the intensive care unit to which he had been admitted as an emergency. He had suffered a cardiac arrest and everybody was worried. But he wanted to recover, he wanted to be present at the ceremony of presenting the Cardinal's hat. He would hold on. We were all amazed by his determination and his courage.

Thursday, 8th December, 1994. A Cardinal in the church of Saint-Louis des Invalides! It was Cardinal Jean Willebrands, special envoy of Pope John Paul II, who presented him with the hat and the ring. Closely observed by his somewhat anxious doctors, Uncle was present at the ceremony up to the time of Communion. He could not stay any longer. He was brought back to his room as quickly as possible and once more attached to his breathing apparatus.

Then he recovered and returned to his room on the first floor in the Turenne wing where his dedicated nursing staff and Père Tournier were waiting for him.

A few days later, I recalled with him this nomination and the emotion that we had experienced in hearing the very warm and affectionate address by Cardinal Willebrands. Uncle Vonet found it difficult to speak but even so he managed to recall the Ardennes, the 1914 war, his diary, the suffering he endured, his Dominican brethren around him and helping him, but from whom he regretted being separated.

Tuesday, 21st February, 1995. Uncle received the cross of an officer of the Légion d'Honneur from the hands of the Governor, General Maurice Schmitt, in the Salle des Boiseries at the Invalides. In a very fine speech addressed to 'Monsieur le Cardinal, my captain', General Schmitt quickly reviewed the religious and military life of Yves Congar, and he concluded: 'Monsieur le Cardinal, yours has been an extraordinary destiny, as a man of the Church, as a soldier. You deserve the Officer's Cross of the Légion d'Honneur for a number of reasons. I am now going to present it to you in the presence of the members of your family, of the former inmates of Colditz, of your Dominican brethren and finally of those who are here around you'.

Monday, 27th March, 1995. Representatives of the Ardennes General Council made a special trip to Paris in order to pay honour to the 'Cardinal of the Ardennes'. He was given a rug worked in Sedan stitch featuring a wild boar standing and looking out. He asked me to fix it to the wall close to his bed.

More will be said about the Ardennes, Fond de Givonne, Kiki, the War, Tere, Mimi. This First World War made a deep impression on Yves Congar and our family to all of whom he felt so closely united.

Thursday, 22nd June, 1995. Uncle Vonet died alone in his room while he was having his breakfast.

Monday, 26th June, 1995. Notre-Dame de Paris. Funeral Mass of Cardinal Yves Congar. He was buried beside his great friend, Frère Marie-Dominique Chenu, in the Dominican vault in Montparnasse cemetery.

Monday, 29th April, 1996. Frère André Duval from the Priory of Saint-Jacques, the Provincial archivist, wrote to me: 'It's here! ... After going through half a cubic metre of cardboard boxes, I have found the five exercise books of Yves Congar's diary of the 1914-1918 war. It's sensational!'

Tuesday, 30th April, 1996. I hurried to Saint Jacques. There I saw for the first time the diary of a little ten-year-old boy, the youngest of a family of four, a little fellow who dearly loved France, a little fellow who was to become a Dominican Friar and a theologian, who was to take part in Vatican II, become a cardinal and be buried with the French flag in Notre Dame de Paris.

It was with deep emotion that I then opened, read, studied those five school exercise books. I was discovering my uncle as a child, I was seeing my grandparents, my family, 'my' Fond de Givonne, because we all have a 'Fond de Givonne' at the bottom of our hearts.

I will leave to the reader the surprise of discovering, through these pages, all that the land of the Ardennes and its civilian population went through during those painful years.

I would like to address a few words to my uncle's many German friends and ask them to realise that this diary was written by a young patriotic boy who expressed himself with great, and at times brutal, frankness. I dare to hope that they will not hold it against him.

We hope that the notes, the appendices and the three important texts which follow the Diary, which has been reproduced as faithfully as possible, will provide the reader with all the explanations he or she will need.

Even as early as 1914, in writing and, a few years later, re-reading his Diary, Yves Congar was almost certainly thinking of the possibility of it being published. This has now happened thanks to Éditions du Cerf and the historical work of Stéphane Audoin-Rouzeau.

I sincerely hope the reader will experience what I myself have felt in reading these five exceptional exercise books.

Dominique CONGAR
Paris, 15 February 1997

EDITORIAL NOTE TO THE FRENCH EDITION

Yves Congar's original French text
has been respected as far as possible
in transcribing it for publication.
Readers should not be surprised to see reproduced
the spelling and grammatical mistakes to be found in the original text,
written by a child aged ten in 1914
and fourteen when the war came to an end.
We have also endeavoured to respect
as far as possible the author's choice of presentation.
All the headings are also his.

Stéphane AUDOIN-ROUZEAU
Dominique CONGAR

SEDAN – Looking down Fond-de-Givonne.

nne

Yves [Vonet] and Marie-Louise [Mimi] on the day they made their First Communion (Sedan, 5th June, 1914).

Diary of

the Franco-Boche War 1914–1915

by Y Congar

Illustrated with 42 drawings and 2 maps …

from the declaration on 4th August, and even from

27th July 1914, to 27th January 1915.

[Cover of first exercise book containing Yves Congar's Diary]

DIARY OF THE HOLIDAYS 1914

[By Y Congar][1]

(for publication)[2]

MONDAY, 27th July 1914 [3]

Today rumours of war were already in the air. A Serb had killed the son of the King of Austria and Austria wanted to declare war on Serbia. This means that Germany for its part would be fighting against France which is in alliance with Serbia.[4] The wives of military personnel were all worked up, there were queues at the banks and at the Savings Bank, people wanting to withdraw their money. Sedan was on edge on account of the false news that was making the rounds in the town. Pierre [5] was in Germany and we were worried. We did not really believe there would be war. The Military are not allowed to go further than 2 km.

Tuesday 28th July 1914

The same as Monday, but worse. Everybody is very worried and upset.

Wednesday 29th July 1914

I am not at all reassured. I can only think about war. I would like to be a soldier and fight. I believe in today's declaration[.] [W]e are going to gather pectoral flowers to make herbal tea. No news of Pierre. I have colic.

Thursday 30th July 1914.

I still have colic. Instead of going to Raucourt, I am going to Grandma's[6]. I shall sleep there. Taïe [7] is ill. The news is worse. I believe there will be war. My thoughts are all going round and round in my head. Anxiety about Pierre. People are beginning

1. Yves Congar's signature as an adult!
2. Yves Congar added his signature to all five exercise books. On the first he wrote: 'for publication'.
3. Note by Yves Congar: 'Written, I think, on 29.7.14'. The author was ten years old when he began his diary.
4. Yves Congar is referring here to the murder of the Archduke François-Ferdinand in Sarajevo on 28th June, 1914.
5. Pierre Congar, an older brother aged 15, who was in Germany visiting his German pen friend.
6. The reference here is to his maternal grandmother. 'Père' designates his paternal grandfather. Without counting these two, the Congar family consisted of six people in 1914: Georges Congar, the father; Lucie (née Desoye), the mother; four children: Pierre (born in 1899), Robert (born in 1900), Marie-Louise (born in 1902) and Yves (born in 1904).
7. Pet name for Aunt Marie-Louise, who never married, and who was Georges Congar's sister.

to believe there will be war. Notes are being exchanged for gold. There is panic in Charleville. The trains are in the station ready to start. And they are beginning to call up the reservists. Sedan is neutral. The President of the Republic is back. There is talk of an interview with the Emperor of Germany on the waters of the Kiel. People are beginning to buy supplies in town. Fond de Givonne [8] is fairly quiet. We would like to arrange for Pierre to come back. Golden five-franc pieces are being given in exchange for the 10 franc ones.

Friday 31st July 1914.

A telegram has been sent to Pierre telling him to come back at once [illiquot[9]]. Tere [10] is getting in provisions. We are alright for three months with the animals, the bread and the vegetables. Motor cars and carts are being requisitioned. The 28th, the 30th and the 147th [11]are leaving for the Frontier. It is very serious. Germany has declared war on Russia[12]. The soldiers are very cheerful but not in our house. My aunt would like to come to Sedan but the increasing seriousness of the situation makes it impossible. The 91st line [regiment] is replacing the 147th.

Saturday 1st August

War has almost been declared. It is very serious. No news of Pierre. Mr Girardin has gone. All one sees is women in tears. At about 4 p.m., Madame Girardin came in tears [saying] the French are at Thionville and have been fighting since 11 a.m. It's a lie. At 4.30 p.m., trumpets were blown throughout Fond de Givonne. It was the general mobilisation. We were all afraid on account of Pierre.

Sunday 2nd August 1914.

We went to Mass although Tere was not too keen on the idea. We went to Vespers while Tere and Papa went to see if there were trains running for Pierre. We too went to see but we saw nobody. That made us all very anxious. The war is coming close.

Monday 3rd August 1914

Pierre has not returned. We are very afraid for him. It is thought that he has been unable to return. In the afternoon Grandma came and told Tere that she had good news about Pierre. Tere guessed at once that he was there with her. She went to look for

8. Part of Sedan, on the road to Belgium where Congar's parents lived. In 1914, the family lived in nº 85 Fond de Givonne, in a very large wooded property. Aunt Taie lived in the 'old house'.
9. The Latin word 'illiquot' means 'at once', without delay.
10. This is the pet name – pronounced 'Teureu' – of Yves' mother and may well be derived from an expression of Robert's who, having developed whooping cough at the age of six, called his mother 'petit rat' [little rat]. With the fits of coughing 'petit rat' became 'Tira' and thence 'Tere'. This was what everybody called Lucie until her death in 1963.
11. French army units
12. Austria declared war on Serbia on 28th July. Russia ordered a general mobilisation on the afternoon of 30th July. On 31st [July], Germany put itself on a war footing, demanded to know France's attitude in the event of war with Russia, and ordered Russia itself to call a halt to its mobilisation. On the afternoon of 1st August, both Germany and France ordered a general mobilisation, and towards evening, Germany declared war on Russia. Germany declared war on France on 3rd August, but the people of the Ardennes did not learn this until the following day. Great Britain declared war on Germany on 4th August.

him and was beside herself with joy. Pierre was hungry and tired. He went off to rest and ate and drank a lot. We were happy that day and no longer believed in the war, but it was very close just the same.

Tuesday 4th August 1914.

We went to Grandma's. Much more at ease, we set about amusing ourselves. In the evening Papa told us that war had been declared between France and Germany and that the German ambassador was leaving Paris. We made war on Hélin [13] .

Wednesday 5th August 1914

In the morning we heard the firing of a cannon. War is all one thinks about. There are 4 regiments in Sedan, the 2nd Cavalry etc. They sent 2 men to Fond de Givonne in search of accommodation for the men and the horses. In the afternoon we took in horses and the person of M. Vernier, Paris adjutant of the 2nd Cavalry military school. He is in Tere's room and his horse Ebreuil and that of his orderly, Historia, under the pump.

Thursday 6th August 1914

Germany has violated Belgian territory;[14] fierce resistance by the Belgians; bridges have been blown up; the Germans retreated northwards after having burnt down, sacked and destroyed, unremittingly etc. Skirmishes en route to Holland, whose territory was violated, after which England declared war on Germany.

Immense conflict: 10 nations shedding blood [15]; the Germans shot the mayor of Sales for having aided the French as well as a chaplain, and several Alsacians, and murdered the President of the French memorial in Metz. There are more men than usual in Metz. No news about the army.

Germany has declared war on Belgium. We spent the afternoon attacking the lads. In the evening we heard that two 15 year old boys wanting to announce that the Germans were on their tail had got themselves shot. There was a skirmish between the French cavalry and the Uhlans[16]. Among the French: no damage. Among the Uhlans: 5 deaths. The Germans have bombarded Liège, which put up a good defence. The Belgians blew up two bridges. There is dynamite underneath the bridges in Sedan. About 67 military ambulance vehicles went along the Fond de Givonne in the morning and 33 in the afternoon, Some Hussar cannons, cars from the Galeries Lafayette in Paris and buses from Paris and 2 military planes. A quiet night.

Friday, 7th August, 1914

The rest of the buses passed by during the morning, as well as two military planes. The war is still being waged in Belgium, and the Belgians seem to be winning. The English have reached Namur in Belgium. Planes are flying overhead. German ships are being stopped at sea. Some of the German ships were bombarding Bône and Philippeville [17]. Gibraltar is fortified. The Germans are bombarding Liège, which is being well defended.

---

13. Obscure passage: 'Hélin' could be the name of a young neighbour with whom Yves played 'a little war' with his brothers and sister.
14. German troops invaded Belgium on 4th August.
15. Nine, in fact, at that point: Germany, Austria-Hungary, Russia, Serbia, Montenegro, France, the United Kingdom, Belgium, Luxemburg.
16. Uhlan = member of a body of Prussian light cavalry originally modelled on Tatar lancers. Ten year old Yves wrote 'Hulan' instead of 'Uhlan'. [Trans]
17. Bône is now known as Annaba, and Philippeville as Skikda.

The Germans are reduced to taking Liège street by street. The French have entered Alsace and captured Mulhouse and Colmar from the Germans, thanks to the battle of Altriech.[18] Liège has not yet been taken. They are fighting street by street. The Germans have 3000 dead and they are asking for 24 hours in which to bury them and there are bodies 1 m. high lying in the streets of Liège. The Germans are going to have quite a pile.

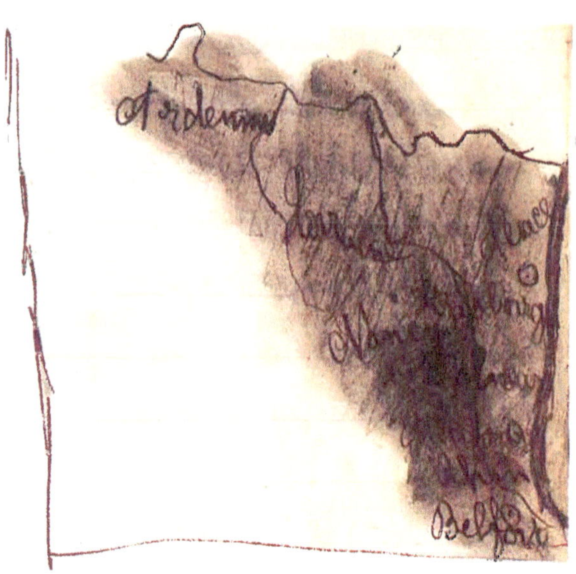

Saturday, 8th August, 1914

The morning brought 3 German prisoners to Sedan. They were grumbling and saying that they did not have enough to eat. They thought they were going to get in as easily as a knife through butter but that's enough, Germany, the blood of your victims cries out for vengeance!! The stalwarts in Liège are still holding out. The Battle of Altriech has been confirmed. Seemingly, the soldiers took the town in a bayonet charge while the cavalry pursued the German rear-guard. The people of Alsace are triumphantly moving the frontier posts which they have uprooted. There was a battle with marbles in Fond Collasse.[19]

Sunday, 9th August, 1914

In the morning we went to Mass. On our way back, Taie picked up a little cat. No further news.

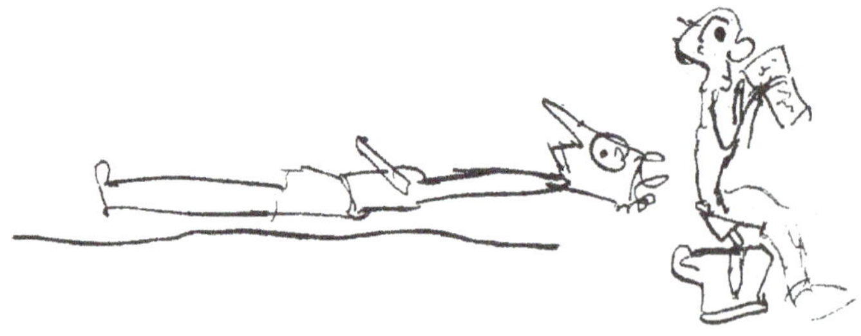

18. Altriech' = Altkirch. The 7th corps had entered Upper Alsace on 7th August and Mulhouse on the 8th, before withdrawing on the night of 10th/11th.
19. Collasse = Colas, i.e. a location in Fond de Givonne where the children often played together and fought one another.

Monday, 10th August, 1914

In the morning, fighting in Longuyon was confirmed. We heard the cannon gun fire. In the afternoon, I was playing with Mimi.[20] All of a sudden, I heard something falling outside. I looked out and saw some soldiers in the process of demolishing our railings, digging holes, and using the earth to create a wall covered with foliage and hiding behind it two machine guns with several thousand bullets. In the end I learned that they were on the watch for a German car which was due to pass over the bridge,[21] and as our garden was right at the corner they could shoot at it from there. Later on, 6 men and a corporal encamped at Fond Colasse. The word is that 7 Frenchmen, including an officer, encountered 22 Germans including an officer. The French officer approached, shot the German officer's brains out and the other Germans fled, leaving the body of their officer behind. The stalwarts in Liège are still holding out.[22]

Tuesday, 11th August, 1914

The soldiers are still on watch. I brought them some food. The corporal was asleep. A German plane and a French one flew overhead; they exchanged fire. Tere is cooking for the soldiers.

Wednesday, 12th August, 1914.

The soldiers left their post. We heard that the German plane had crashed a little further on. There was a storm. A lot of troops went by. Nothing new this evening. A German prisoner went by between two Belgian policemen wearing police caps. The German officer is bony, thin and yellow because he has not eaten for several days. He was wearing a peaked cap. I called out to him: casque à pic chfaing[23] ('spiked helmet coward') since he was passing grenadiers of the Belgian king, Albert the First. They have huge bearskins and several scores of bundles of fuses.

---

20. Marie-Louise, Yves' beloved sister, two years older than himself.
21. Well-known spot on the Fond de Givonne, on the road to Belgium. The bridge crossed the Le Vra stream.
22. In fact, the resistance in Liège happened on 4th and 5th August. The German army had then entered the town devoid of troops on 7th August.
23. The reference is to the German spiked helmet or *pickelhaube* [Trans].

Thursday, 13th August, 1914

There is talk of fighting in Illy and people are saying that the Germans have bombarded Pont à Mousson. We played. In the evening a French and a German plane passed overhead. The French have taken a prisoner with a spiked helmet; he is thin and yellow. He passed along Fond de Givonne. Everyone called out: 'casque à pic'.

Friday, 14th August, 1914

The Germans are bombarding Pont à Mousson. The Belgians are still holding out. I went with Papa to look for news. There was none. A German pilot has been killed. There is news of Jean Stakler,[24] he had fought but was not wounded. There are 12 soldiers at Fond Colasses. The planes are being camouflaged.

Saturday, 15th August, 1914

Mimi's and Taïe's feast-day. No further news.

Sunday, 16th August, 1914.

We went to Mass and played at boats. The light infantry gunners went by. There were a great many of them.

Monday, 17th August, 1914

We played at boats. Nothing special happening. A lot of wounded went by on their way to the station, and on from there . . . Each German plane that passes overhead causes a cannonade and crashes between Florenville and Carignan[25].

Tuesday, 18th August, 1914

We played and got ready to go to Grandma's. The great battle has not yet begun. German planes are being brought down in the town.

Wednesday, 19th August, 1914

A German plane crashed in Carignan. It is thought that this village would be where the enemy army would enter. We can hear cannon fire. German planes fly past. One flew very low. It fell not far away and the French shot the soldiers and the officer who were in it on the spot. The Germans have been driven back to Florenville. Three regiments of artillery have left Sedan. A Hennecart [26] has been sent to Abbeville. He was allowed to remain in Mézières. The people of Sedan are saying that the Germans would like to go northwards.

24. A Congar relative.
25. Florenville (in Belgium) and Carignan (in France) are located north-east of Sedan.
26. A Congar family relative.

~~Friday~~ Thursday 20th August, 1914.

We can hear cannon gun fire. The Germans are in Brussels from which they have demanded the sum of 200,000,000 Francs. They have reached Namur.

Saturday, 21st [August, 1914]

We can hear cannon gun fire. There is fighting in Bertrix[27]. Whole trains are arriving full of wounded people. The supply carriages are returning. Everyone is just waiting. They are in Neuchâtel[28].

Sunday 22nd, 23rd [August 1914]

We can hear cannon fire: Belgian emigration began this morning. Seven artillerymen returned who had left their equipment behind which was then taken by the infantry who say that they were fighting blind and 10 against 1 – then 2 regiments, the 3rd and the 4th and finally the artillery: 2 regiments in good order: a cannon gun, a caisson. The Belgians are continuing to flee. People are saying that the Germans have committed unspeakable atrocities[29]. It is pathetic to see these poor Belgians passing by, some trailing a child in a pram followed by old people walking with difficulty and finally the children carrying a small packet in their hand and driving their flocks ahead of them, while others with two mattresses on 2 carts with crying children on top of them, old people and women looking sadly at their meagre possessions.

Monday 24th [August 1914]

The cannon fire is very loud. The Belgians are still passing by. Something is expected to happen this afternoon. The French are beginning to flee. Catherine [30] has come from Givonne with nothing except the child's pram full of things but without her 3 cows and her colt. They ate with us and they were asked to stay. According to them, there are Uhlans in Givonne wood. To make room for them, we are going to Grandma's. This evening M Douffet arrived from Fond de Givonne. He said: I have left Carignan which is occupied. Bullets are raining down on the railway at night. People are continuing to flee from these unspeakable barbarians.

---

27. Bertrix (Belgium) is located north of Sedan.
28. A mistake on Yves Congar's part. The reference is to Neufchâteau (Belgium) close to Bertrix.
29. There were indeed atrocities there, as in all the areas which had been overrun by the invading armies in the summer of 1914. Recent historiography has estimated that approximately 6000 civilians, mostly Belgians but including also French citizens from the Northern and Eastern départements had been executed by the Germans in the months of August/September 1914. See on this subject John Horne: 'Les mains coupées: 'atrocités allemandes' and French opinion in 1914', *World Wars and Contemporary Conflicts,* n° 171, July 1993, pp. 29-45. Alan Kramer, 'Les ‹atrocities allemandes': mythologique populaire, propagande et manipulations dans l'armée allemande', *World Wars and Contemporary Conflicts,* n° 171, July 1993, pp. 47-67. John Horne and Alan Kramer: 'German 'Atrocities' and Franco-German Opinion, 1914: The Evidence of German Soldiers' Diaries', *Journal of Modern History,* n° 66, March 1994, pp. 1-33.
30. A resident in Givonne, Catherine had been Yves Congar's mother's wet nurse.

81. - SEDAN.

ons du Fond-de-Givonne, incendiées systématiquement par les Boches au moyen de bombes incendiaires en 1914

SEDAN – Houses in Fond-de-Givonne systematically set fire to by the Boches [sic] by means of incendiary bombs in 1914.

==

Tuesday, 25th August, 1914

Here begins a tragic story; it is a sad and sombre tale written by a child who has ever in his heart love and respect for his country and a great and righteous hatred for a cruel and unjust people[31].

==

Tuesday! Cruel Tuesday and day of suffering

doubly marks the time of the evil spell

When will be the day of deliverance

that will put joy and fire in one's heart.

We were just getting up when Grandma came and said to me: Vonet, Vonet, you must put your soldiers away; unfortunately, the Germans are not far off. It was true because I went out as soon as I had put the soldiers away and I heard shooting and saw a plane overhead. I went back in and almost at once, while the shooting was still going on, the 'big ones' appeared[32]. 'They're here. They're here. They're behind us'. I went to the dining room to look out and opened the window. The Uhlans were just coming round the corner from the avenue to the embankment, then we heard the door, it was Tere. At that moment about thirty engineers were passing, following a wagon loaded with sticks of dynamite.

The Uhlans are back. Oh! The wretches; they are passing the window; we heard a guttural order: aarrarrrnncharr[33], they halted and got in line to go to the station when, hearing the shooting from engineers in Place d'Alsace, they turned round, reloaded, and there was an enormous 'puff', or perhaps 2, and 2 horses fell dead in front of the window. Bullets were flying in both directions. The French were shooting a lot. All the Uhlans fell dead; 6 horses in the neighbourhood and 2 Uhlans, 1 Frenchman. At about 9 am, cannon fire began in the 'marfée'[34]. The boches[35] have established themselves in Fond de Givonne[:] 12 Batteries

---

31. This text was to be repeated several times by Yves Congar in later writings. Sedan formed part of the sector of the 11th corps, belonging to the 4th army commanded by General de Langle de Cary, who began the offensive on 22nd and 23rd August, and was forced to withdraw on the evening of the 23rd. On 24th August, the 11th corps, in retreat, passed through Sedan, abandoning the right bank of the Meuse. This setback is part of the wider picture of the annihilation of the breakthrough offensive envisaged by Joffre in the Ardennes. On 25th August, the German vanguard entered the town, but the battle to take definitive possession of Sedan and the Meuse continued until 29th August, the date of the complete withdrawal of the 4th army. On 3rd September, the whole of the Ardennes département was occupied. All the data concerning the occupation of the Ardennes and the town of Sedan in the years 1914 – 1918 are taken from the following publications:

   'Les Ardennes durant la Grande Guerre (1914-1918). Catalogue of the 29th October to 20th November 1994 Exhibition. Archives départementales des Ardennes, Charleville-Mézières, 1994, 296 pp. Pierre Congar, Jean Lecaillon, Jacques Rousseau. *Sedan et le pays sedanais. Vingt siècles d'histoire,* Paris, FERN, 1969, 577 pp. On the situation of the occupied countries in general, and in particular in the North, see: Annette Becker, 'Mémoire et commemoration. Les 'atrocités' allemandes de la Première Guerre mondiale dans le Nord de la France', *Revue du Nord,* June 1992, pp 339-354. 'D'une guerre à l'autre: mémoire de l'occupation et de la résistance: 1914-1940', *Revue du Nord,* July-September 1994', pp 453-465. 'Lille-Roubaix-Tourcoing. 1914-1918. L'expérience d'une occupation', *Tourcoing et le Pays de Ferrain,* nº 22, 1996, pp 56-63.
32. The Congar children formed two groups: Pierre and Robert were 'the big ones' while Marie-Louise (Mimi) and Yves (Vonet) were 'the little ones'. Due to their ages, the 'big ones' were forced to work in a war booty storage depot during the occupation.
33. Yves Congar may have been trying to transcribe a German word: he probably wanted to convey the guttural violence of a military command.
34. Wooded area overlooking Sedan.
35. *Boche*: a derisive term used by the French during World War I, and directed especially at German soldiers. Throughout his diary, young Congar nearly always wrote the word without a capital, a further token of his contempt for the German invaders. For this reason, the French word has been

at Iges, 2 batteries and more or less everywhere (one Boche battery: 5 canons (one French: 4)) the cannon is booming all the time[,] the machine gun and the rifle. We went to the dining room to look out and we heard the Germans hammering with their rifle butts on M Benoit's door to see if there were any troops or form of defence there. They shot M Benoit's and M Dupont's dog simply because they were barking [and] warning the French about the German patrols – another time we heard a patrol passing along our wall and then, in French: 'Silence!!' At midday nobody was very hungry. All that had sealed our stomachs. Our dog has not eaten – in the afternoon the cannon went on booming loudly and the French were firing a lot.

the cannon booms and booms again,
killing men and spreading fear
without stopping the cannon provides
bullets for amateurs

The first German infantry went by. The cannon went on booming. At about 5 o'clock anxiety became intense, the bridges blew up. It was fantastic. However, Grandfather[36], who is over 70, knows about these things and he was wondering whether perhaps it was the town itself that was blowing up (9 explosions). The French, behind the railway bridge, had taken some bales of woollen material from Mr Stackler's and were shooting from behind them, so much so that the cannon balls and the shells were embedded in the soft wool and they were shooting extremely well. From there they caused the Germans the loss of 40 men and unfortunately also a civilian who was shot by? . . . At about 6 pm, the French engineers set fire to Mme Stackler's house.

2. SEDAN – Eglise St-Etienne incendiee volontairement par les Allemands
à leur entrée dans la Ville, le 25 Août 1914.

SEDAN – Church of St Étienne deliberately set on fire by the Germans as they invaded the town on 25th August 1914.

But the Germans, the Boches, wretches, thieves, assassins and arsonists were setting fire to things: our nearby Givonne church, the chapel at Fond de Givonne, Glaire Longyon, Donchery with incendiaries and many more besides[37].

retained in the translation.

36. Yves' maternal grandfather.

37. Yves Congar wrote in red in the margin alongside this paragraph. 'There'. In fact, the Germans did deliberately set fire to the Chapel in Givonne, the old Fond de Givonne, Glaire and Donchery. Twenty-five inhabitants were killed in Sedan and six in Wadelincourt, most of them either executed or burnt in the fires.

In the evening we drank broth which was a help; in the evening, too, Grandfather went to the riverside[38] to have a look. There was an immense amount of smoke. We went to bed but did not sleep, the cannon went on booming then there was a knock on the shutter, I wondered who it could be, then I heard: 'It's me. It's Catherine'. Papa came and said: The church in Fond de Givonne is on fire and the houses by the bridge as well. At 7 pm, we went to sleep at Grandma's[39]; it was impossible to sleep. On Wednesday morning, at about 8 am, the cannon started up again as loudly as on Tuesday, we no longer knew how to keep going. The cannon kept on booming. We were told that on Tuesday evening, they had been driven back to La Chapelle, Wednesday was an exact copy of Tuesday; at 4 pm we went to see the railway bridge; there were 30 bodies lying at our feet, the wounded were being removed, what fierce cries with our bloodied trousers[.] [O]n the way back, we saw some carrying their weapons with a workman leading them, others on bicycles chatting with the locals while the cannon went on booming, but not above the town as on Tuesday but from Noyer[40] à la Marfée. We slept better but still without undressing. On Thursday the cannon was still booming. Tere went up to Fond de Givonne and saw the battle very clearly. She saw the German shells falling on the towpath. At about 3 o'clock we went up to the Fond de Givonne. What a doleful sight! We were all disorientated, but we will get used to it. On the way back a train with more than 400 wagons . . . of . . . Givonne fir trees to Torcy bridge.

Sedan is full of Boches they are taking away weapons [that] we are bringing to them. They are demanding 250,000 gold pieces[41]

Saturday, 29th [August, 1914].

Pierre went to the Avenue as Grandfather is a hostage[42]. The cannon has moved further away.

Sunday 30th [August, 1914]

Nothing new.

38. The river Meuse.
39. The grandparents did not live in Fond de Givonne but in Sedan itself, close to the Avenue Philippoteaux which Yves referred to as 'the avenue' or the 'Venue'.
40. A village close to Sedan.
41. As soon as the German army entered Sedan, the Duke of Wurtenburg demanded that the sum of 200,000 gold pieces be paid the next day. The mayor appealed to the population, and succeeded in getting the money together in a few hours. A further sum of 500,000 francs was demanded on 1st September, under the pretext that the people of Sedan had shot at the soldiers. The town had to pay the same sum again after the sabotage of a railway line during the night of 27th to 28th September. These impositions became more and more frequent in the ensuing months in revenge for the escape of prisoners or acts of sabotage. To these sums should be added the payment of very heavy war indemnities in July 1915, 1916 and 1917, and again in January 1918.
42. As a reaction to the attitude of the people and to ensure that the requisitions were paid, hostages were imprisoned day and night in the Cercle opposite the court house, in groups of ten, then of six. A list of 145 men, with 50 substitutes, was drawn up for this purpose. The system went on until the end of January 1915. Thereafter, the hostages were used in seeking accommodation for the officers and the requisition of furniture.

Monday 1st [September 1914]

The 'big ones' went to see the houses that had been burnt. They say that they are in ruins.

Tuesday 2nd [September 1914]

The town is calm. Papa is a hostage[.] We found an enormous piece of shell in the garden.

Wednesday 3rd [September, 1914]

All calm. At about 11 o'clock in the morning a captain called Caspari arrived asking to place two men with us; 250 men have come and established themselves in the vicinity, 2 mobile stoves, then they saw a herd of cows passing [and] immediately took one, killed and butchered it. They then left us, on condition that we buried the skin and the entrails, the head and the fat. They left at about 4 o'clock, to no-one's regret!

Thursday 4th [September, 1914]

Calm, nothing new.

Hortense Desoye (née Brière), 'Grandma' [and] Frédéric Desoye, 'Grandpa'.

Friday, 5th [September 1914]

We have an officer, Captain Nemnick lodging with us, he takes tea and he calls 8 others to take it with him, he takes it with good burgundy from M Dodelier's, whose kepi and epaulettes he has taken, he orders the cooking of 4 hens, in the morning the orderly devours a whole one. Out of fear he slept with his orderly and a lieutenant.

Sunday, 6th [September 1914]

We went to Mass in the priests' chapel.

Monday, 7th [September 1914]

Grandpa is a hostage. They don't want more than 40. We have heard that they have suffered a fine defeat in Châlons!![43]

Tuesday 8th [September 1914].

Nothing new.

---

43. There is no record of a German defeat close to this town, but it could be that it was in these terms that preliminary reports reached Sedan of the Marne counter-offensive which began on 5th September and which resulted in a general retreat of the German armies between 10th and 13th [September].

Wednesday 9th [September 1914].

Papa is a hostage. We hear the cannon booming.

Thursday 10th [September 1914]

We went to Grandma's. Pork is scarce. We returned home .Towards evening, we had some Boches to stay. They ate our salad and our potatoes; one is from Cologne, one from Silesia, the others from Saxe and one from Aix-la-Chapelle.

Friday, 11th [September 1914]

Nothing new, there is no news.

Saturday, 12th [September 1914]

Today, Grandpa was to be a hostage, but as the Boches are asking for 220, they will no longer be going so often so he did not go. A convoy of wounded on foot and lying on straw in farm carts went through Sedan. It is windy and it's raining.

Sunday 13th [September 1914]

People are saying that the boches were defeated in Blagny (near Carignan). It is still windy and raining. We went to Grandma's.

Monday 14th [September 1914]

There is nothing new. We had a history lesson with Père Pierre, a good man. It is raining.

Tuesday 15th [September 1914]

Still no news, but we are beginning to get used to it. The Boche planes are standing in the open area[44] near Balan. They are clearly visible from the Windmill.

Wednesday 16th [September 1914]

The weather is fine. Mme Deloffre has been to Douzy to get some wheat ground and she saw 800 Uhlans arriving covered in mud like pigs – Ah! If only that were their retreat!! We would accept it cheerfully, but [no-one] asks us our opinion about advancing or retreating We went to Bazeilles where there are shells (1 m. long and weighing 240 kg), others 0.50 m. long and the shells [casing?] of ordinary pieces (75 mm in diameter), as well as barrels of powder. We brought back some bread.

---

44. Wide expanse of grass near the Meuse.

Thursday 17th [September, 1914]

The weather is turning fine. We went to Grandma's. Mr Helin went to Belgium and brought back butter and eggs. People are saying that Rheims Cathedral has been burnt, oh! What rats these Boches are[45]! A Boche plane has been burnt. We hear the cannon from Daigny.

Friday 18th [September, 1914]

We played in the garden. Still no news.

Saturday 19th [September, 1914]

This life surrounded by Barbarians, enemies of civilisation. Can it last for a long time, already a whole month without news, or supplies – Ah! I did not know that the future had so many things in store for me. It will have to be well garnished !!! . . . !!! . . .

Sunday 20th [September, 1914]

We went to Mass, again in the chapel as they have burnt down our church, they have occupied this Brothers' school, 4 come to our new premises –

Monday 21st [September, 1914]

Tuesday 22nd

Nothing new at all

Wednesday, 22nd [September 1914]

The boches did not come down[.] A very quiet day.

Thursday, 24th [September 1914]

We went to Grandma's. We can't hear the cannon, the [month] of October is about to begin.

Friday 25th [September 1914]

Tere makes us settle down to work, we are going to have no bread[46]. What a deprivation! [F]or French people!

45. 'verrat': A common word of abuse in the Ardennes dialect.
46. In fact, from the end of September 1914, the population had no bread and, from 1914-1915, there was no milk except by underhand means and skimmed. Then, meat was no longer available except at certain times, after which it disappeared completely, the cattle having virtually disappeared from

Saturday 26th [September, 1914]

Still no bread. These cursed Boches are forcing us to adopt a new diet.

Sunday, 27th [September, 1914]

Nothing new. We all went to Mass. Our worthy parish priest spoke, the Big Ones went for a walk through Illy[47] where a German 4-star general was killed, then on through Floin [Floing] where 6 or 7 houses have been burnt down, and they came back home without a hitch.

Monday, 28th [September, 1914]

No news, but we could hear the cannon booming.

Tuesday 29th [September, 1914]

Nothing, it was raining, the cannon booming all the time.

Wednesday, 30th [September, 1914]

Fine weather. The cannon booming, Grandpa is a hostage, no other news.

Thursday 31st [sic!] [September, 1914]

Nothing, Grandpa was reported for having wine, oh such 'verrats'[48] [rats] of informers, they deserve to be burnt alive!

Friday 1st [October, 1914]

The cannon is booming very loudly, the Boches themselves are quite disturbed by it, it is being said that we have reached Rimogne and Vendresse[;] if only it were true.

1916 onwards.

In 1915, a black market system organised by Belgium managed to make some things available but this trade, which was harshly repressed, was forced to desist quite soon. A Supply Syndicate was set up under the personal supervision of the mayor: but this system failed to establish itself satisfactorily and the people remained convinced that supplies were being badly distributed and useless items stocked. In spite of food supplies from neutral countries, the shortage of food became more marked during the second half of the occupation. Cabbages and turnips were the basic foodstuff, with dried bran cakes and 'potato flakes'. The bread was black and, on the days that they were open, butchers' shops sold only offal and bones. However, those in need were to some extent helped by the Fourneaux économiques.

47. A nearby village and place for walking, 4 km from Fond de Givonne.

48. Cf footnote 45.

Saturday 2nd [October, 1914]

We are hoping, the cannon is booming so loudly. The German trains have left. Pierre has tooth-ache. He wants to go to M Knott, but he has been replaced by a German dentist. In the end Mr Molard took it out.

Sunday 3rd [October, 1914]

Papa is a hostage. Instead of doing 12 hours at night, 12 hours by day, the requirement now is to do 4 hours at night and 10 in the daytime, which is not fair, however, if it were only that, things would not be too bad – the sun is shining, the cannon is booming, a convoy went by, we went to Mass, no bread, the officers have gone, there is a change of command.

Monday, 4th [October, 1914]

A white frost. Nothing new, yesterday's train returned empty in order to go and be reloaded.

Tuesday, 5th [October, 1914]

It rained a little. No cannon to be heard. Trains passing.

Wednesday 6th [October, 1914]

Thursday, 7th

We went to Grandma's. There are cars, some damaged, some not, waiting to be repaired or not, right in the middle of Place d'Alsace and on the left side of the Avenue. A group of 8 or 10 Boches, all wounded, went by. – We could hear the cannon booming.

Friday, 8th [October, 1914]

Wilhelm, having established his headquarters in Charleville[49], has gone from there, it is being said that the French are in Tournes.

Saturday, 9th [October, 1914]

Maria Bourbon's granddaughter has died. On the way to the cemetery we met a Boche who wanted Pierre to show him the way to Place Turenne, so that he could go from there to Charleville. We refused, but he will not be able to get there as the bridge has been destroyed

49. The German staff and the major Headquarters had been established in Charleville since the beginning of September, but Wilhelm II, with his court, did not arrive until 28th October. He left the town on 5th May [1915].

Sunday, 10th [October, 1914]

We went to Mass – Men fit for military service who have escaped from the French territorial army are to present themselves to the command post; hence, as we have seen up to now, every time they do us a favour of this kind, things must not be going well for them.

11th Monday [October, 1914]

The Théatre des Frères near our little chapel is in flames. Trains are going by empty and returning empty.

12th Tuesday [October, 1914]

Defeat for them: a charming gesture has just been announced for us: those who have cars or bicycles are to bring them at once to the command post, under pain of being sentenced under martial law – the trains which go past empty return empty.

13th Wednesday [October, 1914]

Tere is ill. The cannon is booming very loudly, we will not be able to bake more than twice or three times a week as the Boches have taken the flour for themselves.

BOULANGERIE : BAKERY.

To get hold of a pound of porridge
The duration of the occupation (hygiene).

Thursday 14th [October, 1914]

It's cold and windy. The cannon is very loud even at night.

Friday, 15th [October, 1914]

The cannon is still booming, but much further away. The weather is fine. The housework is still being done. In the evening the cannon came nearer. Once again a ray of hope: the officers are moving around, above all they are leaving [but] we later heard that it was only a change of army corps. What a disappointment!!! . . .

General Impressions

I had read in history: 'The Huns entered France burning everything before them'. Seemingly, therefore, it is legitimate, after 1400 years of civilisation, to find once again in Europe such a barbaric and fire-loving race, this race which in Belgium, in Louvain, in Liège, and throughout the country, chose to reveal its barbarity. The countries that have been invaded could go and complain to the court in The Hague[50] about all the gifts and qualifications of these rotten and barbaric thieves and arsonists. They probably wanted to show us their (so-called hygienic[51] , gentle, gracious and agreeable) way of acting.

In Belgium they have set fire to 2,000 villages;
In France they have rationed our bread and meat for two weeks;
They have taken and even stolen our straw, our copper, ivory and
the property of more than 8,000,000 inhabitants.

They have looted the cellars, empty houses, the fir trees, the nut trees, the telegraph poles, money and small change. Like the Romans and the Assyrians they have demanded a war tribute, men and cattle; in brief, they have treated us as badly as they possibly could under the pretext of making us live hygienically and at our ease; in order to extract a half-penny per family, they have printed false notices and have made the price of bread exorbitant.
Never again in my life, surely, will I see anything so horrible.

This page has been written in order to state something of the truth and should be attached to Wilhelm's back.

Saturday 16th [October, 1914]

Tere is still laid up; we are becoming quite good cooks. Pierre and Robert are going to the classes organised by Mme Dervin. Bread is becoming very scarce. Oh the bastards! It's not hygiene that they are forcing on us in that, they are preventing us from eating: the grocery shops are empty.

Sunday 17th [October, 1914]

Monday 18th

Still no bread Tere is a bit better. It's raining.

---

50. The reference is to the Permanent Court of Arbitration set up at The Hague Peace Conference in 1899.
51. Yves Congar repeatedly makes fun of the occupying forces' supposed claim that the constraining measures they were imposing were necessary steps in the light of their concern for the hygiene of the local people.

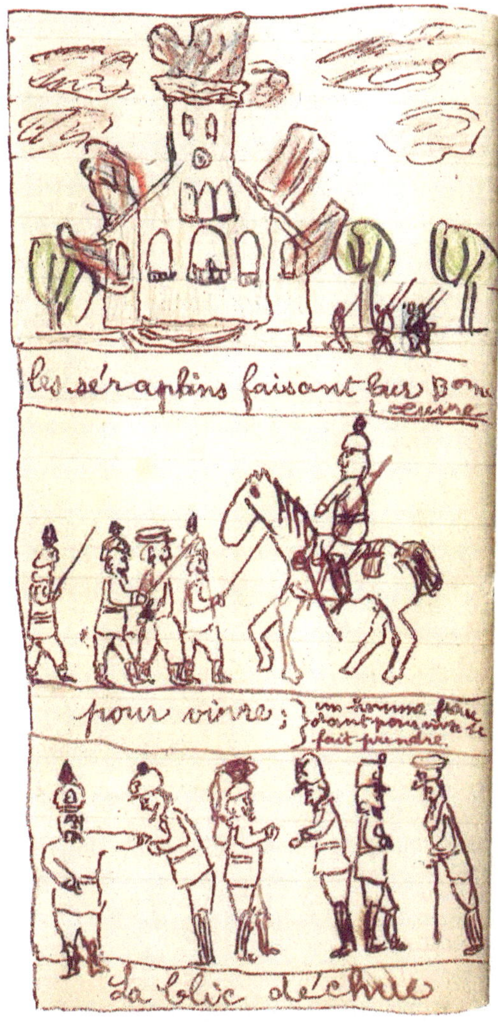

the seraphim doing their good work

In order to live: a man cheating in order to live is arrested

Those on high are brought low.

Tuesday 19th [October, 1914]

No bread. Tere is better. No news.

Wednesday 20th [October, 1914]

The cannon is booming very loudly. Grandpa was in his office writing, then without hearing any footsteps he heard 'knock, knock, knock' and said: 'Come in'. Two Boches (a lieutenant and a soldier) came in and said; 'Haven't you got a telephone?' 'Yes, there it is.' 'Right, we are taking it.' So they unscrewed it and took it; they wrote '. . .' on a piece of paper and went away leaving Grandpa with about ten screws and totally dumbfounded.

Thursday, 21st [October, 1914]

We walked to Noyer but it was raining heavily and we had the wind against us. In the end, having splashed about in the mud for an hour, we could see Noyer very well. We brought back some underpants, a bag and all sorts of little souvenirs.

the officer and the soldier.

Friday, 22nd [October, 1914]

The college has acquired another teacher: M Claudel – the cannon is booming very loudly. It is coming closer. Oh! If only the French could return – in the evening it was very windy.

Saturday, 23rd [October, 1914]

It is now forbidden to turn on the slightest light after 8 pm, on pain of a 500 mark fine[52] – the cannon is even nearer. Oh! What a blessing!! The Boches are afraid they will be coming back. They have fortified the fir tree bridges concealing the cannon guns!!

Sunday, 24th [October, 1914]

The weather is fine. We went to the cemetery. Tere will be getting up tomorrow.

52. Threats of fines, but also of imprisonment or even death, were systematically part of the many prohibitions or obligations imposed on the population by means of public notices.

Monday, 25th [October, 1914]

The cannon was booming very loudly, extremely loudly. A French plane passed over but no-one shot at it – we went for a walk – we went past Glaire, which has been completely torched, or nearly, and we went as far as Iges – there more than 1,500 Boches were killed by 35 Frenchmen. There too 3 batteries who, intending to fire at the Marfée [53], were in fact firing at Donchéry and setting it on fire; we were just about to go when we heard prrprrrem ziiiiii prrrm: a bullet fired at us by the guardian of the bridge– we turned red then white, what a fright, we quickly moved away from there and returned home to tell our story to Tere.

Come on, Michel, it's a question of stealing
They know how to go about it.

Tuesday, 26th [October, 1914]

Another notice has appeared: it is forbidden for more than 3 people to meet together in the street. I now understand why we were shot at: there were 4 of us together: The guard at the bridge must have known about this beforehand and shot at a group of people whom he could see from afar – the Big Ones and Papa are making ready a cellar in which to store our potatoes so that the boches do not take them. Tere got up. Yet another plane has escaped the hands of the Boches.

Wednesday, 27th [October, 1914]

Nothing new. Work on the cellar is still going on; there are some huge stones to be removed.

Thursday, 28th [October, 1914]

There are now only two barbers, one in the town and one at the Fond so we go to Mr Briand. At about 6 o'clock in the morning two planes flew over the Marfée – It seems that a sergeant major has said that they had left Verdun.

53. Cf note 34.

A battle in Argonne.

Friday, 29th [October, 1914]

What a shame! Catherine had managed to keep her foal and the 2 cows, [but] today they came and took away the foal, giving her in payment only a requisition voucher valid for after the war. Pierre has a headache.

the seizing of the foal

Saturday, 30th [October, 1914]

Nothing new Pierre still has a headache.

Sunday, 31st [October, 1914]

We went to deliver the bikes[54].

Monday, 1st [November 1914]

Grandma came and told us that people are saying that we have crushed the 9th army corps in Alsace, capturing 300 cannon guns and 3 standards, that we have achieved a fine success in Sissone, that William has ordered a retreat from the north to Ypres; that they have been beaten in Châlons and that German officers will not in future be receiving more than half-pay and, this is certain, that the German soldiers have entered the church in Sedan 30 at a time in order to swear fidelity to the emperor.

54. Requisitions of all kinds were systematic during the occupation. From the beginning, logically, people were required to give up any weapons, carts, bicycles, cars and coaches. But the Germans later repeatedly requisitioned immense quantities of furniture. In 1916, curtains and household linen were requisitioned, then, in 1918, mattresses which were exchanged for kelp. Garden and farmyard produce were taken to some extent, as well as metals from 1916 onwards thanks to unannounced raids on people's homes. Paper and cardboard were also requisitioned at the end of the war, but also machines and raw materials from steel and textile works.

(Saturday) Tuesday 13th [November 1914][55]

Tere is up – nothing new.

'We swear our loyalty to the Emperor'.

(Sunday)

Wednesday 14th [November 1914]

The cannon is booming from a great distance.

Thursday 2nd [November 1914]

We went to Grandma's. The boches' front line now runs from Sissonne to Louvain.

Friday 3rd [November 1914]

The news that Italy was on our side has been denied but the boches have been defeated in Sissonne.

55. This part of the Diary is characterised by great confusion about dates.

Maison Vivi
Political east of France [Fr.0,50]

Saturday 4th [November 1914]

We don't have a crumb of bread to eat –this clearly indicates that they have been defeated. Oh the rotters! They will let us die of hunger – too bad – after all we are French and if we have to die we shall die, but France will be victorious.

Sunday 5th [November 1914]

A notice has been posted: those who would like 100 kg of wheat flour must go and deliver to the station 800 kg of potatoes. Mme Leclerc did this but they gave her in exchange 100 kg of (potatoes) unkneadable black flour. We have black bread (probably from the Cameroons)[56]

Monday 6th [November 1914]

Tere had three visitors Mme de Rosbot, Mme Bazelaire [and] Mme leDuc. No news. No bread.

Tuesday 7th [November 1914]

It's very cold. No news. The cannon is very loud.

Resistance in the Marfée.

Wednesday 8th [November 1914]

No news. Grandpa is a hostage. The cows taken by the Boches have been brought down from Illy. The poor peasants who have already been burnt out followed behind. Oh! In 10 years time !!!!?

56. This seems unlikely in wartime. Might it be one of young Vonet's little jokes: – bread so black that it must have come from Africa (Trans).

Thursday 9th [November 1914]

We went to Grandma's. It is cold. No news.

Friday, 10th [November 1914]

No news. It's 1° on the second floor[57] in spite of the fire.

Saturday 11th [November 1914]

It's cold and windy. It is thought that there is a wireless telegraph in Sedan connecting us to the French army. We have some black bread. Mr Theâtre found a French corporal's diary on the Marfée of the 63rd. From Haraucourt he went to Bouillon where he was assigned to guard duty in the square in front of the church. From there he went to Balan and finally they were all led to Méssin where they advanced but saw nothing and were shot at. Whereupon they charged in all directions shooting at one another and were ordered to leave – this was the retreat – The people of Sedan is exasperated with the boches !!?

Sunday, 12th [November 1914]

No new developments

Monday, 13th [November 1914]

The boches are continuing to steal the cattle belonging to the peasants who have been burnt out

Looting.

57. Second floor of the house, where the boys had their rooms.

Tuesday 14th [November 1914]

We bought some coke. Trains full of guns and men are passing through the station.

Wednesday, 15th [November 1914]

It is snowing. We went sledging and in spite of the snow we could hear the cannon booming.

the town on Thursday 28th November.

Thursday, 16th [November 1914]

Tere went to the butcher's: no meat. During the night 54 trains went by. We went to Grandma's. The town is a pathetic sight. Some beggars are going from door to door asking for a piece of bread.

Friday, 17th [November 1914]

Grandpa is a hostage so Mimi will go to lunch in the Avenue[58]. Trains are going by all the time; we hear the noise they make all the time.

Saturday, 18th [November 1914]

Nothing new. It is fine and the sun is shining. I have an upset stomach (Mr Goguel[59] came but it is nothing).

Sunday 19th [November 1914]

Tere went to Mass, she is recovering very well. The cannon is booming very loudly, always in the direction of Rheims. No news.

58. Cf note 39 [Trans].
59. The family doctor.

Monday, 1st December [1914]

The cannon is getting very close. It would be great if it returned to Sedan, all covered in mud, out of shape, beaten up, . . . 1 regiment of Uhlans, several cavalry men on foot [Chasseurs], machine guns, bullets, cases of food supplies, hay, thrown

The Retreat!

together pell-mell. If only that could be the great day, they have come from Vrigne aux Bois and Lugny. Grandpa was visited by an officer, but he will not be staying as he would be sleeping on the ground floor but his orderly on the 3rd, so he was afraid.

Tuesday 2nd [December, 1914]

One can't sleep at night. Trains are continually whistling through the Ardennes. Tere stayed on in bed. Mme Brégi came to see her, still with no news of Jean. All the Boches are still there.

Wednesday, 3rd [December, 1914]

No news. Tere is still in bed. I am much better.

Thursday 4th [December, 1914]

Everyone went to Grandma's except Tere and myself. Grandpa has had an operation. He has been pumped out. He is up. Hip, Mr Fery's storekeeper, saw an officer who said he was his cousin and said to him: 'What you are seeing here is a retreat in good order'.

Friday, 5th [December, 1914]

The town is in turmoil: people have got hold of what are said to be extracts from French newspapers saying that the Russians were in Berlin and Metz had been taken. The Vauches[60] have some postcard-size photographs showing all the countries burnt by the boches.

Saturday, 6th [December, 1914]

No news. We have had a German newspaper it says nothing except that the Germans are at Koningsburg and Posen. We went into the town for confession, there is now no confessional.

7th Sunday [December, 1914]

It is being said that we are in Metz. The boches are pitiful, it is being said that the French government has appealed to the Vatican for the Pope to secure peace for us.

Monday 8th [December, 1914]

The king of Saxe is furious with William for having led his men into fire instead of the Prussians; they had a quarrel and William in a rage threw his sabre into a mirror and broke it.

The fighting continues in Flanders and Poland. It is being said that in Alsace we are at Sarrebourg.

In Metz: the occupation.

60. Friends of the Congar boys.

William, Emperor of Germany or emperor of the Boches or the Huns.
The Crown Prince (young man).

Tuesday, 9th [December, 1914]

We can hear the cannon booming. It is raining. According to the Boches, Poincaré has made a speech saying that the war will not end until there is an announcement that Germany has been utterly defeated militarily, to which they replied: 'Then, never'. Mr Cosson, the protestant pastor, is lending the little orphanage chapel to M le Curé [61]. We haven't a crumb of bread.

Wednesday, 10th [December, 1914]

Oh the pigs. This morning an endless convoy of balls of wool stolen from Mr Ringard passed by. Ringard Junior had been left on his own when the Prussians came without a requisition voucher, with nothing, to take the wool. He said to them: [']I must have a voucher, you should have one[']. What will his father say when he returns?

Thursday, 11th [December, 1914]

We went to Grandma's. The big ones changed where the bikes were being kept, they were in the attic because they will soon be requisitioned. The cannon is clearly audible.

Friday, 12th [December, 1914]

In Grandma's. We are obliged to clean the chimneys or pay a penalty, even though there is no chimney sweep.

---

61. The church in Fond de Givonne had been completely destroyed and burnt down during the German invasion. The protestant pastor's offer to the Catholics was a gesture of vitall importance in Congar's memories of this period in his life. He deemed it the beginning of his later ecumenism.

Saturday, 12th [December, 1914]

People are saying that Hirson and Rethe have been recaptured, but we are being told the most outlandish news. It is probably not true but we have made an advance as the following notice has been posted up: 'It is now forbidden under pain of a fine of 1200 marks or 1500 francs to go to Belgium in search of food or other provisions[']. Ah! They want us to starve. Alright then! In the next war our young people will go to Germany and starve them. They will see that they are turning the French against them, so much the better[.] I have never hated them so much. The price of [----------] has gone up: 7½ sous a pound, double the usual price. People say that Mr Bompard has been taken prisoner.

Sunday, 13th [December, 1914]

The protestant chapel is fine but small, but we will be happy with it. Grandpa came to see us, as well as Mme Bacot and her two sons.

Monday, 13th [December, 1914]

The boches came to search Grandpa's house from top to bottom, from the cellar to the loft, the cupboards, boxes, bags. They found nothing [ill.]. They see a box, they give it a kick and say: 'Right, that's books.' In fact, it was books. They send people familiar with the place to do the searching.

28

Tuesday, 14th [December 1914]

Mme Girardin is collecting money to give something to the French wounded for Christmas. There is no fresh news. For a month or two people have been saying that they will have gone by Christmas; now they are saying by the end of February . . .

Wednesday, 15th [December 1914]

The cannon is booming very loudly – so much the better. No other news.

Thursday, 16th [December 1914]

The boches must have been defeated in yesterday's battle. Whenever they have been defeated, a fresh tiresome notice appears. Today all are forbidden, under pain of 6 months' imprisonment and a fine, to leave the town of Sedan, no-one is allowed to go either to Waldelincourt, Bazeilles, Floing [or] Givonne[62] without a travel permit, several people have been to ask for one but were refused[63].

Friday, 17th [December 1914]

In order to have our milk (as our milkman has gone) we had asked someone from Givonne, but she did not come; people are not allowed to move around. The boches (des trous de bals de poules[64]) have taken charge of the mail. Calendars/timetables are being printed. No fresh news. The boches want a list of the hostages. Grandfather's got it and he says he won't give it [to them].

Saturday, 18th [December 1914]

Nothing. There is to be a meeting of the hostages on Monday. There has been no meat for the past two weeks. Slaughtering will now only take place every fifteen days, and there is still no milk.

Sunday 19th (20th) [December 1914]

We went to Mass. We went to the horse butcher. People are saying that the cannon we hear booming is in Buzancy[65] because we can hear it very clearly; people even go up to the dyke[66]to hear it.

Monday, 21st [December 1914]

There is a notice (therefore a defeat): those aged between 16 and 20 years are to present themselves and register at the town hall. Clearly there is no need to repeat the threats of fines {marc[ks]} and prison, but people couldn't care less. The hostages have

62. List of places close to Sedan.
63. Traffic in the town was authorised from 5 am to 7 pm. (German time, imposed on occupied areas, which was one hour ahead of French time and 2 hours from May 1916 onwards). No-one was allowed to leave the town, even to go to the nearest villages.
64. A child's insult invented by Vonet but in a very Ardennais style.
65. 25 km south of Sedan.
66. An earthwork close to the Meuse, not far from the Avenue Philippoteaux.

been brought together. They are going to have to do disgusting kinds of work; they are to go through each area of the town to see if there are any weapons. They are putting Frenchmen against Frenchmen, it's disgusting, that is not work!! Oh the boches, the cows!! . . . !! Grandpa is to do rue St Nicola. Catherine returned from Givonne.

Tuesday, 22nd [December 1914]

Grandpa went out on his search at 8 a.m. It is raining, nothing new.

Wednesday, 23rd [December 1914]

The weather is getting wetter and wetter. Grandpa finished his search as they had settled that this was to be done before Wednesday.

Thursday 24th [December 1914]

It is Christmas Eve and we are rejoicing more this year because [it] is turning out to be [better] than the year that is coming to an end.

It is very cold. Grandpa is a hostage tonight: what an odd kind of midnight feast it will be for him and for us too. There is no Midnight Mass. A year ago one went in one's sabots through the snow with one's little lantern, [and] a wide-brimmed hat, moving over the old road lit up by the lights from the windows to the Church where the flickering light of the candles marked the shape of the altar where, at the bottom of a crib, our Saviour lay: so many voices singing hymns rose towards heaven. Now, on the old road soiled by the feet of foreigners everything is dull and silent, there are the ruins which are still smoking, there is the burnt-out church[67], pasted to the wall is a threatening notice, there is the most compelling reason [of all], the invasion and devastation: the complaints of the unfortunate people who have not a crumb of bread, the hatred of this race who loot, burn and make prisoners of us, the country sealed off from its homeland where our white cabbages[68], our leeks and our goods pass by in the hands of these robbers singing 'Gloria, Gloria'; there is the town which is held to ransom by the conqueror, under the

and the magician Ballo makes this year disappear almost or very nearly with the wave of a sleeve.

67. Yves Congar never forgot the fact that the Fond de Givonne Church had been torched.
68. These cabbages were a speciality of the Fond de Givonne market-gardeners.

French soldier saluting.

before the invasion. after the invasion.

boche saluting.

fiercest oppression and injustice of the aggressor, the undertone of steadily increasing hatred which will soon be overflowing like the water in a vase full to the brim [and] will be capable, within 10 years, of paying back our invader to the full.

Friday 25th [December 1914]

There is a notice: All the carrier and other pigeons in Sedan are to be killed under pain of a heavy fine or imprisonment. Second notice: It is expressly forbidden to leave the town without a passport[; the town] is declared to be in a state of siege, those who leave the town in search of food or other goods and who are caught will be thrown into prison and whatever they have on them, food or provisions, will be confiscated. We went to Mass in the morning; in the afternoon we went up to Algeria[69] where we heard the cannon booming a long way off but unceasingly. People say it is Verdun[70], the fort batteries. We found two little dogs among the rocks[71].

69. One of the high places in Sedan.
70. Verdun is 80 km from Sedan and in fact it seems that it was the artillery of this sector of the front that the Sedanese heard most often during the occupation.
71. The reference is to the rocks on the family property located over an old quarry.

Saturday, 26th [December 1914]

Tere is not very well but it is the result of the intense cold over the past ten days. They must have been defeated because there is a notice: 'Men from 18 to 48 are to report to the town hall: they are prisoners[72], and also because one can hear the cannon booming very loudly from the direction of Noyer.

Sunday, 27th [December 1914]

No fresh news. It is windy and stormy. The cannon is still booming very loudly. Trains are passing through Sedan station. Is it a retreat or a change of army unit?

Monday, 28th [December 1914]

No news. It is still raining and windy.

Tuesday, 29th [December 1914]

The road is a sad sight. Men going down the Fond de Givonne on their way to make themselves prisoners at the town hall, one carrying sardines, bread and a bottle of wine, another bread and a litre of beer. They are said to be going to work in Balan; their wives go with them as far as the town hall, with their children. People are saying that we have retaken Stenay[73] – no news.

Prisoners!!

72. Throughout the district, men from the age of 18 upwards had been liable to be called up since 10th November. In January 1915, men aged between 17 and 48 were deemed to be civilian prisoners. In October 1916, in Sedan, children from 11 to 16 years were also called up and required to work from April 1917 onwards under the supervision of the occupying forces. In November 1916, [this applied to] the entire population.
73. A village situated about 35 km south-west of Sedan.

Impressions of the War

How sad [that] after long months of good fortune
How sad these soldiers lying dead on the field of battle
Had been sacrificed on the field of honour
How sad for these villages rebuilding the walls
Of their poor chimney and the rich altar
[Making them] habitable, good, comfortable and nice
Germany was there watching with a jealous eye
For the favourable moment to come and nest amongst us
To do as the wicked Bismarck had said
Overrun the Ardennes through valiant Belgium
Bleeding white, burning churches and town halls,
Villages, schools, and creating panic amongst us all
It is they who have sought for this cruel war
They wanted it, they wanted it fiercer and more bloody
If only they had not wanted it, these dustbins!!!
– 'He laughs best who laughs last'

'Other impressions'

Germany felt very ready to undertake the war and she thought that France was not, so she looked for a pretext to start a war: the fact that a Serb had killed the son of the uncrushable[74] gave him his opportunity: Austria declared war on Serbia but Russia did not want to allow this little country to be crushed [so] Germany declared war on it, the boches reckoned that the Belgians would not offer any resistance, they violated their territory in order to get into France because France was supporting Russia. Owing to the violation of Belgium, England declared war on Germany, which was not expecting that, or at least reckoned to set Italy against it [ie England], [but it [ie Italy] did not set its troops in motion. However [Germany??] was strong enough to resist for a long time. Nevertheless a day will come when, having exhausted all her resources of food, ammunition and men, she will be forced to give in and acknowledge herself defeated. Amen.

Wednesday, 30th D [December, 1914]

The boom of the cannon is very loud, but it is raining but no frost. The winter is not very severe.

Thursday, 31st [December, 1914]

We did not go to Grandma's. No fresh news.

74. The reference is to the Emperor Francis-Joseph, then aged 84.

Friday, 1st January 1915

We went to the 9 o'clock Mass and paid New Year's Day visits to Taïe[75] and to Mme Girardin. Tere is going into the town for the first time since the bombardment. On the way down we called to see Mme Quinchez. We got there and back without incident. We had lunch in the Avenue and had supper there at 5.30 p.m. with the older boys. After supper the older ones went back to Fond de Givonne with Grandpa. We remained with Tere, myself and Mimi, to sleep there and go back home tomorrow morning.

Saturday, 2nd January [1915]

Tere returned home. She was not too tired. We called on M le Curé.

Sunday, 3rd [January 1915]

No news. As the boches have very little to eat themselves, they have released the prisoners they had taken earlier, telling them to be ready to return. They are completely broke. We went to Mass.

Monday, 4th [January 1915]

No fresh news. Godchaux burnt himself while washing his teeth, he was not in class today. Le Gros came to show us postcards of the countries that had been burnt: of Longwy, etc.

Tuesday, 5th [January 1915]

No news. The boches are becoming boring. There is a new pupil in class: D'epnont.

Wednesday, 6th [January 1915]

No fresh news. The weather is very ugly. It is stormy but it is not a severe winter. According to the Ardennes Gazette[76], M Viviani[77] seemingly made an 'anti' speech in parliament from which they cite passages. They are very angry. Wilhelm replied in another speech which will be reported to us in the next issue of the Gazette.

75. See footnote 7.

76. The *Gazette des* Ardennes, printed and edited entirely in Charleville, the first issue of which appeared on 1st November, 1914, was both a source of information for those living in the occupied territories, and a means of propaganda for the occupying forces. Entirely under the control of the Germans, the editorial staff included such French professionals as the journalist René Prévost (naturalised as a German in January 1918), and from time to time also made use of the cooperation of other Frenchmen such as the Ardennais Henri Laverne who was condemned to death after the war. The print run steadily increased, rising from 4000 copies to 180,000 in 1918, but it would seem that sales amounted to no more than 50,000 copies.

77. President of the French Council from June 1914 to October 1915.

French Russian English Belgian

Thursday 7th J [January 1915]

We went to Grandma's. Seemingly people are saying that France has allowed the Japanese[78] to occupy Annam[79], so that they can come at the Boches (from the rear) so there is a lot of talk in the town. It is Wilhelm's name day on 29th The Boches want to offer him Verdun, 50,000 men have gone there. What a feast day: 50,000 bodies.

Friday 8th [January 1915]

32 lorry loads of hay, probably from Givonne, went by this morning as well as a lot of horned cattle stolen from the peasants. The cannon is still booming fairly loudly.

Saturday 9th [January 1915]

Nothing. We can still hear the cannon booming probably as loudly as ever. It is still very stormy.

Sunday 10th [January 1915]

We went to Mass and afterwards into town; as we were going down Place Nassau, we saw people coming back, we heard the sound of motor cars. It was William II[80]. One car full of officers in front of his, then his with 2 armed soldiers then another car

78. The Japanese had entered the war on the side of the Allies on 23 August, 1914.
79. A former subdivision of French Indochina, now the central region of Vietnam.
80. William II stayed several times in Sedan, as did the Crown Prince in 1917, the kings of Saxe and Bavière and Marshal Hindenburg.

Boche Austrian Turk

Wilhelm II and his helmet.

Guillaume passant en automobile

Wilhelm passing through in a motor car.

with 2 officers and two armed soldiers then two enormous vehicles full of soldiers. He was going towards Bazeilles. We felt that it was in fact himself who was leaving Ardennes because the cannon is booming very loudly.

Monday 11th [January 1915]

No fresh news. Two boches, a doctor and a sergeant, came, according to them, to pay a visit to Mme Girardin. They toured the garden and when they reached the look-out point, they said: 'This would be a good place for a cannon.' No other remarkable incident, no sound from the cannon.

Tuesday 12th [January 1915]

Wednesday 13th

No new developments.

Thursday 14th [January 1915]

Nothing new. We went to Grandma's. The talk in the town is that all is going well for us, that wherever they try to advance, they are driven back (?). One is beginning to have had enough of the Boches.

Friday, 15th [January 1915]

The cannon is booming very loudly. Mme Stackler brought us a boche newspaper which says that the Russians have advanced in the north of Prussia and in Austria and that the Serbs are advancing in Austria[81].

81. On 4th and 5th December 1914, the Austrian army was defeated by the Serbs, so much so that the Austro-Hungarian army was forced to withdraw

Infantry —cavalry—spiked helmet.

hussars—territorial police—infantryman cap.

the boches' headgear.

Saturday 16th J [January 1915]

No fresh news. The cannon continues to boom.

Sunday 17th [January 1915]

No fresh news.

5 heavy bullet magazine.

10 light bullet magazine.

the 2 rifles
1. Boche 2. French

---

to the frontier. Belgrade was recaptured and the territory liberated on 15th December. Was it to these events that Yves Congar was alluding some four weeks later? Moreover, news from the eastern front undoubtedly mentioned the Russian's January offensive in Bukovine and then in the lower Vistula.

Monday 18th [January 1915]

Nothing. Mr Foucher and Mr Benoit are going to Luxemburg to collect food supplies. We are waiting for them to return.

Tuesday, 19th [January 1915]

Wednesday 20th

We can hear the cannon. It is snowing hard. Abbé Toussaint, parish priest of Villers-Cernay[82] had not given up his bicycle. He was notified yesterday to come to Sedan on it today so he set out. On the way he was stopped by the boche guard post. He was told to stop and his bike was taken from him, He sat down in a corner, opened his breviary and read it. The boches then told him to go [but] he raised his eyes and continued murmuring; he did this several times. In the end, one of the Boches said to him: 'Get out, monk. You are fouling the camp with your bike so you can have it back and go.' He left and arrived in Sedan without further difficulty.

Departure. The reading of the Breviary.

Thursday, 21st [January 1915]

We went to Grandma's. Mr Benoit got nothing. He was refused both money and goods. The Boches have brought together all the mayors of the district and told them that they were to submit a petition to the President of the Republic to make peace, to which the mayor of Raucourt, who was the spokesman replied: 'Monsieur, we are Frenchmen. We have suffered up to now, we will suffer to the end, and you will have nothing.' The Commandant exacted from them a fine of 60,000 fr. The town of Sedan has been ordered to give the boches 250,000 frs. It replied that they will give nothing (resolution reached by the hostages).

o-o-o-o-o-o-o-o-o

82. A village close to Sedan.

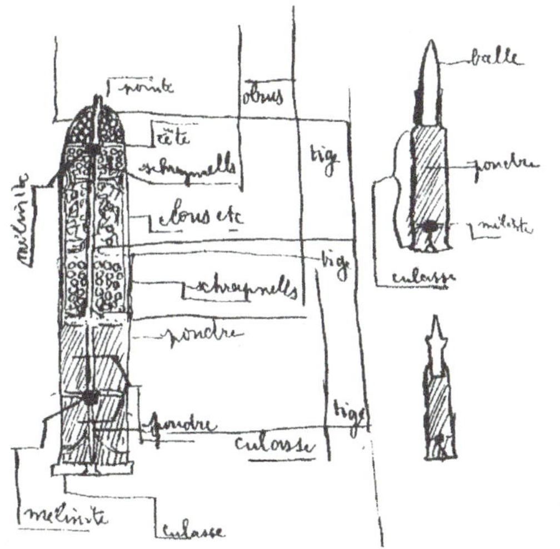

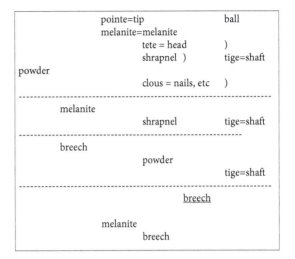

pointe=tip ball
melanite=melanite
tete = head)
shrapnel) tige=shaft
powder
clous = nails, etc)

---

melanite
shrapnel tige=shaft

---

breech
powder
tige=shaft

<u>breech</u>

melanite
breech

Personal Thought [83]

Turn over

Oh! France! Thou Queen of the earth
You leave your children under brutal force
Enduring need. See what they have suffered
And what they continue to suffer under showers of metal.
All are suffering for you and for your flag;
All are ready to die so that you may be victorious;
And all will in fact die, if necessary, tender mother;
All will indeed die because they seek your glory
Your honour and your life and your lovely existence.
All seek it. And all will have it,
Because these Prussians will leave France
And we will all go to them. We will all go there! . . . PTO

Refrain

You, France, our beloved queen
We will all make you great
We have endured suffering
We too will receive honour.

Copyright [84] Y Congar

83. This text appears on a loose undated sheet inserted into the first exercise book. It was therefore decided to reproduce it here.
84. Dts = 'Rights'. Though only 10 years of age, Yves Congar envisaged the possibility of publication at some future date.

The German mobile kitchen and the people needing food.

r Gulaschkanone

WAR SCHOOL

DIRECTED BY

Mme Conpar[85]

Continued from N 1

Diary of

the World War

85 Owing to the difficulties encountered in sending the children to school, Tere gave lessons at home.

Cover of the second exercise book.

Continuation!

scale: 50 cm.
The actual bread : 4 lbs.

End of the 1914 – 1915 War Diary

22nd January Friday

1915[86]

The cannon is booming very loudly especially in the evening. It makes the windows rattle dreadfully.

We hear it in bed at night
They must be very heavy cannons which
have entered the battle because
the shots fired are loud and heavy.

this formidable cannon
does nothing but boom
it makes the houses tremble
destroys walls and towers

Saturday 23rd [January 1915]

Tere made a ground loaf for us, grey green close-knit and sticky but when one has nothing, one makes do with it. There is no bread at the baker's and when, for 4 days and at times for 8 or 10 days we have only 4 lbs of bread – sticky, gluey. black and badly made at 7½ sous per lb for 6 people, we were well satisfied. The French can't be very far away because they are again demanding money and the booming of the cannon is very loud. In many families who have no bread, the coffee grinder is being used to grind corn.

Sunday, 24th [January 1915]

Monday 25th

Tuesday 26th

Wednesday 27th

86. The date reference was added by Yves Congar at a later date, together with his signature on the cover and on the first page of this second exercise book.

Cigarettes please.

Thursday 28th

It's raining. The cannon is not booming as loudly as on last Friday; there is no bread. We have had none since Wednesday 20th. We are making 2 lbs per day[87]. Tere makes a 2 lb loaf; it is very cold, we went to Grandma's.

Friday, 29th [January 1915]

We have a very dark bread; we have had none since the 20th. No sound of the cannon.

Saturday, 30th [January 1915]

It is snowing and very cold. A census is being taken of the inhabitants family by family. Is it to do with supplies, or is it with a view to evacuation or, on the contrary, to leave so much per person and take the rest? This is the great question crossing people's minds just now.

Sunday 31st [January 1915]

We are going skating this afternoon: we were on our way when two men came towards Papa and said to him: 'You are due to be a hostage tonight?' 'Yes'. 'Well, this service has been discontinued' Phew!! The hostages!! In the afternoon two men came to count our hens. Probably in order to take them. We have been told that the new Pope Benedict XV has produced a prayer for universal peace for all Catholics[88].

87. Note added by Yves Congar: 'when I measure it: Tere makes the bread. It is we who grind the flour.'
88. Since the beginning of hostilities, the papacy had maintained an attitude of strict neutrality and never ceased thereafter to work for a restoration of

1. George IIII 2. Wilhelm's helmet.
3. George's cap. 4. Nicolas' headgear.

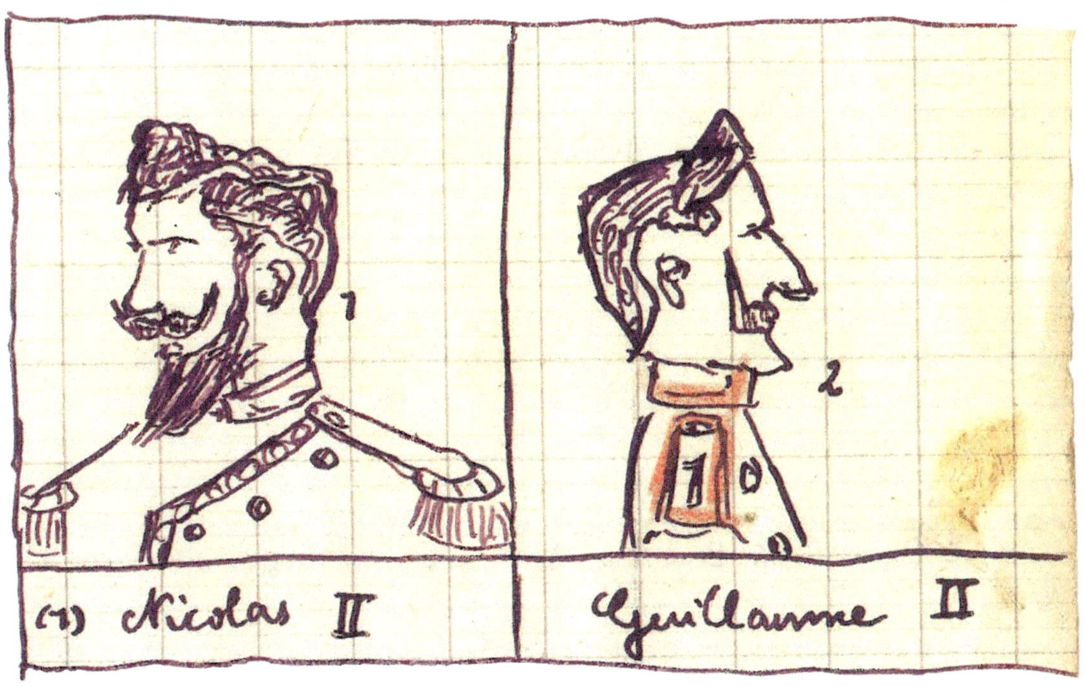

(1) Nicolas II.

Wilhelm II.

scout princes infantryman gunner Uhlan gunner Uhlan

People are fighting, people are always fighting
People are being wounded and killed
There is fighting going on night and day
Under the earth, on the earth and in the clouds.

Monday 1st February 1915

The snow is melting fast. The boches want people to go to the town hall to declare [the number of] pigs, cows, horses and 47 other items (potatoes, beetroot, etc.): what a lot of pigs have been slaughtered today! People are saying that [there has been] a huge convoy of wounded captured by us, including one of Wilhelm's sons. So much the better! If that were true, but he hides his skin behind 6,000,000 soldiers who only wanted to stay at home, this wretch.

Tuesday, 2nd [February 1915]

The snow is still melting and the meadowland[89] is no longer flooded. Nothing new about the war.

Wednesday, 3rd February [1915]

We can hear the cannon booming, but far away. A lot of trains are passing through Sedan station carrying shells, refuelling vehicles, cannons, machine guns, rifles, shot and above all about 60,000 men all going towards Alsace. The weather is fine.

peace. The appeal for prayer for peace had been made by Benedict XV on 10th January, 1915.

89. This extensive area on the right side of the Meuse was often under water, making it possible to skate when it froze over.

infantryman Hussar gunner infantryman Royal Guard Wilhelm French rearguard

The boche army on the run

Thursday, 4th [February 1915]

We can hear the cannon. It is fine. We went to Grandma's. People are saying that the United States are supplying us with flour and the Spaniards with dry vegetables[90]: it would be wonderful to have some good white flour. In Sedan there are two American officers and a civilian to supervise the unloading of the food supplies. Oh what splendid people! A boche wanted to object: he brushed his arm aside, the boche shut his mouth. They have pinned a notice on the door of the mill: 'To avoid diplomatic complications with America, the German authorities are forbidden to enter the mill.' A French plane flew overhead this morning, following the course of the Meuse, flying in the direction of the Marfée, which it observed and then flew off. A German one passed later in the day.

Friday 5th [February 1915]

Saturday 6th

The cannon is audible. The weather is fine. We have some magnificent white bread at 5¼ sous per pound, excellent. Seemingly there is going to be a huge battle between Montmédy and Stenay. The boches are sending troops there.

90. From the early months of 1915, the civilian population began receiving supplies from Spain and America, and later on from Spain and Holland, after the United States entered the war in 1917. Distribution, which was fairly regular, occurred once a fortnight under the direction of a municipal commission, but the quantities distributed remained always well below the real needs of the recipients.

Sunday 7th [February 1915]:

We went to Benediction: to the prayer for peace. Nothing new.

Monday 8th [February 1915]

The felt factory has been set on fire. Two officers and 3 stable hands came to Grandpa in search of lodging, but having seen the apartment they went away. Preparations are still going on for the battle between Montmédy and Stenay where there are some insignificant skirmishes. The rear-guard of the army which is destined to fight at Stenay is at St Valfroy. Their tents are visible from Piermont[91]. We walked as far as Torcy in order to see the fire: it is smoking still. We can also see the St Vincent bridge which has been cleverly blown up. William is said to be in Sedan.

Tuesday [9th February 1915]

Wednesday 10th

We can hear the cannon. It is probably the battle in Montmedy. It is fine and it is raining.

Thursday, 11th [February 1915]

The crown prince is at Abonneau, he created the devil's own row during the night. No fresh news.

Friday, 12th [February 1915]

Pierre is 16 today. One can barely hear the cannon.

Saturday, 13th [February 1915]

Sunday, 14th

We went to Grandma's and people are saying that the boches have been defeated at Montmédy, and in Alsace: in a rage, the boches have requisitioned shaving brushes and they are demolishing the walls of the college (the courtyards) so that their wounded can take exercise; weather fine all day.

Boche
Down with
the German

Frenchman
Greetings, Soldier of France

Monday, 15th [February 1915]

No fresh news. Weather fine.

91. One of the Sedan heights.

Torchons = tea towels.
Cuvettes = bowls.
matelas = mattresses.
Argent = money.
Crèche = day nursery.

The Sedanese Ransom.

Tuesday, 16th [February 1915]

The gazette is absurd: to be used outside (see the collection[92]). We are getting flour from the United States. The weather is wonderful. There was a meeting of hostages: they began by trying to frighten them by telling them that German officers were working in Morocco under the supervision of Blacks [sic!]; also, since 4,000 men are to be accommodated in Sedan, they requisitioned: 4000 mattresses, 8000 towels, 4000 bowls, the orphanage, the Brothers' school, Guérin etc.[93] and the town of Sedan was ordered to give 140,000 francs. But the hostages decided to give nothing.

Hail to you, Soldier of France!
Valiant defender, full of courage!
Hail to your fine army!
You, our much loved fatherland!!

Oh this cursed race!
These Germans with fierce eyes,
I reflect on the black eagle,
The unkempt beard hiding the mouth,
The flat and deceptive head;
You violated loyal Belgium
In order to get into the land of Gaul
Germany in your critical position
Say: 'I am defeated' and for the first time
I could say: 'I believe you'.

92. Once the war was over, the three Congar brothers organised a war museum in the family house. Cf A WARTIME CHILD, by Stéphane Audoin-Rouzeau, footnote 14.
93. It was on 10th February that these requisitions were made in order to accommodate 4000 young recruits. The figures Yves Congar gives are correct.

17th February [1915]

One can hear the cannon booming very loudly and the French cannot be far away because a French plane flew overhead. The Boches shot at it fiercely and for a long time. This plane was followed by a German one.

Thursday 18th February [1915]

We went to Grandma's. They are saying in the town that the boches have been badly beaten in Creil. So much the better.

The Franco-Boche War in 1915.

Friday, 19th [February1915]

No fresh news. The noisy cannon has gone silent.

Saturday, 20th [February1915]

Robert went to Mr Tehatre who says that the Russians have lost[94].........., the Austrians ...., the boches ...., the French ...., the Belgians .... and he maintains that the strong French towns ought not to have yielded their walls, their men, foodstuffs, munitions or at the very least ought to have destroyed their flag, as I am destroying this one

94. Yves Congar left blank spaces here, presumably with the intention of inserting the figures later.

The End of the Flag

It was war time, and the town that had been under attack
For two months was exhausted and almost without resources
The surrender was about to be signed
When there came to me, worn out with running,
A young man, dripping with sweat,
Tanned with the sun, tall, thin, with blue eyes,
Looking sad, with lowered eyes in which glistened a tear.
He said to me: 'Colonel, the General wants you'.
'He wants to sign the surrender'.
'He wants to surrender the weapons, the town, the soldiers,
'the provisions, the rest of the ammunition!'
And the soul of the soldier: 'he wants to surrender the flag'!
He did not finish the last words.
I then said in the voice of a soldier:
'Montignan[95], bring me the flag'.
Then he brought the treasured flag.
A fire was lit with the shafts of lances,
And slowly, in the presence of the soldiers with uncovered heads
Under the waning moon, the Colonel moved forward
And held out this shred towards the blazing fire.
It burnt. Increasingly high flames rose up towards the heavens,
And approaching the circle of the soldiers
Whose tears filled their eyes,
He said to them: 'Let us surrender' and he embraced them!

Yves Congar (1904 ....?) [96]

Sunday, 21st [February 1915]

We went to Mass. The United States want those who wish it to be repatriated. There is talk of repatriating Mme de Kerlero de Rosbot.

Monday, 22nd February [February 1915]

At 3 a.m. in the morning, quite a lot of French people, prisoners, went by. The boches are idiots, they were playing the French marching song, played as it would have been played by a 3 year old African. We hear the cannon booming.

95. Note by Yves Congar: "Montignan: imaginary (name of the standard bearer)'.
96. Yves Congar here envisages his own death, which eventually took place some 81 years later in 1995 (see preface).

Des flammes plus hautes s'élevaient dans les cieux.

'Increasingly high flames rose up towards the heavens'.

Thoughts

In our town of Sedan they have paraded their spikes, their platform, their cannon balls, their black eagles, they have paraded their flags, they have cried out 'Hurray, Hurray', they have sung victory, they have shouted out; in our botanic garden they have played their melancholy music, they have soiled our roads, our houses, our Ardennes, they have spilled the blood of innocent people, they have carried their incendiary torches all through the countryside, they have taken our crops, our property, but that is enough. 'Deutschland'[:] the blood of your victims cries out for vengeance[97].

Tuesday 23rd [February 1915]

No fresh news. We can still hear the cannon booming quite loudly. We don't quite know from where exactly.

Wednesday 24th [February 1915]

The cannon is still booming very loudly. In Champagne the boches have been to steal the sheep which, having been abandoned, and dying of thirst, are mangy. They often kill some of them and put the rest to grass. Today they are grazing in the Fond de Givonnais fields.

97. In the original, the rest of the text printed below, together with the following poems were written in parallel, in accordance with a complex arrangement, with the entries for Tuesday 23rd, Wednesday 24th and Thursday 25th February. For the sake of coherence, we have grouped them all together here, before resuming the diary format.

The Imperial seal.

German Barbarities[98]

At the time of the invasion: 8am on Tuesday, August 25th , the French had left 2 soldiers in Givonne: Mathurin Raff and François Travert and a third, too, was left whose surname was Quinquin. Raff and Travert were killed but poor Quinquin suffered quite a different fate: seized hold of by these barbarians he was then the spectator of this act of barbarity: Mr Distribué tied to the tail of one of the Uhlan's horses, in such a way that, having been dragged along like that, his head left his body and was shattered in pieces.

But that is not all. These barbarians do not stop at soldiers, they have seized hold of civilians. After cutting off the fingers of a wounded person who, having been shot in the face was hiding his face in his hands, they took him in order to make an assault on the station bridge without themselves getting killed, being shielded by the civilians that they held in front of them. One was killed.

Poor Quinquin.

98. The three texts entitled 'German Barbarities', 'Thoughts', 'Refrain', and 'The death of a hero' were written by Yves Congar in such a way as to be parallel to the rest of the diary which at this point is divided into two columns. For the sake of convenience, we have grouped them together and printed them in sequence.

In Fond de Givonne, Mr Pouteaux emerged from the cellar in his room. He wanted to leave before the invasion, so he went to see if the road was free. At this moment, the barbarians entered his house, took hold of him, placed him against the wall of his house and killed him.

The boches thought that there were machine guns in the Church which they had burnt down, they took hold of civilians, made them kneel down in order to shoot them twice, but after burning the Church down, they let them go.

Like so many others, the Vauché family of carpenters wanted to escape before the invasion. The Uhlans were approaching; the mother and father and 3 of the children had already gone across the fields, but two teenagers, one aged 19 and the other 17[99] wanted first to look after their rabbits; they did this, then returned for a moment to the house. The Uhlans heard them talking, came in and shot them on the spot. One of them died instantly and the other died 10 days later in hospital.

Mr X…., a mason, was in his house at the moment of the invasion. When they came, being thirsty, to knock at the solid door, he did not want to open to them, they set fire to it, the mason being inside, and he was nearly burnt alive, but escaped across the fields.

Still at the moment of the invasion, Mr Jacquemart was at home when these barbarians came in, took hold of him and led him along the Boulevard de la Rochette [100] and, against a tree, they cut off one ear with a sabre and then let him go.

Before leaving for France, Mr X…..A….. was on his way to see to his horses. The Uhlans saw him, aimed their rifles, there was a round of rifle fire and his dead body was seen to fall into the dew.

Mr Fix in Wadlincourt was in his cellar when the battle took place. When he heard knocking at the door, it was the 1st Infantry. They told him they were going to shoot him and then the shots rang out. Mr Fix fell onto his daughter at his wife's feet, who both witnessed this act of barbarity characteristic of the Germans.

Not only that, but the present-day Huns also attack animals. At Mr X….'s, the animals were in the stable when brutal force descended on the unsuspecting house in the form of fire, theft and pillage and with its senseless force made the roof beams bend under the fierce fire and cast over the victim's burning house a fierce and wild look of satisfaction while these animals struggled to free themselves from the flames but the doors were closed so they were roasted in their stable.

If these proofs of barbarity are not sufficient to show the French who have remained close to their mother in 1914 and 1915, let them go to the Ardennes in Belgium and the North, they will see right violated, their brothers under attack, their country defiled, their property disappeared and everywhere they will find this proverb: 'might over right'.

99. Later correction in pencil: 17 and 14 years.
100. One of the streets in Sedan.

'Thoughts'

Oh France! You Queen of the earth,
You leave your children enduring brutal force
Succumbing to need! You see what they have suffered
And what they are still suffering under hands of metal.
All are suffering for you and for your flag
All are ready to die so that you can win;
And all will do so, if they need to, loving mother.
All will do so, of course, because they yearn for your glory,
Your honour and your life and your glorious existence.
All wish for this!! And all will have it! ...
Because these Prussians will leave the soil of France,
And we all will go to theirs.... Yes, we will all go there! .... !! ..

Refrain

You, O France, our beloved queen,
We will all contribute to your glory.
'We have been enduring suffering,
'We will also grasp your honour '
I will insult their eagles and their songs
Their flags and their empire
Words of Victor Hugo rightly repeated here:
This is what the German barbarians are like.

The death of a hero.

The aim was to overcome the assault position,
These Bavarians were to be overcome or put to flight.
General Levert was directing operations,
Sensible, always prudent and at the same time helpful
He gave the order: 'Fix bayonets'!
And under the rain of bullets and the machine gun
The 7th Battalion was seen to disappear
under the thick smoke covering the battle

the boches come down the slope, it is necessary to brake.

Thursday, 25th Feb. [February 1915]

We went to Grandma's and were going out into the garden when we heard a low hum mixed with and followed by a fierce and heavy fusillade which seemed to come from all sides of the town at once but without result, but later in the evening we heard that [the plane] had come down at ....X but when the boche soldiers who had been away from their post got there the Frenchmen who had been inside had been got out and hidden in the village so the boches threatened to bomb and shoot people, etc.

It's a French bird
hail to you, good friend
fill us with hope
my very dear one

Friday, 26th [February 1915]

We hear the cannon booming. No fresh news.

Saturday 27th [February 1915]

M.....r. no fresh news...We hear the cannon booming.

Sunday 28th [February 1915]

The kitchen has been dark for three days: we are using candles to light it as we have no gas.

Mme de Rosbot.

1st March. Tuesday 1915

Deutsch kaput.
No sound of the cannon. The boches have suffered a huge defeat by the Russians in Poland [101]

2nd March Tuesday [1915]

Wednesday 3rd

No fresh news. The boches are kaput everywhere according to the information from Sedanese sources that are brought to us.
Mimi is sick.

Thursday 4th [March 1915]

Friday 5th

Mimi is still sick and in bed. We are going to Grandma's, we can hear the cannon.

Saturday 6th March [1915]

Mme de Kerlero de Rosbot and her antics.

101. Yves Congar is clearly here referring to the Russian counterattack on the Nieman at the end of February 1915 which forced the Germans to withdraw. In March, the Russian offensive began on the Lower Vistula, in Bukovyna and in eastern Galicia in the Carpathians. The Russians captured Przemysi on the 22nd March.

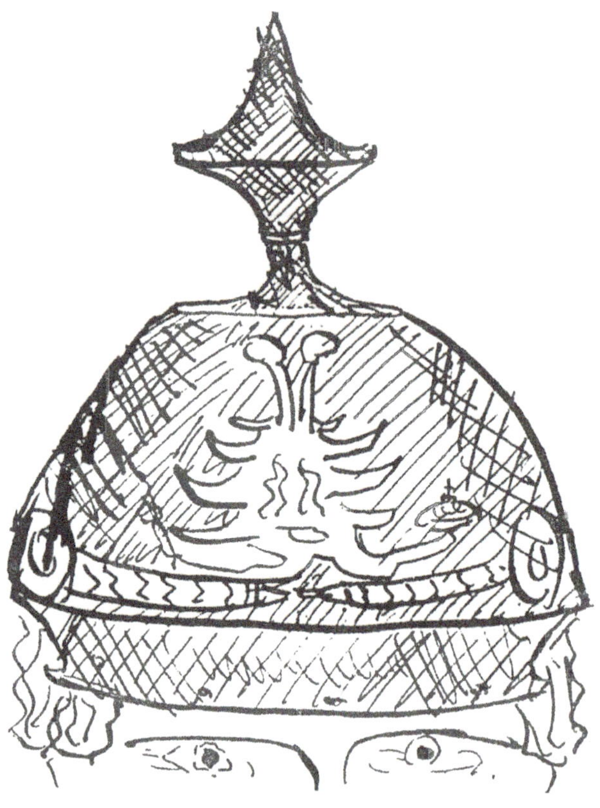

Sunday 7th

Mimi is getting up[.] [I]t has snowed.
The wind is blowing. We will probably be eating frogs tomorrow. Mimi is getting up.

Monday 8th March [1915]

No fresh news. The wind is blowing.

Tuesday 9th March [1915]

There was a huge storm. No news.

Wednesday 10th [March 1915]

We hear the cannon booming quite loudly. Same weather.

Dear Frenchmen.

Thursday 11th [March 1915]

We hear the cannon. Tere went to the Avenue.

Friday 12th [March 1915]

People of Sedan: Rejoice, your brothers are not far away, keep hoping. We are going to have gruel, fresh supplies!! .....! It is wonderful! Sugar, salt and the gruel we so much loved as children, hooray, hooray! It is from the boches. We are being given some supplies after such a long time. People are saying that there is fighting above Rheims, a historic city.

Yesterday I was going to Grandma's with Robert and as it was my custom on other days to upset the boches I set about doing so[;] then in the Rue du Ménil I saw one; Robert went 'pchiiiteiiite' at him so, believing that Robert had spat at him, I planted a huge blob of spittle to the right of his chest to serve as a souvenir medal of the campaign. He looked at me for a long time but as he was only an ordinary soldier, he said nothing to me.

Saturday 13th March [1915]

We hear the cannon booming very loudly, the boches are searching Raucourt[102] from cellar to attic.

Sunday 14th [March 1915]

No fresh news. The dull sound of the cannon is less marked, we still have no fresh news.

Monday 15th [March 1915]

No news. Played in the garden.

Tuesday 16th [March 1915]

No fresh news.

Wednesday 17th [March 1915]

We have been told, and moreover there is no doubt, that the production of the gazette is to be transferred to Charleville, since the French are almost certainly advancing as we can hear the cannon booming very loudly; morale is quite good in Sedan. They are coming for the hens; a little poster has been put up (see among the war souvenirs[103]) stating that they will collect them in 3 days! Hence everyone is saying that it is because they are leaving Sedan and even that they will not have the time to collect them, that they will have left before then. In fact we hear the boom of the cannon all the time oh! If they could only come back here, we would willingly give everything one possibly could! 3 days! It is not much, after all. Let's move on to a new chapter: let us move on to

18th March 1914 [104] Thursday

We went to The Avenue. The Boches have hung huge nets on St Vincent bridge because they suspect people are sending messages in bottles by the Meuse; these bottles are then taken to their command post, so the Sedanese are throwing bottles with 'Deutsch kapout' [Germans kaput], à bas les boches [down with the boches], etc. and Grandpa threw one in with 'Dreck für Deutsch' [Germans are dirt].

Friday 19th March [1915]

We hear the cannon booming all the time and people are saying that the French have killed about one thousand boches.

---

102. Village close to Sedan.
103. Cf footnote 92.
104. Clearly, 1915 is meant here.

Saturday 20th March [1915]

No fresh news. We can hear the cannon but it is a long way off and . . .

21st Sunday [March 1915]

The cannon has become much louder[105]. It appears to be in Charleville. The weather is fine.

22nd Monday [March 1915]

The cannon is still audible. The weather is fine.

Tuesday, 23rd March [1915]

The cannon is still quite loud. Troops went by {(3 regiments) in the direction of Daigny}.

God with us.

The devil with you.

24th March Wednesday [1915]

The boches marched past with musicians at the front, always in the direction of Daigny (cars, lorries, etc), the town is quickly full of life, people are saying, and hoping, that they have been defeated.
About belts [106]

Got mit Uns![107]

You dare, you Germans!
No! the devil with you.
Liars, thieves, wretches!

105. 'less loud' deleted.
106. Reference to the design of the German belt buckle.
107. For 'Gott mit uns', ie 'God with us'.

'Got mit uns! This word in your mouths
after 1900 years of civilisation
we see this fierce people
inscribe this precious word on their belts
'Got mit uns'! These sacred words,
these words of the Roman church,
We see them made into a sacrilege
by this Germanic horde
'Got mit uns', horde of boches!
We are going to put bullets into you.
You will dance like tramps
or in the oven: on a stove.
'Got mit uns' You see quite clearly
the word does not match the action
your God, for you, is nothing,
nor the church. We see it.
'Got mit uns' Huns! brute beasts!
who don't know what you are saying,
when you do see your fall
you will say: 'der teiffel uns mit'[108]

Thursday, 25th March [1915]

It is raining and windy. In the morning the town was crammed with boches: 9,000 men plus the garrison, so that the place was crawling with 'grey worms' as they are called now because of their grey-green uniforms and that the more that are killed, the more they re-appear: just like grey worms, in fact.

Friday, 26th [March 1915]

We can hear the cannon, but not very loudly, and above all in the evening. There are trains passing (still quite a lot) but empty, presumably because they have nothing left to put inside but among them all some are almost full, they are going towards Givonne (Belgium). They must be hard-pressed because they have requisitioned bales of wool to protect them in the trenches: they are short of things and, something that has never happened before, 'The Marfée has been occupied'![109] How delightful! So we shall be seeing these dear Frenchmen again, so much the better. Oh, one would endure whatever was necessary and even more if it were to result in our being freed.

108. Note by Yves Congar: 'The devil be with you'. The correct spelling and syntax is: 'der Teuffel mit uns'.
109. Cf footnote 34.

Saturday, 27th March, [1915]

We hear the cannon and morale is good because people are saying that the boches are leaving Sedan and people believe it because a lot of vehicles have been going up and coming down laden with hay; it is thought: 1) because when the boches are leaving they have an urgent need to take everything from us and 2) they try to take everything before they go. So much the better!

Sunday, 28th March [1915]

No fresh news. We hear the cannon and about 300 armed boches came down: probably, they are short of men and are sending the few that they have managed to recruit in the villages 'under fire'.

Monday, 29th March [1915]

No further news. Always the boom of the cannon and always the boches on the way down.

Tuesday, 30th March [1915]

We can still hear the cannon booming rather loudly and there are still boches coming down (as reinforcement). The area is in a state of defence and the men have been divided up as follows:

Cheveuge	1200 men	Vrigne	3,100 men
Floing	1,200 men	Sedan	2,000 men

including the trenches in Douzy, chiefly close to the bridges and the railway: in Daigny and in Mocelle (La Rapaille) so we all the more believe in the longed-for return of the French, but on the right bank.

31st March [1915]

Tuesday

Wednesday

Nothing new. We hear the cannon and Madame Pageot has prophesied that we shall be set free on 29th April, so may this month pass quickly! And let us live it well as we wait!

Farms by farm! The war of attrition

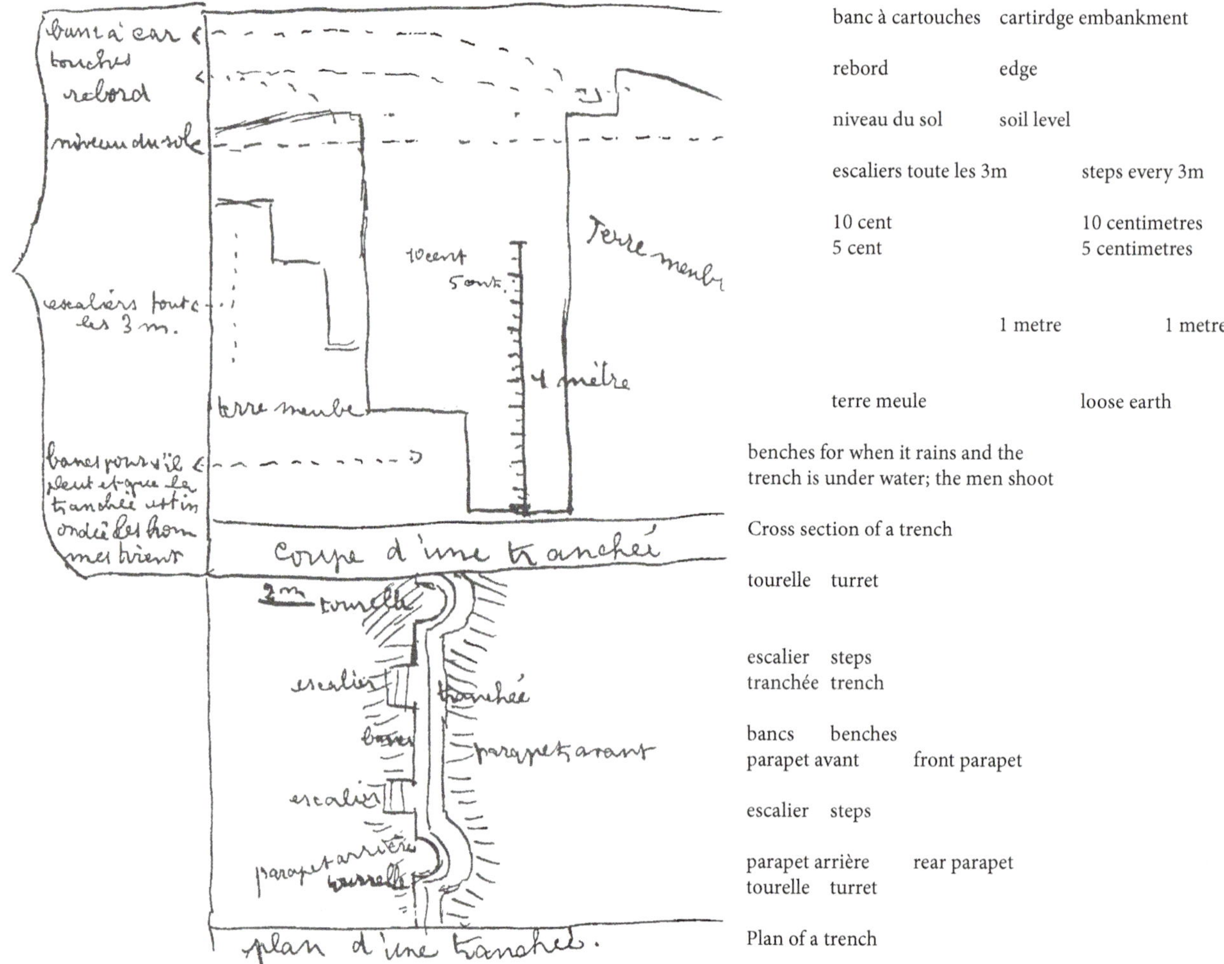

Thursday, 1st April [1915]

No fresh news other than that it is being said that the French have retreated a little in Alsace; they would appear to be in Tannes (?) (close to Belfort). We hear the cannon booming a bit.

Friday, 2nd April [1915]

The cannon still booming a bit. Still no fresh news; it is annoying and this diary must make very dull reading but: it describes 'life in the occupied countries' and if it is disagreeable to read, life 'in the occupied countries' was disagreeable to live.[110]

110. Remark confirming that Yves Congar was writing in the hope of being read.

Saturday 3rd [April 1915]

Absolutely nothing, nothing, nothing. The same for Sunday.

Monday, 5th April [1915]

No bread. We made some because it is probably our Easter Monday when, normally, we would go walking, we celebrated etc. Today it is the 'German occupation', alas, such sad words!!

6th April, Tuesday [1915]

Today we have 100 grs of bread per person and tomorrow this ration will be even smaller. Ah!

7th April [1915]

Nothing at all [not] even bread so we ate swedes [choux navets].

Thursday 8th [April 1915]

People are saying that the French in Verdun made a sortie and are advancing all along the line, so everything leads one to believe that Madame Peugeot's prophecy will prove true. It is hilarious: people are saying that the blacks are charging the boches with bayonets and that they have not the time to retrieve their dead because, as they advance, the blacks are eating the dead and the wounded. Seemingly, the boches have retreated 13 km. It's a foretaste for the 29th![111]

Friday 9th [April 1915]

No sound of the cannon – no other news.

Saturday 10th [April 1915]

Nothing else. Still no sound of the cannon.

Sunday, 11th April [1915]

Still no fresh news: this 'still no news' keeps re-appearing because there really is nothing new except the vexations of all kinds to which we are subjected.

Méfiez vous au chat qui dort!

Beware of a cat that is asleep.

111. The reference is to 29th April, the date on which it was hoped that the Germans would be leaving.

Monday, 12th April [1915]

At last we can hear the cannon, fortunately.

Tuesday 13th [April 1915]

Fine weather. We can still hear the cannon, but rather faintly. Rosbot came and put on an act: she is crazy: Madame you are not French! . . . !! . . .

Wednesday 14th April [1915]

Thursday 15th April

The boches are odious, they have probably been severely beaten and the French are advancing because at 6 o'clock a French plane came. It followed the course of the Meuse and flew over the Marfée then flew off in the direction of Bazeilles. The boches are still trying to re-capture Verdun; they have sent 50,000 men there under the command of Wilhelm II and we can already hear the cannon booming in that direction while still more trains are transporting what they need (cannon, food, munitions, bombs, shells, bullets, shrapnel, riflemen, bayonets, horses helmets, buckles, flasks, haversacks, tents, saucepans, bomb launchers, crates, vehicles, . . . etc.)

Mme De Rosbot.

Friday 16th [April 1915]

A French plane came and dropped 20 bombs. People are saying that another destroyed the station in Charleville.

Saturday 17th [April 1915]

We can still hear the cannon. The boches are taking the pigs, cows, horses, etc. they are forcibly evacuating part of the town: 1,200 people are in desolation leaving their homes to be pillaged, all their possessions; it is sad to see the town. All the way through, surrounded by the songs of the barbarians, women are weeping, others in groups with men are talking animatedly, the women are distraught, the men all worked up[112]. It is sad to see. Oh these boches! These barbarians, making use of their physical civilisation for the benefit of their avidity and their cruelty.

112. On 15th April 1915, the Germans decided on forcible emigration to Switzerland for all inhabitants of the area ['département'] who were unable to work, principally old people and women with children. At the end of 1915, 1,800 indigents were evacuated from Sedan. The town, which had a population of 16,000 in 1912, had no more than 10,000 by October 1915 and 9,800 at the beginning of 1918. (plus 800 non-natives: foreign workers, mostly of Flemish origin, as well as evacuees from the North or from Champagne).

Wilhelm and the Crown Prince.

Sunday, 18th April [1915]

So the boches are short of money: they have levied a tax on dogs, poor creatures, at the rate of 5 fr per month (60 fr a year). Poor Kiki[113]. We may well have to kill him. Oh these boches, watch out in ten years, 5 %: 50% in 10 years, at a rate of 1,000,000,000 fr = 1million 500,000 francs. The reason why they are forcing people to leave is that a French plane dropped a bomb on Wilhelm and it landed about 100 m. from him. They say that if it had hit him, they would have burnt down our town and several others.

Monday 19th [April 1915]

We hear the cannon. The boches are already forcing the poor French people to leave; what despair if a French plane had not flown over the station; poor people.

Tuesday 20th [April 1915]

The platforms are crowded, they want everyone to leave except the hostages. Since there is something happening, the crowds gather, thereby increasing people's unhappiness instead of waiting resolutely and calmly, but it is excusable: after what we have seen, one can always expect worse to come from them.

113. Kiki, the famous dog that featured in all the exploits of the Congar boys, the dog about which Yves Congar still spoke to me fondly at the Invalides in 1995 [note by Dominique Congar].

Wednesday 21st [April 1915]

The train carrying the emigrants has gone to Bazeilles and returned. Tere saw the Crown Prince and Wilhelm on the way back from Les Amerois.
X see page 2 because there is no room on this one [114].

Thursday 22nd April [1915]

No cannon, wind, the emigrants are leaving.

Friday, 23rd April

Nothing, no cannon, wind.

Saturday 24th April

No cannon. St Frederick. Grandpa's feast day.[115]

Sunday 25th April

No cannon. Weather fine.

Monday 26th April

No cannon.
We have some white bread, it is delicious.

Tuesday 27th April

No cannon.
Long live Spain and the United States.

Wednesday 28th April

No cannon.
Long live France and her allies.

Place Turenne as it is now.

114. Note added by Yves Congar: 'This means that on that day things were being hidden'. The writing shows that this note was added by Yves Congar at a later date. The page 2 referred to is no longer in the notebook which tends to confirm that, to begin with, there were some additional loose leaves which have not been preserved. Throughout his life, Yves Congar followed the same procedure in his writings
115. Frédéric Desoye (1845-1920), the father of Lucie Desoye, Yves' mother.

Sedan, Platz Turenne.

HOTEL DE LA CROIX D'OR
INSTALLATIGN MODERNE

Thursday 29th

Friday 30th

It is thought that the Russians are advancing because 6 aeroplanes have left from here, [and] 100,000 men in the direction of Nez [Metz] via Bazelles.

1st May Saturday [1915]

We hear the cannon booming quite loudly and we again have white bread.

2nd May Sunday [1915]

We hear the cannon booming so loudly that everybody agrees that there must have been a major battle: we went to see the boches' trenches at the blow-out near La Moncelle. We smuggled back 3 rolls of barbed wire.

Monday 3rd [May 1915]

People are saying that the French won yesterday's battle. We again have white bread.

Tuesday 4th [May 1915]

The cat has had 4 kittens, we are keeping one, Titi, the kitten. No fresh news. It is grey with black stripes.

Wednesday 5th [May 1915]

Nothing

Thursday 6th [May 1915]

175,000 Russian prisoners. It's written up by them in chalk everywhere, as well as 30,000 horses [116]. Oh I am going to die, the boches are crazy.

Friday 7th May [1915]: nothing.

Saturday 8th May

No sound of the cannon.

116. Reference to the combined German-Austrian offensive in the Spring of 1915, which resulted in the invasion by the Germans of the northern Baltic provinces at the end of April and which, in the south, after the collapse of the Russian army at the beginning of May, was to lead to the recapture of Przemysl on 3rd June and of Lemberg on the 22nd.

Sunday, 9th May [1915]

Monday 10th May

No cannon. Weather fine.

Tuesday 11th [1915]

Wednesday 12th

The boches are retreating, they are falling back, the cannon is getting nearer. Nothing else.

Thursday 13th [May 1915] : nothing

The boches are still in retreat. It's raining. Nothing else.

Friday 14th [May 1915]: nothing

Saturday 15th [May 1915]

Gloomy day, sad day. My dog was put to death.[117]

Poems about his death

Poor Kiki

Poor Kiki has been killed
I will never see him again
poor martyr of the fatherland
such a good dog: 'poor Kiki'

with a calm but trembling hand
we laid him in the ground
I am sure he had a soul,
and even a complete one.

1. Kiki, towards my heart, let out a loud call
when on your treasured tomb a final farewell will be laid,

117. The Congars had decided to kill the dog rather than pay the taxes imposed by the Germans.

I am there, thinking of you and weeping for you
always close to your heart and close to my loved one.

2. when on the brown tomb a tricolour rag
was laid by our hands on this sad threshold[118]
you, good dog, you trembled then
to see before you two children mourning your loss.

3. - my spirit was wholly shrouded in black
and before you, sombre and sad victim,
I did not raise my eyes, for fear of seeing you
judge of our action alongside your crime.

4. and I dared not speak in this lonely place
until, far from you, you cannot hear me,
except to say that I was going to look for the tombstone
for you, true hero, so good, so beloved, so loving.

5. now here below I suffer and I sigh
I weep at the thought that you were a martyr.

Y Congar.

1. My poor little dog, he has gone,
I will never see him again
and very often I think of him
and of the life he lived.

2. I think of him with bitterness
I sigh over him and I cry [119]
I think as I write with my pen
To tell you about my sorrow [120]

3. Farewell, my dear and faithful friend
Farewell my beloved Kiki
now that you have gone
I weep for you and will go on weeping for you [121]

118. An earlier version had been: 'was laid by our trembling hands'.
119. Earlier version: 'during the day and at dusk'. There is a draft of the poem annexed to the 2nd exercise book.
120. Earlier version: 'to tell you in verse about my sorrow'.
121. Earlier version: 'I have wept for you'.

4. in writing these few words [122]
I have wept and I have sighed
farewell my dog, my lovely 'coco'
I will think of you often.

Memoir
The Martyr

It was today, 15th May, a sad day but one to remember, for today took place the martyrdom of a hero who died for the fatherland. At about 3.30 in the afternoon, the vet came; the dog was given a piece of meat which he devoured, then his mouth was fastened with a string as tight as possible, his paws were held and poison was injected into his heart, and we then buried him while he was still warm.

Sunday 16th May [1915] [123]

We hear the cannon. We continue to be without news. It really is the end.

Monday 17th

Tuesday 18th May [1915]

Nothing at all. Above all we hear the cannon and the occupation is being unduly prolonged as the 29th has already come and gone.

Wednesday 19th [May 1915]

We hear the cannon a bit but unfortunately our bread is grey right through, dense, heavy and flat, but we eat it avidly as we are hungry. An officer of the armoured Uhlan imperial guard came to see Mme Girardin who will be leaving shortly, and as he brought her 1 loaf and 2 legs of mutton she gave us one.

Thursday 20th May [1915]

No fresh news, the cannon continues to boom. Mme Girardin will soon be leaving for France [124].

Friday 21st [May 1915]

We hear the cannon. Mme Girardin left with 1 sister, 1 doctor, 2 soldiers and Alexandre for Chavouse and France; in 20 hours she will be very happy, more than the late Toto.

122. Earlier version of the beginning of verse 4: 'In the evening as I bury my head, in my damp pillow:
123. The word 'Renewal' in a more mature hand was written at the head of the page at a later date.
124. For Yves Congar, 'France' evidently denotes the unoccupied parts of the country.

Saturday Sunday 22nd and 23rd [May 1915]

The cannon. No fresh news.

Monday Tuesday 24th and 25th [May 1915]

Cannon. A lot of mines are exploding but we do not know where!

Wednesday 26th, Thursday 27th, Friday 28th. Saturday 29th [May 1915]

We are still hearing the cannon and quite loud. There is probably a fierce battle being fought [somewhere].

30th May [1915]

We hear the cannon booming quite loudly, No other news except that a ridiculous notice has been posted up.

31st May [1915]

Another month of occupation, and we are about to commence another one, Ah, it is becoming very long-drawn-out, with new sufferings every day! There is still no fresh news, except that we hear the cannon booming louder than ever.

1st June 1915.

We placed a tombstone on Toto's grave:

1. when on these treasured remains
   we tremblingly placed a stone
   in the presence of the birds who chirped away
   in the rocks and in the ivy
2. in view of the war and its evils
   before heaven, before God,
   before this precious flag
   here in this sad place,
3. I solemnly swear for the life
   of my dear dog, my good Kiki
   Fatherland! I will always be faithful to you.
4. and although at this moment I am not a soldier
   I will serve you by suffering the death of a hero
   go, my dog, do your duty, go! Go!
   leave your companions and leave this flag
5. good beast, bleeding victim of the war
   your portrait is always engraved in my memory

the little cat Kiki and its tattooing.

for you were very dear to me, yes! dear! very dear!
and even dearer since you were put to death[125]!

6. on the innocent tomb of a hero of France
3 bouquets of pure white flowers rest on his heart
one represents purity, the other deliverance
and the third, forgiveness of his executioners.

7. Still in my breast I feel this heavy weight,
And he, on his heart, feels me thinking of him.
this dog is no more, now he is dead
but he remains engraved in my heart.

Y Congar.

Toto, my dog who is now dead, go to the fatherland
for which you gave so willingly your poor life.
make for this Standard, make for the dark red madder,
make for your country, make for France.
head for the capital admired throughout Europe.
go quickly, run, trot, gallop,
jump. Go towards the Gauls, towards the Latin race,
go towards this nation, this divine nation
you well deserve it, hero of our Ardennes
flee this horde here, this German horde,
die so that your soul may go to its place
die in peace and be worthy of the race
elder daughter of the Church, daughter of Science
and this race I speak of, this race is France.

Y Congar.

2nd June 1915.

No fresh news. We can still hear the cannon to some extent.

Thursday 3rd June [1915]

Nothing. The cannon is louder.

125. The original version, deleted by the author, had been: 'since you have left me'.

Friday 4th [June 1915]

Nothing. The cannon continues to boom very loudly.

Saturday 5th June [1915]

The cannon is still booming very loudly and we also hear fierce explosions of mines. We were playing when a boche telegraph infantryman (with a black cap and red band) came to our house and put on an act: 'You kids have thrown a stone over the telegraph wires' and he drew out of his pocket a length of cord with a stone at each end, as illustrated here [126]. He did not want to let it drop, he was convinced that it had been us, and moreover a neighbour had told him so. In the end he went off, so that was probably the end of the affair.

the stones and the piece of string.

the lads display tricolour flags etc.

Sunday, 6th [June 1915]

We hear the cannon booming very loudly. Nothing else.

Monday 7th June [1915]

We were on our way down into town when we saw Pauline arriving, who said to us: 'Go at once and warn your parents, there is a Uhlan on his way to your house. This was true and I was racking my brain to try and guess why this Uhlan was coming to our house. Then he demanded to see the entire household and lined everyone up in front of him, including Mme Georges whom he had brought along as interpreter and Mlle Yvonne Gippon who had just brought the milk and Tere, Papa, Taïe, Mme Douffet, Mr Douffet, Mme Douffet [M]édart (who was absent), Mlle Douffet, Pierre, Robert, Mimi and myself, and he asked us one by one , producing a battered piece of string which we recognised as the one from the other day, whether one of us had thrown the string which someone had seen being thrown. On receiving a negative reply, he put back the evidence of his conviction and departed, convinced that it had not been one of us. The French are in Ripon and St Marie near Vouziers.

Tuesday, 8th June [1915]

We hear the cannon fairly close to us. This proves that the French are advancing, all the more so since 'they' are tightening the knot even more: not only cutting off our grocery supplies, but they have caught some smugglers coming from Belgium. Moreover, they have sold us, for the entire town and its suburbs, 15,000 people: 'Guess what?'! . . . half a head of veal!' . . . ! . . .! It is laughable! Oh! These boches! Oh! . . .

---

126. See the drawing in the margin. Yves Congar's drawings are often very close to the text to which they refer.

Wednesday, 9th [June 1915]

People are saying that the French have dropped bombs on Stenay. We hear the cannon booming very loudly.

Thursday 10th June [1915]

We hear the cannon booming. The kids who up to now have been marching out with rifles on their shoulders, red kepis, the tricolour and nurses etc have now been forbidden to do so under pain of a fine and we are even ordered not to play at soldiers at home. It's disgusting, because the ban applies to us too.

Friday 11th [June, 1915].

The cannon is booming quite loudly. People are saying that the French have crossed the Meuse at Stenay. We went to Grandma's.

Saturday 12th [June 1915]

No sound of the cannon. Tere is not well; she has a bad migraine. No news.

Sunday 13th June [1915]

Deutsch kapout

Yesterday the boches took 10 hostages: Mmes Dupont, Doin, Benoist, Metzguer, the Cosson boy, Molard, Abbot Ninin the German [127] . . . etc. The cannon is booming very loudly from the north and people are saying it is in Nieuport.

the 12 hostages bide their time

Monday, 14th June [1915]

They have recaptured two hostages and if people don't want them to be sent to Germany the town will have to pay out 15,000 marks, and in the meantime the 12 hostages are biding their time in the meadow in Balan [128]

Tuesday 15th [June 1915]

The boches are abominable. We don't hear the cannon but they must have suffered some reverses as they are making us suffer in all sorts of ways. It is really awful.

127. Note by Yves Congar: 'The reasons: The German (the Abbé) because each religion must be represented. Nini, (son) for nothing. Dupont (wools) because he had brought some newspapers. Doin (Prof) for going to Carignan (with a passport) by another route. Benoist (Prof) because he allowed the Marseillaise to be sung. Metzguer (interpreter) because one of each religion is needed. Cosson (pastor) because one of each religion is needed. Molard, doctor, because he was a military doctor.' In fact, this event corresponds to the general practice, after 21st April, of selecting hostages from among the notables in each commune throughout the *département*.

128. A neighbouring commune, to the east of Sedan.

Wednesday 16th June [1915]

No sound of the cannon at all. The authorities are imbeciles[129], they have paid the 15,000 marks.

Thursday, 17th [June 1915]

No news. No cannon booming. The hostages were released yesterday.

Friday 18th [June 1915]

No news. No cannon booming. It's windy. We picked the herb-tea leaves.

Saturday 19th [June 1915]

No news. No cannon booming. It's windy. We picked the strawberries and the lime.

Sunday 20th [June 1915]

Nothing. No cannon booming. No fresh news. We went to Vespers.

Monday 21st [June 1915]

No news. No cannon booming. We have no meat. We are suffering.

Tuesday 22nd [June 1915]

No news. No cannon booming. No fresh news. Still no meat.

Wednesday 23rd [June 1915]

No news. No cannon booming.

Thursday 24th [June 1915]

No news. No cannon booming. The boches came to pick our cherries for themselves: it is disgusting: they even took the cherries I was keeping for someone who was wounded.

---

129. The town council had been reduced to ten members during the fifty-one months of the occupation, including those councillors who had been mobilised or evacuated. The deputy mayor, M Grandpierre, acted as mayor, assisted by some leading citizens of good will and some interpreters. On the whole, this town council proved itself to be rather weak: it is true that in Sedan it was dealing with particularly harsh German authorities in comparison with the other towns of the *département*.

Friday 25th [June 1915]

No news. No cannon booming. They came to our house to look around but they did not take anything, fortunately (song).

Saturday 26th June [1915]

No sound of the cannon booming. We have had no meat for 17 days: it is miserable and today we have l kilo of tripe; after having taken our animals they do not want to let us have the thousand-millionth part. It is disgusting, oh these cursed boches!

the authorities Alexander Muller

Sunday 27th June [1915]

Fortunately there has been no further requisitioning of fruit: they have not taken any from here and it is thought they will not go on doing so, but they have requisitioned, oh, guess what ....shallots and garlic! ......!!

List of the things taken by the boches: [130]
Money:
Wool:
Sheets:
Men:
Clothes:
Cabbages:
Leeks:
Wood:
Flour:
Coffee:
Chicory:
Sugar:
Chocolate:

130. Yves Congar had left this list blank; he did not fill it in at a later date.

Monday 28th June [1915]

Still no sound of the cannon; the town is in a panic; it is thought they are going to take the currants and other fruits!

Tuesday 29th

Wednesday 30th June [1915]

No fresh news. We still do not hear the cannon, and we don't know if it has been seen.

Thursday 1st

Friday 2nd July [1915]

No fresh news. No cannon. We went to Grandma's. People are saying that 14 carriages of prisoners went by!

Saturday 3rd

Sunday 4th

Monday 5th

Tuesday 6th

Wednesday 7th July [1915]

Nothing new. We remain without fresh news and it is horrid. From time to time we hear the cannon a bit even quite loud, and the next day, without being able to explain it[,] we hear nothing.

Thursday 8th [July 1915]

Madame Benoist's maid has been arrested and fined 31.50 fr. for having tried to eat a rabbit on the dyke. It's shameful! It is nothing when you read about it, but when you actually see it, it is a torture.

Friday 9th [July 1915]

Nothing new, as yesterday.

Saturday 10th July [1915]

It's disgraceful!! The town has been fined 1,000,000 marks! Lille 3,000,000 and Mézières 900,000. Lille say they have nothing left. Mézières refuses point blank and Sedan gives in yet again and demands money from the shopkeepers. It's disgraceful for French people to be giving money to be used in killing their brothers! [131] Oh! Oh! Take care the vase is filling . . . not only that

131. These very heavy fines were imposed in retaliation for the destruction of insulators on the Sedan-Bouillon line.

but I would give 5000 fr. to anyone who could find a litre of milk in Sedan except in the houses occupied by the boches! Watch out Muller, Alexander. [132] Take care, there are loaded revolvers in Sedan! . . . and . . .!

Sunday 11th [July 1915]

No fresh news. We are waiting to see what the mayor will do.

Monday 12th July [1915]

As regards the million marks, we are waiting to see what Charleville will do. The boches are closing the iron circle around us. We have made our own beer. There is no doubt that it is war that reduces you to making one's own bread and one's own beer.

13th July Tuesday [1915]

Nothing, as yesterday.

Wednesday 14th July [1915]

We held a parade: flags flying, etc. I was leader; it went very well and the spectators were delighted.

Oh, France, on this day of glory
you say to us: March then! Old men and children
and, starting from your presence, inspiring victory
We marched out with our heads held high with our triumphal songs
We joyfully sang the Marseillaise
being transported by our warlike songs.
How happy we were! How much at ease
in resembling our old troopers
and raising on high the tricoloured flag
as if we were carrying the statue of France
at dawn, at sunset, at the rising of the sun,
everywhere: it was joy impregnated with [a desire for] revenge.

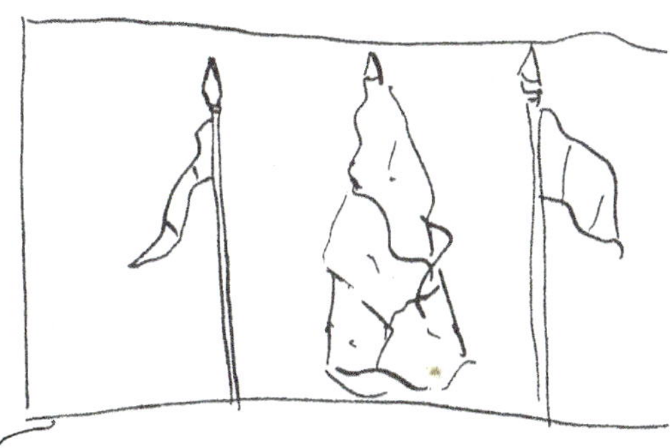

Y Congar.

France, our Mother, our native country,
on this anniversary of your freedom

132. The headquarters [Kommandantur] had been installed in a bank at nº 2 Place Turenne, under the command of Colonel Heyn, then of Major Von Metsch. But those effectively in charge were Lieutenant Muller and the interpreter Alexander. As they multiplied, the occupation forces ended up by occupying a total of 117 buildings, including 10 hospitals and 10 barracks.

We sing (to the tune of the Marseillaise)
France has 2 regiments
that have never known fear
they live ever in hope
in glory and in honour

Always trusting in God (repeat).
This regiment which nothing deters
in the battle everywhere
is on duty and in celebration
in the cities, towns and villages
To arms, infantrymen, arm yourselves with courage
and be worthy of these heroes
who carry the flag.

'Forward march!

Thursday 15th

Friday 16th

Saturday 17th

Sunday 18th

Monday 19th

Tuesday 20th

Wednesday 21st July [1915]

We hear the cannon booming quite loudly from the direction of Verdun but above all in the afternoon from 4 pm onwards. It is incredible, a constant booming noise, we go about like souls in purgatory, like dishwater. Oh, what a life one lives in occupied countries.

Thursday 22nd [July 1915]

The boches are horrible and probably done for because they are taking the copper everywhere even in the villages that were burnt down. They are still demanding a fine of 1,000,000 marks! It is dreadful. Oh what wretches they are!

Friday 23rd

Saturday 24th

Sunday 25th

Monday 26th

Tuesday 27th

Wednesday 28th July [1915]

The question of the million marks is still unsettled and people are really desperate because we have no more than 160,000 frs. and they have said that if they do not get it, they will loot the town. We still have no news except that life in the occupied countries is not very hygienic (see the Gazette des Ardennes).

Thursday 29th [July 1915]

This morning (what proves that the French are advancing is that a plane flew overhead) we began to hope again, and people are saying that the French will return before the question of the million marks has been settled.

Friday 30th [July 1915]

Yet another French plane flew overhead this morning. Things are moving; come on then, my little boches, wait patiently for a good thrashing. Moreover, the mood in Sedan is quite good and the boches are so angry about it that they are coming to collect the copper and screws left in Sedan, even the screws from the telephone. They came to Grandpa's and placed the bell from the telephone on the table; then, seeing a basket of apples, they took two each. During this time, Grandpa, whom the boches whose backs were turned could not see, took the bell and put it behind his back and then went to hide it. The German then looked for the bell but he could not find it.

Saturday 31st [July 1915]

Tere went to see Grandma. The men aged between 17 and 40 are leaving today for Vouziers, there, undernourished, having 7 pfennigs per day, the men of the town are each required to supply 2 steres [cubic metres] of wood per day: it is appalling.

Sunday 1st August [1915]

There is a boche plane which has returned from the front and flown by Mr Karhl [sic] . . . X, which landed at Bazeilles. He will leave again this evening. No other news.

Monday 2nd August [1915]

We have had no gas for 4 or 5 days. We eat by candlelight! There are a lot of boches quartered in the town.

Tuesday 3rd August [1915]

Wednesday 4th

Thursday 5th

No fresh news except that we have neither potatoes nor gas nor news and that only the United States are thinking of us as supplies are due to arrive tomorrow and I will describe it all.

Friday 6th [August 1915]

Saturday 7th

The supplies have come. Well, you go to the grocer's shop with your bread card; there [you find] a hundred or so people milling round the door and shoving baskets at one another in order to be first. More and more people keep coming, and you join them[;] you are punched 6 times, 4 times pushed at with a basket, then all of a sudden a great big man arrives: 'eh im' faud la plasse moi' ['Make room for me'] accompanied by a punch, a thrust with his elbow, a thrust with his basket, another with his knees, and there he is in front by the door, you are squeezed into this mass of executioners and you are lucky to escape with your life.

Sunday 8th [August 1915]

Nothing.

Monday 9th [August 1915]

It's disgraceful: there is a notice. Everyone must bring to the town hall all the money one possesses: all of it. It's disgraceful.

Tuesday 10th and Wednesday 11th August [1915]

Grandpa took 80 frs. in units of 5fr. We have more bread and I find it quite nice.

Thursday 12th [August 1915]

We had a discussion with Servais. He is completely overwhelmed and will do no more soldiering.
The Uhlan, Christian, has only to capture 2 more smugglers in order to win a gold medal. This Uhlan is all out to take women prisoners. One day he sat on the embankment, put his hand to his head saying: 'great misfortune 6 women to go to Belgium and I took none'.[133]

Friday 13th and Saturday 14th August [1915]

No fresh news. Cannon booming.

Sunday 15th [August 1915]

No sound of the cannon. People are saying that the boches already have 140.000 frs. The boches are taking cartloads of wood, about 800 cubic metres per day!

Monday 16th August [1915]

We went to the 4 to 6 literary and scientific [lectures]. The Gazette des Ardennes says: In Berlin a pound of horsemeat costs '5fr'! [so] even dearer than here! (see Gazette nº . . .). In the evening I went down to the end as I usually did. The lads were there and they said to me: 'Vonet, just look, doesn't it look like an airship?' Oh, yes, it must be one surely; the airship seemed to be floating, as we viewed its outline . . . I went back up at a run and called Tere. She came and we looked[;] it was floating and moving away etc. ahah, it is a good sign for us to see an airship here! Oho, you boches, just look. But can we be sure that it really is an airship? Oh, but what else would it be? But no, the cloud moved away and what appeared in its place? . . . The moon !!! Oh what a lovely airship. If the people on the moon only knew that we took them to be an airship!

Tuesday 17th and Wednesday 18th [August 1915]

Nothing. Tere is in bed.

133. In execrable French! (Trans)

Thursday 19th [August 1915]

There is a meeting at the town hall of the Municipal Council in order to decide what to do about the money. They were in session for two hours and during this time a Company with bayonets at the ready stood on guard in Place Turenne. It's unfortunate. The cat had her kittens in my bed: I shan't be sleeping in it but I shall sleep with Mimi instead!

Friday 20th August [1915]

Supplies are due tomorrow! No news.

Saturday 21st [August 1915]

No news. We went for the supplies, no salt this time.

Sunday 22nd [August 1915]

No fresh news. Le Gros gave a cross to the Church.

Monday, 23rd [August 1915]

Today's rumours are dreadful: Joffre has been killed: Poincaré assassinated. A revolution in Paris, the administration changed. It's idiotic.

Tuesday 24th August [1915]

There is a meeting of the [K]ommendantur of the Ardennes in Sedan and the regional chief is here: Reddern. We hear the cannon booming.

Wednesday 25th August [1915]

Memorable date. A year ago we heard the cannon booming very loudly!

1. already a year of occupation
For 365 days
we have heard the cannon
always, always, always.

2. yes already, already, already
for a year
we have not glimpsed a soldier
belonging to the good French nation

3. already already a year of horror
already a year of suffering
a year since our poor heart
has not seen its beloved France

4. Already a year since the barbarians
have soiled French soil
they will be leaving soon, because
they can no longer remain here.

Thursday 26th August [1915]

We celebrated the anniversary with a review. A soup offered in the workroom was much appreciated.

Friday 27th [August 1915]

We have read Albert's[134] proclamation, which is admirable, truly splendid, and contains some very fine and very consoling words!

Saturday 28th [August 1915]

We have gas [again] after 3 weeks without it! But there is so little that we cannot light it; the air has to escape first but tomorrow we will have gas.

Sunday, 29th [August 1915]

We have gas and we hear the cannon booming quite loudly; some men will probably be released.

Monday 30th August [1915]

We are still hearing the cannon, which is good, but there is no news which is very disagreeable!

Tuesday 31st [August 1915]

Nothing

Wednesday 1st September [1915]

Nothing except that we are still hearing the cannon and I don't know quite what it is that is eating me. It's disgraceful: two anniversaries with them: 1st September 1914 and 1st September 1915!

Friday, 3rd September [1915]

We went to Grandma's and we saw the wounded passing in motor cars and on foot, about 15 per vehicle, on top of one another and the blood seeping through their bandages with no doctors, dirty, etc.

134. The reference is to Albert I of Belgium, deemed to be the 'king-chevalier' by public opinion during the 1914-18 war.

Saturday 4th [September 1915]

Our grains (wheat, oats, etc.] go to the Garenne [135] where the boches thresh it, put it in sacks, and bring it back down while the lads get a knife, cut holes in the sack and the women gather it up on the way, so that on arrival the sacks are empty.

Sunday 5th [September 1915]

Nothing, still no fresh news except that we hear the cannon booming.

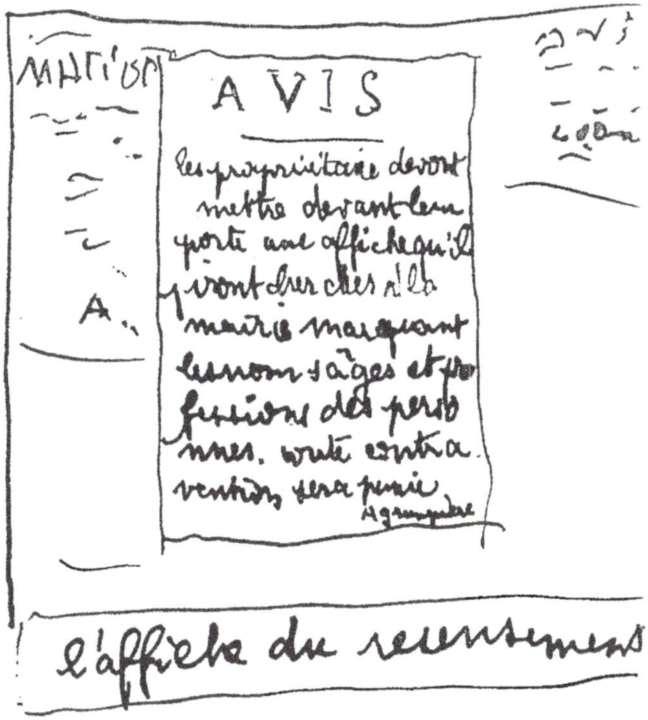

NOTICE

Owners are to display on their door a notice to be had from the town hall listing the names, ages and professions of the inhabitants, any failure is subject to penalty.

The notice about the census

Monday 6th [September 1915]

Mimi is 13 today. No fresh news.

135. Name of location overlooking Sedan.

Tuesday 7th [September 1915]

There is a notice: see the illustration and you will see more or less what it says [136].

Wednesday 8th and Thursday 9th [September 1915]

Nothing. No cannon.

Friday 10th [September 1915]

Nothing.

le hulan chargeant la foule à coups de sabre

The Uhlans attack the crowd with sabres.

Saturday 11th [September 1915]

200 officers have arrived in Sedan. They are in lodgings all over the town! It's a good sign.

Sunday 12th [September 1915]

We have neither meat nor milk. I wonder how one can live in Sedan. Grandpa went to Givonne to look for milk to smuggle. He brought back 2 litres. Wonderful.

Monday 13th September [1915]

We are hearing the cannon and trains are running continuously.

---

136. Text of the notice reproduced alongside the text in the original:
'Notice about the taking of a census'.
NOTICE. All householders must place on their door a notice copies of which they are to collect from the town hall, indicating the names, ages and profession of all: failure to comply will be punished.'
It was on the basis of this census that, throughout the occupation, the Germans were able to levy men and boys.

Tuesday 14th [September 1915]

We got up at 6 am and went for the potatoes in order to pinch them [ill.]. We came back at 8 am. soaked to the skin, like sponges! because it had rained and we had continued to dig them out, but we brought back a good quantity! Long pink ones. We'll be going back.

Wednesday 15th [September 1915]

I went for potatoes on my own. I brought back as many as yesterday, Magnum. We went twice again in the afternoon and brought back a lot of long yellow ones.

Thursday 15th [September 1915]

We went back for more potatoes and brought more. The boches came and took all our apples; they only left a fifth on each tree. It's shameful to take the apples.

Friday 17th [September 1915]

I went back to the potatoes with the wheelbarrow. I had got as far as the arch when I saw a crowd of people; I was wondering what was happening and I saw 300 women, men and children taken with wheelbarrows or sacks. I put mine behind the wash-house and mixed in with the crowd to watch the people pass; there were about one hundred of us when the Uhlan appeared on the scene, gave a few kicks and told us to clear off, drew his sabre and galloped his horse at the crowd, 2 people were hurt. It's disgraceful. I fled with Gentener (?) into the fields, I had a narrow escape!

Saturday 18th [September 1915]

We did not go back to the potatoes. Some people were released. No news.

Sunday 19th [September 1915]

For the whole town there are only 4 legs of meat. Neither meat nor milk, yet again!

Monday 20th [September 1915]

We have neither potatoes (because they take them all), nor meat and [to complete the picture], also 2 litres of skimmed milk which is going sour!

Tuesday 21st September [1915]

No cannon[,] no French[,] no milk[,] no meat[,] no potatoes[,] no bread! Thus are we hygienically cared for as regards diet!

One hides the little one has

Wednesday 22nd [September 1915]

No fresh news. Mr Douffet knocked and said in a low voice: 'Madame, if you have any potatoes, hide them as all the houses will be searched for them tomorrow['] so we hid the few we had[,] so were up till 10 pm that evening!

Thursday 23rd [September 1915]

Early in the morning 2 French planes flew over. We are swimming in hope! The boches searched all the houses and recorded all the potatoes they found and buy from us in order to sell them back to us, they did not come. It is 13 days since the boches entered brestlisof in Poland. Yesterday [ill.] [I] saw a boche newspaper which said: 'The Russians have established their head-quarters in bresticof which means that the [front] lines are in Galicia[137]! One continues to hope! Long live France!

Friday 24th September [1915]

We hear the loud booming of the cannon, German booms and French booms. The boches came for the potatoes, there are 50 kilos and they noted down 40K. (for them to take and sell back to us) it's unfortunate! People say that Vouziers is on fire! And certainly this cannonade is for us, so things are going well, very well, Sedan will be set on fire like Vouziers if necessary but it will be retaken! . . . One hopes! [138]

137. In fact, it was the Austrian army which had headed northwards and occupied Brest-Litovsk on 25th August. Yves Congar was perhaps referring here to the Russian counter-offensives during the month of September.

138. With the 2nd exercise book there was a map/chart bearing the number 5 and the name 'Frégaton'. The explanation is in a later style of writing 'Chart [made by] a member of an anti-boche association founded during the war; nicknames were used; this chart belongs to Henri Faquier' (a local friend of the Congar boys).

DIARY OF THE WAR 1914–1915

Third exercise book

Saturday 25th September [1915]

We continue to hear the cannon booming as loudly as yesterday but it is raining. People are saying that after a general stampede, the young people, seeing Vouziers burn at their feet, wanted to save themselves. 1) some escaped; 2) some went to Germany as prisoners; 3) some joined the French. Mothers of families whose sons are in Vouziers are frantic, running everywhere and asking where their sons are; no news.

Sunday 26th [September 1915]

No fresh news. We heard the cannon booming in the morning, then it stopped and began again after 4 pm, making everything rattle and hurting our heads abominably.
German dispatches and newspapers: 'The French offensive began 20 hours ago'. 'The French offensive covers the entire front and has been repulsed nearly everywhere[‘] (which means that they are withdrawing)[139]. Yesterday we made a bet with François Vauché (a ball or a picture) that the French would be here by Christmas (in 3 months' time). People are convinced that 'the young people of Vouziers are in the fodder store'; 'that the boche magazine is in Chalerange'; that 'Vouziers has been evacuated, that the cannonade is to our advantage and that it is killing a lot of people on both sides. A lot of wounded are arriving in the town. 150 were evacuated to make room for 5000 more. In Sedan there was 1 French and 2 Russian prisoners. The Frenchman, who was born in Bazeilles, had urged the Russians to escape. They succeeded, the Frenchman went to hide in Bazeilles where he was recaptured with his two companions and thrown into the fortress. A woman seeing them from her balcony called out 'Good luck', so she was fined. French prisoners passing through the station called out 'Keep hoping, and see you soon'.

139. The reference is to the French offensive in Champagne, which began on 25th September. Between the 25th and 28th, French troops in fact met with success along the entire front before coming to a halt. A second attack on 6th October encountered a second setback on Oct. 7th, on which date German counter-attacks began and continued all along the front until the beginning of November.

l'Enterrement des Patates !

The burying of the potatoes.

Monday 27th [September 1915]

We do not hear the cannon, or very little, no fresh news. There are lots of cars on the platform and Grandpa stayed because he was afraid they would want him in the undergrowth as has already happened 4 times.

Tuesday 28th September [1915][140]

We can still hear the cannon booming very loudly, but it has changed position. The weather is very fine. People say that in Charleville they have meat at 20 sous and butter at 30. It's half of ours: 56 sous and meat at 2 francs per joint when there is any [and] there is not ¼ of a crunchy biscuit in Sedan and in the whole of Sedan.

Wednesday 29th [September 1915]:

Mr Péret came to inform us that we are required to take our potatoes to the mill warehouses tomorrow: 40 kgs; we prepared 30! Even that is too much, much too much for the Boches, these Boches! Nothing for them, nothing!

Thursday 30th [September 1915]:

We went to deliver our potatoes, 20 kg on an army stretcher! We went to the Magasin du Moulin and it was closed! We will have to go back in the afternoon. It is detestable and we have to pay 3 francs and 45 centimes for that! It's disgraceful!

140. The name of the month was added at a later date.

Friday 1st October 1915.

Classes begin again. To begin with I went to the 6th but as there is no 5th I shall be going up to the 4th where I shall be fine: with the 3rd.

Saturday 2nd [October 1915]

No sound of the cannon; wood is still being brought down. A load goes by every day and sometimes several times a day.

Sunday 3rd [October 1915]

Still no sound of the cannon. They are still bringing down cartloads of wood. (Monday being the same as Sunday I have not written anything).

Tuesday 5th [October 1915]:

No sound of the cannon. The boches are demanding money[141], otherwise '. . . 'Emigration' . . . !' For shame, Wilhelm; for shame, you who claim to be descendants of Charlemagne, and you, Wilhelm, who call yourself protector of his crown and his name. But be quite sure, little emperor, that the Great Charlemagne, 11 centuries ago, would not have done such a thing; he would have said to the occupied people: 'Come, fill your houses with these foodstuffs and your spirits with this word: 'Charlemagne respects the vanquished!' 'Be quite sure, Teutonic people, that your conduct is cowardly, shameful, and that you ought to blush at having 'this dog' as a leader, and in fact on the other side of the Meuse: Vigne aux Bois, Donchéry, Torcy etc. have been evacuated, why? Seemingly because the French airmen would tear up the rails! It's idiotic on the Boches' part! So much the better! 'Keep at it, airmen, blow up the French railway lines!'

Wednesday 6th October until Friday 18th of the month [1915]:

No fresh news, we continue to attend classes; we have decided from now on that, in the evening, from 8 to 9 pm, we will read: so we will read: 1) our classics; 2) prose novels.[142]
It has snowed a bit.

Thursday 19th [October 1915]

Nothing-

141. This time it was a fine exacted in revenge for railway lines having been unbolted.
142. This reading took place at home under the supervision of Tere, Yves Congar's mother.

Friday 20th October [1915]

We hear the cannon booming. We are fed up of the war, because if the boches do not produce any new notices, the old ones still apply. We have read Molière, and are now reading Corneille.
What we have had.[143]
We have had potatoes at last when the supplies came, at last!
We have had bread, white bread, when the supplies came.
We have had a notice, about death by shooting, at the command HQ.
This notice says: 'anyone who hides soldiers will be shot'.

Saturday 21st [October 1915]

No fresh news. We hear the cannon.

Sunday 22nd [October 1915]

Nothing.

Monday 23rd [October 1915] –

We went to the distribution of supplies.
Let's have a brief look at the prices:

litre	oil	100 fr	before the war =32 sous
litre	chicory	44 sous	before the war =
litre	paraffin	4.50 fr	before the war = 7 sous
litre	millet	4.50 fr	before the war = 8 sous
litre	coffee	4 fr	before the war =
unit	1 candle	16 sous	before the war = 2 sous
pound	sugar	24 sous	before the war = 7½ sous
kilo	cocoa	10 fr	before the war =
1	eggs	9 sous	before the war = 2 sous.

In conclusion, everything is over-priced; the following are no longer available:
Milk – Sugar – Chocolate – Paraffin – Butter – Cheese.
For 10,008 inhabitants there are: 300 litres of milk plus [more like] white water.
Moreover, when the hospitals (which are supplied regularly) receive supplies, there is almost nothing left over (including the hospitals, there is a tenth of a litre per person).

Monday 23rd October [1915]

Nothing – the distribution of supplies.

143. This list appears to be in the form of a poem, though it is not certain that this was Vonet's intention.

Tuesday 24th [October 1915]

Nothing. Mimi is giving up German and will be taking English instead. The second winter will go by and, on New Year's Day, we will still be hearing the guns.

Wednesday 25th October [1915]

We still hear the cannon to some extent. Nothing else.

26th-27th Thursday – Friday [October 1915]

Cannon (very little). Nothing.

Saturday 28th Sunday 29th [October 1915]

Cannon – nothing.

Monday 30th Tuesday 31st [October 1915]

We hear the cannon booming very loudly.

Butcher's shop
The queue to secure some lights. [animal lungs]

December – 1st December [1915]

Life is always the same. I am going to try and give you an idea, and so I shall describe a day under German occupation.
At about 5.30 a.m.[144], one has to go and join the queue at the butcher's (when there is any meat) then, returning at about 8 am,

144 .At a later date, Yves Congar had inserted a 10 in place of the 5, thereby introducing a contradiction of what follows.

it is with great difficulty if you have managed to secure 1 kilo of lights, of *gorgeron*, or *gosillon*[145]; then one drinks what one has, milk if one has any . . .

One goes into the garden and wonders what we are going to eat. . . oh, the days when we saw a slice of meat on the table, a plate of potatoes, half a litre of milk, we gathered round the table looking round with wide-open shining eyes, saying: 'oh, oh, we have something to eat' and we were full of joy.

Sometimes we are visited by a boche.

At such times I go to class: classes in wartime, in the family, we have as teachers:

Monsieur Doin: History, Geography, French, Latin, Ethics.
Mr Claudel: French, Latin, Greek.
Mr Lacroix: French, Latin, History.
Mr Laroche: German.
The Abbot: German, philosophy, logic.
Mr Tuot: French, Mathematics.
Mr Gérault: Mathematics, geometry, arithmetical optics, physical electricity, chemistry.
Mr Collin; mathematics.
Mr Bouvier: English.
Mr Titiert: Natural sciences.
Mlle Pacot: kindergarten [infants]
Mlle Charlier: kindergarten [infants]

We normally return at noon – there we eat (if there is anything to eat) then we go out into the garden, we have tea, we work, we eat, then we go out into the garden for a bit and then we go to bed.

That particular day, we had heard the cannon booming very loudly and the trains going past all night.

The Boches in our place.

145. Probably local dialect words for some inferior form of meat.

1) men, train and cannon
are the foundations of the war
add in compassion money
you will have your fill
2) one wears everything out, during the war
men and money in profusion
all that, one hardly takes any notice
collisions, wounds and blows,
3) all that for sale during the war
the uniforms are in tatters
and patched in all kinds of ways
the men at the front are in rags.

(Yves Congar – 'during the war')

Thursday 2nd December – Friday 3rd – Saturday – 4th. Sunday 5th [1915]:

The cannon all the time. No fresh news.
Oh, my childhood pen
You could never write
all that I feel
and all that I would like to write . . . (Yves Congar)

Monday 6th [December 1915]

What joy! Alleluia: the boches are 'kaput'
they have been thoroughly routed!
A good meal! They have never had one like it! It is more than likely that the cannon we have been hearing for the past week is to our advantage – (in any case, I never doubted it).

Tuesday 7th – Wednesday 8th – Friday 9th Saturday 11th [December 1915]
No fresh news. The cannon continues to boom.

Sunday 12th [December 1915]

My sister has been called a 'postulant' oh! oh! The cannon continues to boom – no other news.

Monday 13th [December 1915]

1. Germans! You are fostering hatred
in the hearts of the people of Sedan.

and your good and human soul
finds it best to deprive us of milk
2. But just you wait!
In 10 years' time it will be
capital, interest, in gold
will be returned to you in cash!

In fact, for 10,008 inhabitants, we have 300 litres of milk. When the hospitals, day nurseries, charitable organisations and small children have been served, all that is left is the . . . 'the skin' (to suck)

Tuesday 14th – Wednesday 15th – Thursday 16th – Friday 17th – Saturday 18th – Sunday 19th [December 1915]

The same situation –the cannon still booming – nothing else. On Friday, Mme Rosinfeld lost 2 daughters in a few hours and the little boy is sick – they are to be buried on Sunday. It is so sad!

Monday 20th – Tuesday 21st – Wednesday 22nd – Thursday 23rd – [December 1915]

No fresh news. The cannon continues to boom.

Friday 24th [December 1915]

Christmas Eve! Once again with them this Feast, the next will be in Germany I hope because, after all, I have had enough of these boches . . .
The second Christmas once again with them! Oh, no, it is too much, and I have had enough. What more can I say? That they exasperate me, that it is shameful, vile. That next Christmas will be joyful, and then, afterwards? Always the same thing: all that I would like to say can be summed up in two words: hatred and revenge. Just that. You can detect beneath that a humiliating situation, and you will have a glimpse of life in the occupied territories.

Saturday 25th December [1915]

Christmas! Christmas! . . . Nothing.

Sunday 26th December [1915]

We went to see the crib in Fond de Givonne.

The Crib in the Annex.

Monday 27th – Tuesday 28th – Wednesday 29th

Thursday 30th – Friday 31st [December 1915]

The end of the year and beginning of another with them -oh well, they are going to fire shots to celebrate the new year: 'in France', in Ardennes' 'in Sedan'.

Saturday 1st January 1916.

In fact, in the evening, I went up to bed with the Big Ones and, towards midnight, shots were fired at a distance, then there were horses galloping, the firing came nearer, we heard the bullets whistling past: one bullet penetrated a beam of our house – we heard it embed itself in the wood – then nothing else except horses galloping – all of a sudden the devil of a racket – then little by little everything died away except one thing: my rage: I was pinching myself convulsively and I was foaming oh! I was growling inside myself, with my teeth clenched and I was breathing noisily and jerkily – I was furious.

Sunday 2nd January 1916

Really and truly, the United States are rather spoiling us – the supplies included tobacco for the men and chocolate for the women.

Monday 3rd [January 1916]:

We have some good news: 1) England has voted in favour of compulsory military service [146], and 2) Baghdad has been captured [147] – Well done!

Tuesday 4th Wednesday 5th Thursday 6th Friday 7th Saturday 8th Sunday 9th Monday 10th Tuesday 11th Wednesday 12th Thursday 13th Friday 14th [January 1916]

No fresh news about the war. No sound of the cannon. On Saturday 8th we withdrew the kings [from the Crib]. In Sedan there is not a single string for a violin.

Friday 14th [January 1916].

They have discovered a new kind of hygienic procedure! The following notice has been posted up: 'We inform the public that as the furniture in the officers' quarters has been damaged, they are to be replaced by surplus furniture that will be collected from the owners' dwellings'. It is disgraceful for the mayor to sign such notices.

---

146. In fact there was no conscription in the United Kingdom prior to this date, the English army having consisted up to then of professional soldiers reinforced by an immense number of volunteers (2,500,000 between August 1914 and January 1916).
147. In fact, between the end of November and the beginning of December, the march up the Tigris which the British forces had begun in 1915 had come to a halt and the British had been driven 250 km to the south, to Kut-Al-Amara which was being besieged by the Turks, and which fell on 29th April 1916. The town would not be recaptured by the English until February 1917 and Baghdad did not fall until 11th March.

Wilhelm and his son

My diary of the war is too long – it is becoming monotonous and the war too – so I will take advantage of this period when events take a long time to relate to jump from Saturday 15th January to Thursday 2nd March:

We hear the cannon booming accompanied by the loud sound of mines exploding. A piece of sad news: we have no potatoes!
Some good news to offset the above. The Russians have taken Erzeroum[148] so the boches, who never miss an opportunity, are saying 'Hooray! We have taken a fort in Verdun'[149], but we know about that trick; the truth seemingly is that they have taken a few farms following a fierce attack that they had taken a month to build up to, with immense losses, during which they were driven back. Oh! My aunt's house must be trembling. She has taken in a toad, a real toad, Mr Kurt Bendix, a doctor, oh sublime piece of luck!

And another piece of luck! We have found some French newspapers! French newspapers, mind you! They were surely dropped by plane[.] Oh! Oh! We are so pleased. We are finding them everywhere, everywhere they are appearing all over the place!

From 4th to 16th March [1916]!

We are again finding newspapers, and the boches have invented {a system} whereby they sell us chickens provided we give them eggs. I hope no-one will give them any. No other fresh news.

Joachim is getting married. May the anger of the Most High fall on him and his progeny! The night curfew extends to 8 a.m. now. To entertain themselves, Taïe,[150] and Mme Dâle meet in the evening at the home of our respectable baker, Mme Tuot.

The French newspapers.

148. Driven back by the Russians in the Caucasus, the Turkish 3rd army in fact lost Erzeroum on 16th February 1916. On the other hand, on 8th January 1916 the Allies managed to withdraw from the Dardanelles after suffering a total set-back.
149. The German attack on Verdun had begun on 21st February. The Douaumont fort fell on the 25th.
150. [cf footnote 7].

From 16th to 23rd March [1916]

Deserters are being shot. We hear the cannon booming very loudly, but one particular incident is notable: There were some officers on the Avenue. On the opposite side were some soldiers who had returned from the Front and were due to return there. Some cows were passing by; the soldiers clicked their heels and gave them a military salute, but when the officers passed, the soldiers did not salute.

'Les Soquettes'[151] is reserved for officers, but now the soldiers enter it without permission. When they are looking at the notices they cry out that it is false! That they are sending them to the Front and that the officers laugh during this time. We see them throwing weapons and bags in the street, insulting the officers. Just recently, there was a battle between officers and soldiers. Muller received bangs on the nose:

'Germany is on the wane'.

German Soldier.

Thursday 23rd – Friday 24th – Sat 25th – Sun 26th Monday 27th – Tuesday 28th Wednesday 29th [March 1916]

We hear the cannon booming very loudly. We sometimes manage to smuggle a litre of milk from Givonne. There is no fighting except at the Front, in the streets of Sedan, Place da la Halle; at the butcher's shop one can wait from 10.00 am to 1.30 pm in order to get n° 160 or 200! Sometimes the women fall down in a faint. In the evening, we stay up until 9 p.m. Tere reads and we listen, our readings are very interesting. The Turks are very unwell but their doctor, Germany, is also ill; as for his aide-major, Austria, he is too old and has gout! We steal from the boches the straps from behind their vehicles which they keep in front of the covered market. All is well, we are fed on hope and on rancour: those are our only supports.

151. A well-known café in Sedan, located in Place Turenne in the centre of the town, and close to the Meuse.

No straps.

Thursday 30th Friday 31st [March 1916]:

No fresh news, always the same old life . . .

Saturday 1st April 1916

One plays practical jokes today, although the cannon keeps on booming, all we think about is April fool tricks!

Sunday 2nd– Monday 3rd– Tuesday 4th– Wednesday 5th– Thursday 6th– April [1916].

There is a notice saying that all the French papers that have been found are to be brought to the 'Komandoche', naturally under very severe penalties; also 4 not very serious accidents.

Friday 7th – Saturday 8th – Sunday 9th [April 1916]:

The cannon is booming a great deal.

Monday 10th – Tuesday 11th – Wednesday 12th [April 1916]–

No fresh news – no sugar.

Thursday 13th [152] .... Tuesday 18th [April 1916]

Some boches have arrived with ovens from the Fond. We have had one staying with us, whose name is Baetzatel.

From Tuesday 18th to 29th (Thursday) April [1916]

No news except the Feast of Easter which I will write about later on.
Until the first of May, no fresh news except that people are saying that the boches have suffered a defeat in Verdun[153].

> They have suffered a defeat
> and we continue to hope
> indeed, we can even begin to say
> victory, victory, Victory.

The nose gets longer.

1st MAY ... 1916.

We hear the loud explosion of bombs – we shall surely know where, but the most important thing is that Papa is ploughing our land and has begun planting.

up to Thursday 18th May [1916]:

The bombs have hit the train station in Bouillon, wounding 2 or 3 boches, and de-railing 2 or 3 wagons and an engine! We have run out of oil. Our boche is really very funny, he is a roisterer and a libertine but he is not wicked.

---

152. Yves Congar's 12th birthday [Trans].
153. On the contrary, in April 1916, the battle of Verdun got bogged down in local actions on both sides of the river Meuse, without gain to either side. The same was true in the following month. In June, however, there occurred the last German successes in Verdun (the Vaux fort fell on 9th June, and Fleury on the 23rd).

from Friday 19th to Thursday 25th May [1916]

Nothing other than bombs and the cannon, in other words deaths . . . !
Yesterday, the patrol was hardly able to stand as they had drunk too much. I will tell you a story.
We were going up to the second floor when we heard shouts of Ah! Ah! Oh! Oh la la . . . [!] We looked out and [saw] the patrol passing: [they were] drunk and hardly able to stand; the first soldier fell holding out his arms to the other two. They took him by the hand and then fell little by little; they managed to pick themselves up; curious heads appeared at the windows, [and there were] bursts of laughter while the patrol continued on its way zig-zagging along, the soldiers stumbled, fell, dragged themselves along, leaned on their rifles, on the window shutters;
the laughter redoubled, an officer, a roisterer (the one from Mlle Faucheron's who, with our own, had returned at 2 am saying that they were going to die, that they would never drink again, and were sick) also fell down on the pavement opposite, we heard the heavy sound of his fall, he cried out: 'Matâme! [Kill me] To me, soldiers, I am dying' The soldiers had not the strength to go to him, they continued on their way, dragging themselves along and the officer sitting on his bottom on the ground, the object of the hilarity of the spectators . . .

There is talk of an attack on Verdun.

From 25th May to 15th June 1916.

We hear the cannon booming. 'Oh! Well, things are moving' – 'What?' – 'Don't you know?' – 'The Russians, for goodness sake' – 'Oh! And what are they doing' 'My dear, since the beginning of the offensive they have taken 116,000 of the Indomitable's soldiers prisoners! . . . ' – 'Ah! The Indomitable's old skin, he will want revenge' – Such are the remarks that people are making to one another. In fact, this was announced by the boches .... The number of prisoners taken was 164,000! . . . Things are going well [154].

from 15th to 22nd (Thursday) [June 1916]:

No fresh news:

22nd June [1916]

The French have taken 113,000 prisoners in Verdun; Madame Hocane (?) has been reported to the authorities and forbidden items have been found in her house. She has been sentenced to 6 months, until December!

From 22nd June to 1st July [1916]:

No fresh news – The number of Austrian prisoners continues to increase.

Today, Saturday, there is a lot of coming and going, cleaning of pathways, bringing of hangings, flowers, vases, planks, tables, lace, pins, carpets, barrels . . . etc. A visitor arrives: 'But what's going on?' 'Ah, it's true, you don't know, well, we are going to have a procession and we are making altars of repose, you can go and look; the traveller goes, we make pathways, we set up

154. The reference is to the Brusilov offensive which began on 4th June over a 350 km wide frontier and which enabled the Russian army to penetrate well into Bukovina, after having crushed the Austrian armies.

the tripods, the hangings, a continual coming and going enlivens the meadow [155]; in the end, the visitor leaves, dazzled. The next day, at the same time, between 2 lines of children and young girls wearing veils, followed by 4 altar boys, M. le Curé, wearing his chasuble and holding the host over his heart, slowly approaches the front steps, the children and the young girls follow and form a group, the Blessed Sacrament had been placed in our dining room: the procession formed up: first, the young girls wearing veils and singing hymns, then came the children, then the little girls throwing flowers, then the Blessed Sacrament, the young people and the rest of the faithful. The procession went twice round the meadow and finally stopped in front of the red altar of repose. On Saturday, before 4 pm, we had set up a red altar of repose for the Sacred Heart, it was a red and white cubic block, on which rested a raised structure filled with flowers and candles, it was made of red silk and lace, on top of which was a very high plinth supporting the Sacred Heart, both decorated with flowers, and below the altar of repose there was an abundance of ferns, flowers and ivy.

The first blessing was given there, then we went to the second altar of repose: this one had been made in 2 hours, with nothing, and it was the nicest of the 2, a second blessing was given there, the singing came to an end, the Te Deum was intoned, the 'Tantum ergo', etc . . . and then the procession returned as it had come. This procession made such an impression on me that I have described it here, the fervour with which one prayed for France, the attitude of recollection, the enthusiasm with which the altars of repose had been made, the single thought that united the spirit of all these people made me think of France, of the country that had been invaded, of revenge, made me dream of new horizons, a future, a mad dream, crazy, then a puff of smoke and that's all. [156]

from 1st July to 10th July 1916 –

No fresh news other than that today everyone has received an order to report to the town hall tomorrow to collect a questionnaire; just one word escapes us: 'at last! . . .' In fact, it is the first time that we have had some news, and we were beginning to get impatient. [157]

155. A stretch of grassland alongside a path on the Congar property.
156. Yves Congar was perhaps here referring to his vocation.
157. No correspondence was allowed either with unoccupied France or with the other occupied areas. So-called questionnaire-cards without envelopes were however permitted from time to time, but not on a regular basis.

Tuesday 11th until 14th July [1916]

. . . no news

14th July 1916.

The 14th July has come! Yes! ... splendid sun, black flags, peaked caps, all mixed together ...

Officer Sister Soldier

To celebrate our 14th July, we have something which comes from the fatherland: an example . . .
In fact, Mr Busson, manager of the gas works in Sedan supposedly convicted of spying and communicating with [unoccupied] France by carrier pigeon (in fact Mr Busson was related to Joffre and irritated them because he often expressed his opposition to the war laws) has just been shot. That is how the country sends to us for the 14th July the most precious thing she has, for it gave to Mr Busson the sublime courage which must serve as a model for us, he died with the (very Christian) words 'Long live France' on his lips[158].

What more is there to say? Nothing. All that I would like to say, I have already said . . .

158. M. Buson, the manager of the gas works, had in fact sent news to his wife in non-occupied France by a carrier pigeon which was intercepted by the Germans. He was shot behind the station on 13th July.

Aus dem Lazarett Turenne in Sedan

Turenne College converted into a hospital.

15th July [1916]:

The boches have banned access to the cemetery for 5 days as they are afraid there will be patriotic demonstrations, but as soon as the cemetery is opened again, we will go there to take flowers to Mr Busson, assassinated on the evening of 13th July 1916 by order of the German command. (in the evening) (Mr Delozaune was with him).

16 –17 –18–19–20–21–22–23–24th July [1916]

Nothing very special has happened, except for one thing: owing to the assassination of Mr Busson, the boches have put up shameful notices ordering the French almost to deny their country. Madame Ofuinchez's (?) maid called Sauvage and a neighbour of Mme Clarisse were talking together on the pavement. Five so-called French women who work in the sewing rooms against their country passed by, of whom 3 in particular were far from respectable. They stopped in front of the notice and burst out laughing. The 2 French ladies who had been talking together, were revolted at this and said 'I would much rather go collecting dung from the roadside than work for those dirty boches'. But the 5 hussies turned back in their tracks and went straight to the commandandoche [sic!]. The next day, this notice was posted up:

By a resolution of the council of war on the 27th inst.
The following have been found guilty of publicly insulting the German army and the workers working for the German army:
Mme Marguerite Clarisse, 2 rue du Ménil, Sedan
and Mlle Aline Sauvage, cook, 4 rue du Ménil
In addition, the latter endeavoured to encourage the said workers to give up their work.
For this reason they have been sentenced to 2 months' imprisonment less time on remand –

Signed:

Adèle Tellier –	rue Carnot	nº 3
Henriette Verlaine	rue Tiers	nº 5
Jeanne Leclers	rue Rovigot	nº 11
Charlotte Nouviaire	place de la Halle	nº 17
Madeleine Richard	Fond de Givonne	nº 36

here goes for the 15–16–17–18–and 19 July [1916]. now

We have decided to meet together with some friends every two weeks. We will put on comedies, play music, etc.

Thursday 20th July to Thursday 17th August 1916 –

Three major events have taken place just recently. Quite often, French aeroplanes fly over. One day we were in the vegetable plot when Robert said: 'Oh, there will be planes to night.' That evening, we were already asleep when we were woken by an unusual noise: 'the bombs'[.] – '[Y]ou Parisians, you do not know about bombs! [159] – a terrible din in the middle of the silence of the night, then you hear a very clear voice . . . the noise goes on, when suddenly the boche cannons bark lugubriously in the night, it is a revolting cacophony, the dull noise of the bombs mixed in with the noise of the cannon, the shrill rattle of the machine guns; we could hear the bullets whistling, if you looked out of the window the air was streaked with flames, fiery trajectories, we guessed there was a plane overhead . . . after 2 minutes, nothing . . . 3 minutes later, we heard a throbbing in the air and we could say to one another: 'It's there . . . ' Then, the cacophony began again, then afterwards . . . then nothing more . . .
The first time, the bombs fell on Maltournée [160], a house was left without windows, then in the fields all around there were huge holes, and the vegetables in the area had been torn to pieces or burnt.
But, not long afterwards, we were woken during the night by tremendous booms from the cannon, 'more bombs'. The thuds were terrific, [and] as earlier on, in between the thuds we clearly heard the sound of voices then, this time, the sound of breaking glass and [other] noise[s]. Then we heard Papa, who was probably going to see . . . shortly afterwards he came back: 'the bombs are falling to within 40 metres of us [161] . . . there were hundreds of broken windows . . . the next day we went to see the damage: the façade of the Vautel house has collapsed, 2 bombs on the Raux dwelling . . . behind, about 2 m. from a house, a hole measuring 2m by 5 . . . in a garden, an enormous hole . . . on Mon Idée [162], a bomb had fallen on a narrow path, Robert rescued 2 rabbits. And no-one killed . . . in one case a fragment had penetrated a bolster . . . In the Raux' house, there was shrapnel in the children's bed . . . but none of them was injured . . . There was a man living on the ground floor in Mr Raux' house; this man

159. This passage has a note in the margin, written in a different and later hand, 'They learned it later'.
160. Located on the road from Sedan to Givonne.
161. The first figure written, and then crossed out, was 100 metres.
162. One of the high places surrounding Sedan and overlooking the Congar property.

UNIVERSITÉ SEDANAISE

4 à 6 artistiques et littéraires.

Matinée du 24 Août 1916

PROGRAMME

L'Arlésienne de Bizet { Menuet. / Farandole. (piano 4 mains) – Mlles Y. Laro et M. Congo

« Sur la Jeanne d'Arc de Fremiet » de Deroulède – Mr Y. Congar.

Mélodrame, de Piccolini (violon) – Mlle M. Laroche.

Le Piano – (poésie) – Mlle M. Vauché.

Bonheur parfait / Marinari } de Schumann, (piano) – Mlle M. Congar.

Le sabre du Colonel – (monologue) – Mr J. Vauché.

Final, de Haydn – (piano) – Mlle Y. Laroche.

Un grand soliste (dialogue).

Messieurs R. et Y. Congar –

La nichée sous le portail, poésie de V. Hugo – Mlle M. Laroche.

Souvenir, de Drdla (violon) – Mr H Facquier.

La vieille horloge, de Botrel – (poésie) – Mlle M. Congar.

Samson et Dalila – (piano 4 mains) – Mlles Facquier.

Le vieux ménétrier – (intermède) – Mr P. Congar.

En écoutant tomber la pluie – (piano) – Mlle Y. Facquier.

On cambriole.

Saynète de P. Ginisty.

Mlles Y. Laroche et M. Vauché – Mrs J. Laroche et F. Vauché.

Un rêve de P. Déroulède. Mr C. Stocanne

Programme for a show arranged by the Congar children and their friends at the suggestion of Yves' mother.

The Boches in the Ardennes.
In order to keep warm, the inhabitants gathered wood in the forest.

(Sedan, Fond de Givonne, winter, 1916).

ns les Ardennes
vont chercher le bois à la Forêt
onne, hiver 1916)

is so very deaf that, the next morning, he was amazed to see his ceiling on the ground, shrapnel in his room, his window panes broken, his furniture overturned . . . he had heard nothing, in spite of the fact that within 1 m. of him, shrapnel was raining down and 5 bombs had exploded round him . . . it was miraculous! Then a third time, the bombs fell in the priests' garden[163] . . . not much damage, but . . . now we are sleeping downstairs in the dining room which, being a wartime dormitory, is filled at night with the sound of snoring.

17th August to 6th September 1916.

Russian and French victories have been announced[164]. Romania declared war on Germany 2 days ago; the boche newspapers maintain that 300 Romanian cannons have been captured . . . Have the Romanians actually got 300 cannons? . . . plus a great many prisoners. On the contrary, it would appear that it is the Romanians who have penetrated well into Austria if, however, they manage to hold onto it. But these boches don't care much about that, just think, they need to capture strong towns, castles (in Spain)! So, they announce that they have taken a strong place with prisoners[165].

6th September 1916 to the first of October 1916 – no fresh news.

1st October 1916 to 10th October 1916 –

We have had an artillery officer lodging with us. 'It seems' that the cannons are to follow. For some time we have been amusing ourselves by making toys as prizes for the catechism classes. The milk supplies are pathetic: we have no more than half a litre of milk per day for six people, when we have it and what is more, the milk goes sour –

11-12th October –

13-14th, 15th 16th 17th

18th-19th-20th-21st

22nd-23rd-24th October 1916

We go regularly to the vegetable plot and it will soon be ready. Two things have happened: 1) a defeat for the boches in Verdun – 2) boys aged from 14 to 16 are to go to Macdonald[166] to learn a trade if they have not already got one.
We have gone back to school and we are entitled to biscuits: 24 per month!

163. A walkway along the length of Sedan castle.

164. Yves Congar may here be alluding to the relative French success in the Battle of the Somme which began in July 1916, or else to the halting of the German offensive in Verdun which occurred in this same month of July. The recovery of territory lost by the French since February only occurred between October and December 1916.

165. Romania entered the war on 27th August 1916, and its army immediately went on the offensive in Transylvania. Towards the end of September, the Romanian army suffered a serious defeat. Bucharest was taken on 6th December.

166. Military barracks built in 1770 and later called after a famous French general who was born in Sedan in 1765.

From Sunday 29th October to Saturday 18th November [1916]

Children from 11 to 14 years have been summoned to Macdonald[167] in order to learn a trade if they are unemployed. I have been summoned [but] I won't describe the scene as it would take too long. Recently, there have been some French aeroplanes, the boches shot at them for a long time, then when everything was over, the alarm bell rang and the gas went out. There is no need to tell you that the boches rushed into the air raid shelter. We have had no gas for the past two days and we are giving ourselves light with what's left of the paraffin in order to do our homework and an old smelly candle in order to read.

The boches want to make Poland independent [168] by installing a German king! . . . it makes you laugh in their faces.

People are now obliged to declare their coppers, bronzes, zinc, etc . . . and woollens! Grandpa is very upset; he had held onto them up to now, and now they are to be taken from him! The warehouse is going to be used! . . . It's a shame.

No other fresh news, except that Mimi is also going to have biscuits.

From Saturday 18th November to 8th December 1916.

It's disgraceful; I am incensed: the boches are taking all the sheets, pillow-cases, serviettes, tablecloths, etc . . . we are to bring a list of all these items to the town hall! . . . [W]e are declaring only 18 pairs of sheets.

Our family now has an extra member! A noble cousin called Arthur Pletz (!). this dear cousin has sent us news of Mr Girardin, Mme. Girardin and Mlle Girardin. We are very pleased! . . . Madame deloffre has received a photograph of her husband. Today, the 19th, we heard that Romania had declared war on Germany, 8 days later Bucharest was taken, but we put no faith in this last piece of news which is idiotic.

There is an important piece of news. We are all to be photographed. The photograph, costing 13 sous per person, will be attached to an identity card and the said identity card will be taken by the said person whenever he leaves his 'domicile'. If, during the operation consisting in your being photographed, the said person or rather the said Patient on whose stomach the German authority will have stamped a number corresponding to that on the identity card moves, the said patient will be sentenced by the said German military authority to a fine of 2 marks[169].

Today, 7th and 8th, the boches are testing grenades.

Friday 8th December to Sunday 17th December 1916

Germany has proposed peace [170]

Each country is going to send a representative to The Hague to discuss the conditions.

In reply to this proposal the French have captured 7,500 men and 28 cannons at Verdun

167. See footnote 166.
168. On 5th November 1916, Germany and Austro-Hungary decided to turn the Polish territories taken from the Russians into an independent kingdom of Poland.
169. Yves Congar kept the Personal Ausweis issued to him on 1st January 1917, bearing the number 01504. He was thirteen years old.
170. The reference is to the German peace proposal of 12th December 1916, which was rejected by the Allies on 30th December 1916.

From 17th December to Christmas 1916.

Yet another haul! Copper, rabbits and chickens. Rabbits and chickens are uncapturable:

Ils sont insaissables	they cannot be seized
mais non pas insaisis.	but they are seized just the same

Yet more boche prisoners taken at Verdun: 11,000, which is quite something, plus some ground; it is always the way: 'little by little, the bird makes its nest'.

CHRISTMAS, 25th December 1916.

No snow –I have nothing else to say . . . It would be superfluous! All that I have to say, I have already said, anything I might say would be pointless. Just realise this: when I do get to Germany this will be my motto:

'no mercy, no quarter'.

End of the year 1916

For the rest of the diary, see
exercise book nº 4 [171]!

171. This last page of exercise book nº 3 was twice countersigned by Yves Congar, as he did in the other diaries. Similarly, the back cover. Yves Congar seems to have been sure, from the beginning, that his diary would one day be read.

Diary of the 1914–1918 War

By Y Congar born on 13th April, 1904

Who witnessed the war.

Written in Sedan

Fond de Givonne n 85.

Ardennes in the year 1917

... from 1st January 1917 to .....

‹I will insult their eagles,

Their caps, their emperor'

(V Hugo)

Cover of the fourth exercise book.

Wohnort: SEDAN
Domicile:

Listennummer: 01,504
Geprüft:

Stempel der Kommandantur

Personal-Ausweis
Certificat d'identité.

Name: Congar Yves
Nom

falls verheiratete Frau oder Witwe: Maedchenname:
pour femmes mariées ou veuves: Nom de jeune fille

Geboren am: 13 avril 1904
né le

zu: Sedan
à

Staatsangehoorigkeit: Française
Nationalité

Wohnort: SEDAN
domicile

Strasse: Fond-de-Givonne Nr. 85
rue

Beruf: s.p.
profession

Groesse: 1 m 57 cm
taille

Besondere Kennzeichen: Néant
signes particuliers

Eigenhaendige Unterschrift: Congar
signature personnelle

Dieser Personalausweis berechtigt nicht zum Verlassen des Wohnorts.
Ce certificat d' identité n' autorise pas à quitter le lieu de domicile.

Ausstellungsort: SEDAN
Délivré à

Datum: 1 JAN. 1917 191
date

Der Unterzeichnete haftet fuer die Richtigkeit obiger Angaben und die Identitaet der Person.
Le soussigné est responsable pour l'exactitude de la déclaration ci-dessus et pour l'identité de cette personne.

Unterschrift des Buergermeisters oder seines Vertreters
Signature du maire ou de son adjoint.

Cachet de la mairie.

Stempel cachet

1501

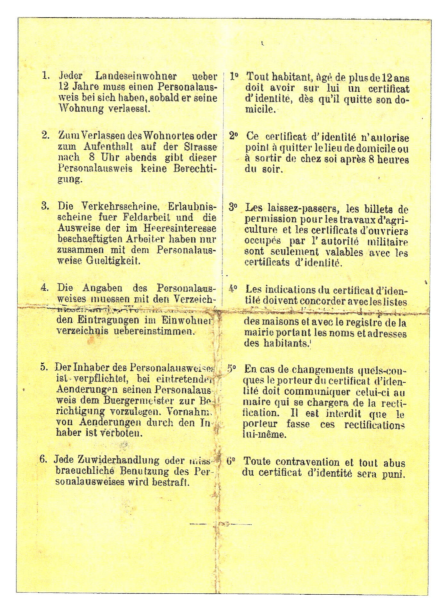

1. Jeder Landeseinwohner ueber 12 Jahre muss einen Personalausweis bei sich haben, sobald er seine Wohnung verlaesst.

2. Zum Verlassen des Wohnortes oder zum Aufenthalt auf der Strasse nach 8 Uhr abends gibt dieser Personalausweis keine Berechtigung.

3. Die Verkehrsscheine, Erlaubnisscheine fuer Feldarbeit und die Ausweise der im Heeresinteresse beschaeftigten Arbeiter haben nur zusammen mit dem Personalausweise Gueltigkeit.

4. Die Angaben des Personalausweises muessen mit den Verzeich- [illegible] den Eintragungen im Einwohner verzeichnis uebereinstimmen.

5. Der Inhaber des Personalausweises ist verpflichtet, bei eintretenden Aenderungen seinen Personalausweis dem Buergermeister zur Berichtigung vorzulegen. Vornahme von Aenderungen durch den Inhaber ist verboten.

6. Jede Zuwiderhandlung oder missbraeuchliche Benutzung des Personalausweises wird bestraft.

1° Tout habitant, âgé de plus de 12 ans doit avoir sur lui un certificat d'identité, dès qu'il quitte son domicile.

2° Ce certificat d'identité n'autorise point à quitter le lieu de domicile ou à sortir de chez soi après 8 heures du soir.

3° Les laissez-passers, les billets de permission pour les travaux d'agriculture et les certificats d'ouvriers occupés par l'autorité militaire sont seulement valables avec les certificats d'identité.

4° Les indications du certificat d'identité doivent concorder avec les listes [illegible] des maisons et avec le registre de la mairie portant les noms et adresses des habitants.

5° En cas de changements quels-conques le porteur du certificat d'identité doit communiquer celui-ci au maire qui se chargera de la rectification. Il est interdit que le porteur fasse ces rectifications lui-même.

6° Toute contravention et tout abus du certificat d'identité sera puni.

Diary of the War by Y. Congar 1917

1st January 1917.

No fresh news except that, like last year, we met together at Mme Quinchez'. There we forgot for a while the nightmare of the war, but this nightmare took over all the more the following day.

2nd January 1917:

Barbarity! Shame! Vengeance! Hatred! . . . When in Germany a woman, an old man, a child pleads for mercy from the conquering French, you will reply: 'January 2nd', and you will kill. In one stroke is too little.

January is better!

-(V Hugo)

Romanians! [172] men! Prisoners! The wounded . . . have been massacred. For days and days on end, the boches have been dragging prisoners through the mud of their towns. These men have fought, these men have given themselves up, and the boches have dragged them dying of hunger and exhaustion for weeks on end, they threw them into a station for 18 days[173] without food . . . They have driven them on with rifle butts, the wounded were falling, and those who fell died! . . . Today is the day on which these corpses who had been soldiers arrived in Sedan.

They were dragging themselves along, and those who were just about able to walk were holding up the dying . . . when food was thrown to them, they gathered the little strength they had and threw themselves on it four at a time, and then it was a battle between them , the strongest knocked down the others and snatched up from the mud an apple, a piece of bread . . . during this time, a boche grabbed his rifle in both hands and rained blows with his rifle butt on the back of a wounded man like a woodcutter with his axe . . . Another held with a trembling hand his jaw that had been broken by a blow from a rifle butt, while from the windows the officers laughingly threw to these weeping men their empty cigarette boxes, on which the Romanians pounced [174]

....

172. This presence of Romanian prisoners in Sedan is clearly related to the collapse of the Romanian offensive after the month of September 1916. All the witnesses agree with that of Yves Congar concerning the fate of the Romanian prisoners who in effect were condemned to a slow death by malnutrition. The town was to be ordered to pay 50,000 marks in compensation for the sympathy it had shown and the assistance it had provided. It should be pointed out that the way in which the Romanian, Italian and Russian prisoners were treated, differed from that meted out to the French and English prisoners: these differences in treatment, as yet not fully acknowledged in the histories of the First World War, would seem to derive from an 'ethnic' hierarchy established by the Germans between the different peoples against whom they were waging war.

173. This figure was altered to 14 at a later date.

174. In connection with this episode, there is, in exercise book n° 3, a loose sheet written probably in 1923 which runs as follows: 'I later learned of the betrayal of which these poor Romanians were victims. Sturmer, the president of the Russian Council, in connivance with Germany, allowed the Russian Dorna Vatra (Bukovine) army to remain idle and did not provide the support troops that had been promised to G[eneral] Iliesco, the Romanian leader, thereby provoking the retreat of the Romanian armies to Sereth and the conclusion of a separate peace (ill.). Stienon: The Romanian mystery Take Jonesco: Souvenirs, 1919.

They were falling down dragging themselves along, some not getting up again[175] . . . men! To see men crying! brothers beating one another! Dying of hunger . . . no, it is a dream . . . the reality is before your eyes, there is the reality: men dying of hunger . . . before your very eyes . . . what use are the bread and apples that you throw to them, just look, they throw themselves onto it, here, a policeman takes the bread and marmalade and throws it into the ditch . . . this bread which might have kept a man alive . . . look there, a wounded man stopping his blood with his hand, which is pouring out and turning the ground red . . . the wounded man stops . . . then falls, a sentinel beats him in the small of the back with his rifle butt and kicks him in the stomach . . . look, see there, a corpse, a woman holds out a piece of bread, she is given a blow with a bayonet and there, in the window an officer laughs and says 'Romania Kapout' . . . see over there 3 soldiers, 3 corpses fighting over an apple, a Romanian officer comes along, thrusts one aside, knocks back another and knocks down the third and takes the apple, look there, a soldier whose blood is pouring out is crying, holding his hands up to heaven, a woman throws him some bread, he throws himself onto it but the blows of a rifle butt knock him down and he falls bleeding to the ground . . . one of his brethren, in order to get hold of the bread, hurries up but a kick brings him to the ground, he rolls over, a comrade comes along and there, in the mud, begins the battle under the blows of the rifle butts, the man who has just fallen is mutilated, he dies [176]?................................

Just look, embed this picture in your hearts, this dream which is truly terrible in that it will be repeated a few metres further on . . .

And in the evening, one heard, while walking in the streets, a series of cries, laments and, seeing blood at their feet, we said to ourselves: 'the Romanians'.

3rd January, 1917 – Some people have been arrested who, because they had hearts, had thrown food to the Romanians, a crowd of people has been arrested and fined either 50 or 100 marks. I admire the replies of some of them who like Mme X . . . the baker have told the boches who were asking for bread: 'I have none' 'Yes, but you gave some to the Romanians'. 'I have bread for the French and for the Romanians, but not for you'; or like Mr X . . . who abused them for half an hour. However, the boches are afraid there will be an uprising as they are going to evacuate several thousand of the Romanians who are in Sedan.

4th January 1917. Friday 6th Sunday 7th

The French have declared that there will be no peace with Germany unless it is defeated. All the occupied countries who have nothing to eat are unanimous in being prepared to suffer everything, on condition that they achieve victory, we will endure our suffering to the end for the sake of the fatherland and no truly French heart will complain when it is a question of safeguarding the well-being of the nation. – The boches have invented a new way of getting hold of foodstuffs and money, all the hens must pay their tribute: one egg per hen and per week, or 55 cm per hen and per week; fortunately Tere did not declare hers and we will pay nothing and give nothing. There is no doubt that they are looking for money, even without the help of the shameful denunciations. Recently two boches called on Mr Deglaires, the veterinarian, and gave him news of his brother and sister. Mr Deglaires was not sufficiently cautious. He received the news and thanked them for it. Then in the course of the conversation with them, he was led to the subject of the news: the boches asked him when he had heard it, from where, the date and so on . . . then, perceiving that Mr Deglaires was conducting a secret line of communication through Belgium, they took him to the Kommandoche and Mr Deglaires is now in prison. It would appear that there are French people who have denounced him – we

175. Above the dotted line, added in the same later handwriting already referred to, are the words: '3 people dead in the street'.
176. Here the question mark and the underlining seem to have been added at a later date.

Soldier Officer

even know who; yes! A fine job these informers are doing: 55 people in prison as a result! Mr Deglaires, his brother, his sister and 52 others who were involved in maintaining the line of communication!

There is no longer any point in recording day by day, event by event, the things that are happening under my eyes, it would be too boring and moreover, I won't do it; it is sufficient for you to read these lines to give you an idea of how we are managing to live.

Flamands be

The Boches in the Ardennes.
Flemish Belgians in line – Removal of the tram lines in Sedan.
(Fonds de Givonne, Spring, 1917).

.es Boches dans les Ardennes
:olonne - Enlèvement des rails du tramway à Sedan
onds de Givonne, printemps 1917)

A monotonous life, repeated day after day, constant humiliations, not enough to eat, deprived of real news for 3 years, fed up of constantly hearing the same noise, the boom of the cannon. Seeing only boches, always boches, a state of moral exhaustion, a bodily lassitude made all the worse on account of being unable to leave the town, always on the qui-vive and under an unjust regime; here you have quite a rosy picture of life in the occupied countries. Calamity after calamity, humiliation after humiliation: [N]early 35 cm of snow, a fierce frost which causes the deaths of hundreds of Russian and Romanian prisoners, the Belgian prisoners who work on the road, mal-nourished and inadequately clothed, digging a ground which is as hard as reinforced concrete, the seizure of the dairy cows and the horses, the shooting of 400 Belgians who were refusing to work, hunger, lack of gas, the deafening boom of the cannons, a 20° frost, reduction in the bread ration, the withdrawal of biscuits from the schools, the closure of the college, the death of friends and the lack of news of one's relatives, the death of near relatives whom one loved, always the enormous number of deaths among the Russians and Romanians, the order to blackout the windows so that no light shows outside, the threats of imprisonment and fines in marks, the wretched bread, yet more news of deaths in all classes of society, the lack of food and, when you do find some, at an exorbitant price if the seller does not want an exchange, because now it is exchange or nothing.
a lot of people forced out of their homes to make space for Messieurs the officers, a revolution in Russia [177], unrest among the people on account of the lack of food, thefts in the cellars and the fields, the compulsory requisition of items made of copper, bronze, works of art, zinc, etc. subject to a fine of 5000 marks and 6 months' imprisonment, 9-month imprisonment of the Pingard's son for having struck a boche who wanted to force him to work etc . . . etc . . . All this is not designed to make one love this atrocious , monotonous, inexorable life! . . . I would never get to the end if I wanted to describe all the humiliations of which we are the victims – the worst of all is still the monotony, to be without news for 3 [whole] years. Being locked in, it is dreadful, indescribable, it causes a moral lassitude, a lack of drive, of energy which gnaws at one's spirit and prevents one from thinking! Oh when will this war be over! – (21st April)
One could endure everything except this moral lassitude if one had enough to eat, but what have we got apart from the rations? Nothing! And then, the compulsory requisitions, the requisition of items in copper. Against the French! Yes, we are forced to do it! Oh, you French, do not come and say to us after the war: 'It is shameful, you semi-boches, who are working for them' because we will reply: 'Why were you so cowardly as to abandon the soil of the fatherland[,] you who had sworn to defend it until death?' I really have nothing special to tell you because, when I began this diary, I thought I would be doing it for 3 or 4 months, and lo and behold this horror called war has been going on for nearly 3 years:[178]

Can't you hear in our countryside
the mooing of these fierce soldiers´
who come right into our arms
to take away our sons and our companions!

177. The reference here is to the abdication of Nicholas II and the formation of a provisional government on 15th March 1917. Until the summer of 1917, people continued to believe that not only would Russia continue the war but [that it] would increase its effort: in May 1917, a communication from Kerenski to the army ordered them to free Russian soil and, at the beginning of July, Broussilov conducted the last Russian army offensive in the direction of Lemberg over a 150 km front.. This was broken during the latter half of the month.
After the Bolshevik revolution of 7th October, which accelerated the process of the internal break-up of the army, the Russians demanded an armistice on 26th November and it was signed in Brest-Litovsk on 5th December, 1917.

178. There follows a sentence which has been crossed out: 'Having taken from us everything that we possess materially, the boches are still taking our young people and . . . '

Yes, they are taking our sons away from us! yes, they are taking our companions from us[,] they are requisitioning the young people of Sedan, in all classes of society[,] to go, in a temperature of 41° [179] to dig excavations for 14 hours at a stretch beyond Glaire, yes, they take hundreds of young girls to go out into the burning sun to make hay and weed the beetroots!! What an abyss! What a responsibility for these army chiefs.

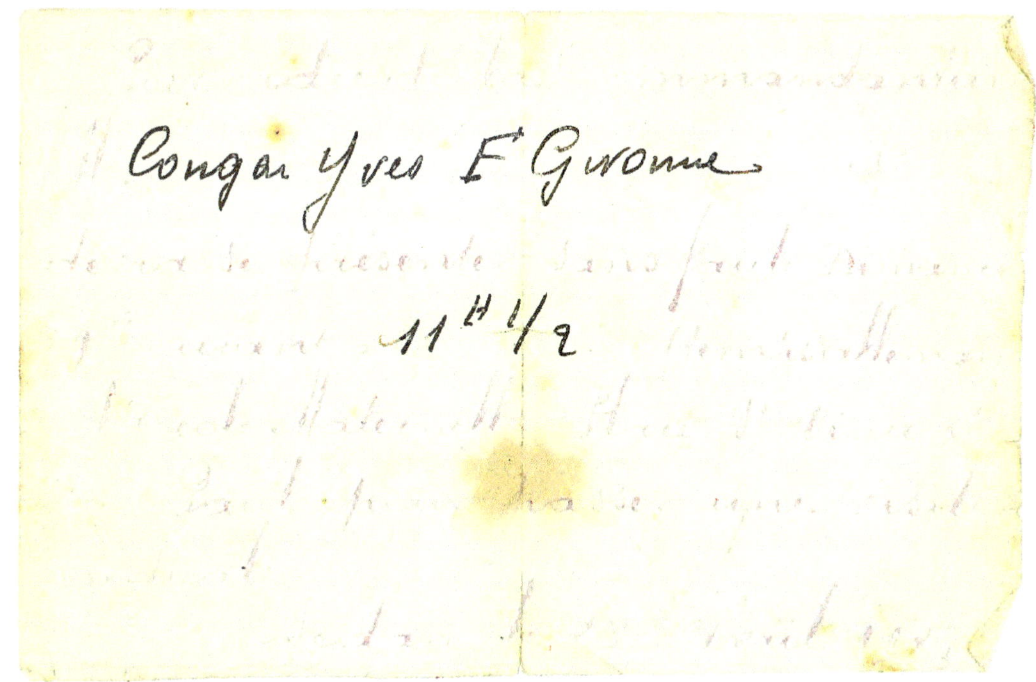

Congar Yves F Givonne

11 H 1/2

By order of the Commandantur
M Congar Yves F Givonne N° ...
is required to present himself without fail on Sunday the 9th inst at 11.30 am (German time) at The Infant School, Place St Vincent de Paul to undergo a medical examination.
Sedan, the 28th April 1917.'

19th March – 14th April, [1917]:

We have retaken Coucy, the castle that the boches blew up. America has declared war on Germany[180], it is a great blessing because even though America has not got vast numbers of troops, its immense resources will be a great help to us; here too we must make sacrifices for the Fatherland, because who will make sure we receive our rations? Apparently about a hundred women armed with old shoes and brooms went to the town hall in order to force the mayor to distribute the supplies that the American events are forcing him to hold back! What sort of people will there be after the war, then? What a hold the police will have to impose in order to keep the crowd under control!
In order to make up as far as possible for the lack of supplies, the mayor of Sedan is arranging for land to be distributed to the inhabitants for them to cultivate themselves[181]. Thus, both rich and poor, all working for a common end, for the sake of life, are

179. This reference to the high temperatures when the author was writing in the Spring might make one think that he was here referring to events which can only have occurred in the previous year, in 1916, In fact, however, the passage from 21st April – 14th May 1917 shows that this was not so.
180. The United States entered the war on 5th April 1917.
181. Two hundred square metres per person were distributed to those who wished, the seeds being supplied free of charge. But the yields were often very

stooping to work. One sees the classiest of people going along the Fond de Givonne pushing a wheelbarrow: a car is a luxury, because most people only have children's push chairs. This spectacle, so sad if you think about it, nevertheless has a certain pleasing piquancy to it. The search for items of copper has begun in Balan and La Cassine[182]; one is obliged to declare everything one possesses made of bronze, copper, tin, zinc, etc. and show it to a Jewish expert, no need to say more about the person who will determine the value.

14th April to 21st April 1917.

Not much to report. The boches have very little to eat[.] Germany is sinking, and people generally are saying that we will not have to face another war-time winter

21st April – 14th May:

This year the Archpriest of Sedan will confirm the children on the 13th – with a temperature of 37° in the shade.
Great events: the treatment meted out to girls has been extended to boys. Everybody must report to [P]lace St Vincent de Paul in order to be assessed as fit or not for work, and it is being said that these people have the inexhaustible capacities of men! These young people, mercenaries at 2-3 Fr per day, are going everywhere in a torrid heat to work for the enemy, on inadequate rations and working 14 hours per day.

14th May – 21st May 1917:

My brothers are working. Pierre at the Station and Robert in Dijonval [183]; so they are separated from each other, and although Pierre's work is both harsher and dirtier than the work at Dijonval, Papa is trying to bring them together; as regards Pierre's work, I remember quite a lot about it, and I am entrusting it to my memory so that I can call it to mind when I recopy in these pages the idiotic and mind-deadening works that 'German hygiene' is offering to our young people.

21st May – 1st June 1917:

No fresh news. The Russian revolution, far from adversely affecting our brave allies will work in their favour because the party which has the upper hand wants all-out war. Moreover we keep on hoping and the boches are very low: the morale of most of the soldiers is very low and one of our rationed biscuits (50 gr) costs ½ mark in Germany.

1st June – 3rd June 1917:

Once again this year, the procession of the Sacred Heart will be in our place, all of us, burning with zeal, will be setting to work, because our work will not only be for our own benefit, but also for France, our fatherland which we want to be great and victorious: the grass will be cut, the pathways weeded, the wreaths made, the ornaments made ready as if a fairy hand had touched all the objects with her wand.

---

disappointing, due to lack of experience on the part of the population.

182. Balan, neighbouring commune to Sedan, La Cassine, the western suburb of the town.

183. Famous cloth factory established in 1646 by Fabert.

The wages at the station are 4 fr, while Robert's is 48 sous, but these payments could never make up for the boredom the Big Ones are enduring on account of this forced labour.

9th June [1917]:

Robert has at last been admitted to the Station; the work they are doing is worthy of I know not who. Most recently they unloaded a wagon filled with bones, there were cockroaches all over them, the bones were already green and decorated here and there with shreds of rotten flesh swarming with vermin and the rotten flesh smelt, while the juices issuing from all this rotten stuff was being turned into vapour by the heat of the 47° temperature and was filling the wagon with a fetid stench. [Moreover], being obliged to touch these horrors and this filth with their hands, these baccalauréat students from Turenne College, deprived of Virgil and Homer, were able to savour the delectable juices of rotten bones and putrid flesh.
One of the greatest concerns and distractions is the collecting of old books, pieces of leather, material, nails, etc . . . but not of foodstuffs. The workers are all filled with the same zeal and wreaths of ivy and bouquets of flowers appear as if by magic to decorate our altars for the procession.

Sunday 10th [June 1917]

It is the great day of the procession. Early in the morning the garden was filled with people, the platforms were prepared, the wreaths were hung in place, the carpets rolled out, the pretty decorations were joyfully suspended, a noisy and happy throng of young people examined all the preparations, the sun itself helping those working for the good God and encouraging them with its golden rays, the whole garden was filled with life when suddenly a few drops of rain, then . . . a downpour; the raked paths became torrents, the paper wreaths drooped their heads sadly. Joan of Arc, whom we could not protect, lost her colours, on all sides it was a headlong flight, each one seeking some kind of shelter; what a shame, such a lovely procession and everything was all ready, in vain we waited until 5 pm, no ray of sunshine came to say to us: 'Come now, the good God only wished to try you'; the procession was put off until the following Sunday.

Saturday 16th June 1917:

We began again to work for the procession although there was less enthusiasm: the Big Ones were working all the time at the station, the heat was unbearable, and it was under these temperatures that people were going, shovel and stick on their shoulder, to cultivate the earth which was to nourish them. However, these workers are not rewarded as they should be; people steal things from the fields and the people under pressure, having gathered the peas, do not consider potatoes beneath them. None of that encourages us in any way, all the more so in that 50 grs. of bread are to be taken from us just when we have most need of it to help us recuperate from the gardening, the work and the heat. But in spite of all this, we will not give in and the boches will not have the glory of having made us say: 'Have pity!' No, we will stand up to them and will suffer for the grandeur of France!

Sunday 17th [June 1917]:

It is the day of the procession: walking in front are the altar boys leading the procession, then the children, the smallest at the front, followed by the girls from the sewing room and the girls' choir chastely wearing white veils and singing the Lord's praises, then came the little girls, all dressed in white who, digging into a large basket, were scattering flowers before the Blessed Sacra-

ment, gleaming in the hot summer sunshine: It was carried by M le Curé who walked slowly over a carpet of roses, and sheltered under a superb canopy; a battalion of young people followed, and their male voices, like the voice of the new France, mixed in with the young voices of the Children of Mary, rose towards heaven in religious unity; finally, the crowd of the faithful, deeply recollected, brought up the rear of this pious and worthy procession. There were 3 temporary altars, one dedicated to Our Lady, where white was mixed in with blue in perfect harmony, another to the Sacred Heart where the superb red hangings were highlighted by the whiteness of the lace, and the 3rd was dedicated to Joan of Arc, to France. How many prayers, wishes, appeals were addressed to heaven throughout that day. Undoubtedly, God will reward this fervour by granting to France a period of prosperity and victory.
Apparently, Greece is in revolt and France has triumphed in the Balkans [184]. So much the better, and may the boches depart from our midst!

Sunday 24th [June 1917]:

The boches are calling up more people to work in the fields. Mlle Stocane and Mlle Thoéry have been ordered to help with the haymaking! Moreover, at the college some of the students have been ordered to go out to the surrounding area to cut and remove the leaves from the nettles in order to make cloth! . . . Robert is to do his exam tomorrow. Let us hope he does well and that it counts!

Sunday 1st July 1917.

We have picked a lot of green peas which are very good; the new carrots are also excellent. However, it is shameful the way people, under the pretext that they need to live, destroy the work of others and steal from them what they have toiled to produce; we ourselves have suffered from this ignominy; we estimate the damage to have been 30 potato plants! The town hall is becoming concerned, and some of the gardeners are authorised to keep watch at night for their own benefit! We suspect the boches of the theft from ourselves because, from the highest to the lowest ranks, they steal everything. Our doctor's orderly himself steals foodstuff from his officer that he has purchased in his name in order to sell it on. Poor Germany! As for Russia, the revolution that the German newspapers depict as being the key to peace only succeeds in embedding them deeper in war: the offensive is about to recommence. May God protect this enterprise and confound the barbarians!

Saturday 7th July 1917:

The Big Ones are relaxed at the station; they have no work, and in fact 5 of them including Rouy and Brégi have been released completely: let us hope that they too may be released completely. Today the Big Ones went walking in the property and went as far as the Lecomte wood, poor wood that has suffered much from the hand of man![185]

---

184. On 12th June, the Allies secured the departure of King Constantine of Greece. Thereafter, their position on the Eastern front was much improved.
185. The winters during the war were extremely cold in the Ardennes, while there was a chronic shortage of fuel. There was very little coal available and the people tried to alleviate the situation by taking wood from the Garenne and Lecomte woods.

Sunday 8th [July 1917] –

The harvests are quite good in our garden blessed by the processions: the peas are coming on very well and, although for us too, getting enough to eat is an ongoing problem, we are feeling sorry for the poor people from the town who come early in the morning to line up at the doors of those who have ground to cultivate. It would be difficult to describe these queues for you: a score or so of people with bony arms are waiting at the door: holding string bags because we can see through them what people are carrying, little by little the people enter into a barn where a peasant weighs out their meagre provisions of vegetables,; but although getting in is difficult, how to get out is much more so, people press forward as you pass 'What have you got?' 'Are there any vegetables?' 'Let's have a look';' 'and potatoes'; 'Are there many people?' 'There are carrots'; 'Oh, what lovely leeks'; 'how much for a bunch of turnips?' 'Whose place have you come from?' – Ah, the poor people who during the winter [186] were having to eat nettles! When will we see an end to these abominable things? May this emperor, the cause of all our ills, endure the most atrocious torments and may Germany be erased from the map of Europe!

Sunday 15th July 1917

The Big Ones are continuing their forced labour under the supervision of detestable corporals. Rouy and Brégi whom we thought were so lucky have been taken on again and are working at the Grosselin factory making oil cakes, a disagreeable job if ever there was one.
The Varnéville (?) organs where the priest in charge is in Balan have gone to the Kreigsbeutesammelstelle[187]. Rouy and Brégi, following a petition, have been released, Jean Laroche[188], too, on the pretext of helping his father in the print works has also been given his freedom. Really and truly, what a life we live here in Sedan under the heel of the foreigner who himself is very poorly fed.

Sunday 22nd [July 1917]:

The Russians are advancing in Galicia and the cannon is booming quite loudly on our side. We are obliged to fight an unceasing war with the boches who are invading our garden, and it is with considerable pity that we put them out; it is becoming boring to have nothing to write in this diary: no fresh news, it is really distressing.

Sunday 29th [July 1917]:

Serious troubles in Germany[189]. The people are fed up with the submarines which on paper are sinking hundreds of ships but are, in fact, producing very little effect[190]; after the serious debates in the Reichstag [191] and the troubles in Berlin, William having been wounded, Bethmann Hollweg, the great orator, has resigned and a nonentity, Mikaëlis[192] has replaced him as Chancellor!

---

186. Above the word 'winter', the word 'Spring' has been written in a later hand.
187. For:'Kriegesbeute samelstelle' (Central war booty depot).
188. A friend of the Congar children. His sister, Gabrielle Laroche, was to marry Pierre, Yves' older brother.
189. Yves Congar is making a double allusion here to the great wave of strikes in Germany during the months of July and August, as well as to the dismissal of the Chancellor Bethmann-Hollveg on 12th July, on direct orders from the supreme authorities.
190. Yves Congar is here referring to the resumption by the Germans of outright submarine warfare, beginning on 1st February 1917. This produced considerable results against the British Navy during the first half of the year 1917, before encountering a serious setback in the months that followed.
191. On 19th July, a majority in the Reichstag voted in favour of a peace resolution proposing the renunciation of all territorial gains.
192. The correct spelling is 'Michaelis', who was imposed as chancellor on 14th July 1917 by Hindenburg and Luddendorff.

In the town a sensational notice has been pinned up: the seizure of everything there is in Sedan, copper, bronze, rubber, buttons, zinc and drainpipes, iron, aluminium basins, saucepans, bath tubs, candlesticks, fire guards, fire surrounds, rubber stoppers and motor cars! Germany is very low. Also displayed is an order governing the cutting of wood, Thursdays and Sundays are the days selected, so this morning, very early, a procession of carts and wheel barrows wended its way towards the wood and came back down towards evening, loaded to the brim. At the station, there has been quite a theft: books; Pierre put them to one side, then, with two companions, he went to collect them: this sudden addition to his library delights him, being, as it were, a small compensation, he who loves books, which is but small compensation for the fatigue and the time wasted in this forced labour. Really, what a responsibility the leaders of Sedan are heaping on themselves; we can only hope that, later, we will punish them severely and we will wreak our revenge on Germany!

July 1917 – has come to an end – Thursday 2nd August 1917:

Pierre has a well-deserved holiday, because the work is tough and our food is not very nourishing. They are now loading up the bells and organs in the region, and they have asked the arch-priest to de-consecrate those of St Charles [193]. Poor idiots! Most of these bells have a glorious past, they have seen the reign of the Great King [194], they have proclaimed the glory of the conquerors of Valmy, their cheerful peal rang out at the proclamation of the empire, their funereal knell marked the moment of the [18]70 invasion, and now, by order of an impious emperor, these sacred objects which marked the time for our souls, are destined to be used for vile purposes.

Sunday 5th August [1917]:

We have learned with dismay that the distribution of food, already so parsimonious, is to be even further reduced. The boches had wanted to have the potatoes for 10 fr per 100 kilos [but] those who had grown them not wanting to sell them at this ridiculous price, are refusing to supply the vegetables. In order to get hold of some[,] people are offering amazing prices: it has happened that vegetables are costing 30 sous per bushel (instead of 4). Bread too is going to be reduced to 290 gr. per day: really and truly, for people working, for men, it is very little; the soldiers have more than double this (750 gr.).

Sunday 12th [August 1917]:

China has declared war on Germany [195]. It is a good thing because even though the Chinese soldiers will not be a great help to us, the low-paid workers that they will secure for us will be a great help. It would seem that the boches, who are short of soldiers, are going to retrace their frontier by withdrawing everywhere by 25 km. Oh, may these 25 km multiply! Grandpa had succeeded up to now in keeping his warehouse intact, and it cost him a great deal, after keeping them safe for 3 years, to be forced to declare his balls of wool which had become very valuable. It is today that they are going to be taken from him. People are talking today about gas: apparently the boches are going to cut it off everywhere: this has already been done in Torcy; really, with all these unpleasant things we are faced with, they could spare us that; how are we to light up without gas and without electricity? The bells of the region are continuing to be turned into war booty [Kriegsbeute] where Pierre and Robert are wasting their time in amongst the rubbish and are not doing their studies and are wearing themselves out 'for the king of Prussia'.

---

193. Central church in Sedan.
194. Louis XIV, known as Louis the Great or the Sun King.
195. In fact, China declared war on Germany on 14th August.

Wednesday, 15th August [1917]:

Things are ready for the procession: a superb altar has been erected, mounted on a huge and imposing platform, the garden has been filled from early morning by the young girls who are coming to put the finishing touches to the wreaths: the garden has been transformed: not a single weed in the paths, garlands of banners made of a combination of ivy, roses and other natural foliage, have been carefully suspended in the trees which had been carefully trimmed back, the grass in the meadow has been properly cut: everywhere there is a great bustle, the sky is blue, although some clouds are visible on the horizon, and finally, at the last moment, the altar is feverishly completed: everything is ready:, the altar decorated when, all of a sudden, there was a downpour, the water ran in rivulets along the ground and everyone went indoors for Vespers, people's faces registering their consternation, and it was with a downcast look that we celebrated the Office; but deep in our hearts we were still hopeful and prayed earnestly that we could repair the damage in the twinkling of an eye and begin the procession. The Blessed Virgin took pity on us and sent us a ray of sunshine to encourage us. In the twinkling of an eye, the banner was brought out [196], and the trestle made ready [197]: the sun sent by the blessed Virgin dried the trees and the procession formed up, the steady verses of the parish hymn rose up to heaven and were addressed to the Most High like the mist that rises from the earth, the Magnificat, sung by the sweet voices of the Children of Mary summoned the Christian to prayer; one felt a desire to kneel on the earth and opening one's heart to embrace and to love everything around us; in conclusion, after M. le Curé's sermon on the blessed Virgin and a blessing[,] the singing of the young girls accompanied the statue of Our Lady to the place where her Son dwelt. Everyone being exhausted after such a full day, and having tidied up the things that could not be left, we had a rest, because the Big Ones will tomorrow have to return to their customary toil.

196. Note by Yves Congar: 'The new banner bought by the parish was painted by Mlle Misset.'
197. Note by Yves Congar: 'The white and gold trestle had been made and painted thanks to Mr François Vauche, a well-known driver in the parish.'

21st August – Tuesday [August 1917].

A hundred French prisoners passed through the station.

Friday 24th [August 1917]:

The French offensive has succeeded [198]: it seems that we have advanced at 4 points. The next day we learned that our advance had been accompanied by prisoners: 7,000, people are saying, whereas on the Italian front [199], 10,000 Austro-Hungarians are prisoners.

Saturday 1st September 1917:

Disastrous day on which, half a century ago, the French army came up against the German army: memorable date and one which calls for vengeance. Fortunately, the boches did not celebrate it to any great extent [200].

4th September [1917]:

They claim to have taken Riga [201]. What a story! Wilson [202] has sent a strong reply to the Pope's proposal in favour of peace[203]. It is very hot. Robert and Pierre have fierce colds.

Friday 14th [September 1917].

The boches are again claiming that they have taken RIGA. Apparently there has been a change of ministry in France: Mr Painlevé is said to be the new Prime Minister [204].

Monday 17th September 1917:

The headmaster has submitted a request on behalf of his workers: we are impatiently waiting for the reply. There are some glimmers and it seems legitimate to hope for a release in the near future.

---

198. The reference is undoubtedly to the French attack on both sides of the Meuse, which was launched on 20th August over an 18 km front and which penetrated to a depth of 3 km.
199. The reference here is to the eleventh battle of Isonzo which began on 18th August and which resulted in an Austrian counter-attack that began on 24th August.
200. The reference is to the 'Sedentag', a national feast day in Germany since the German victory over France in 1870-1871, which commemorated the French defeat in Sedan on 1st and 2nd September 1870.
201. The reference here is to the German attack on Riga which began on 1st September, the town itself being entered on 3rd September.
202. President of the United States who was re-elected as President in 1916.
203. The Pope's appeal for peace dated 1st August 1917, to which the Americans replied on 27th August, saying that they could not trust 'the present rulers in Germany'.
204. Painlevé succeeded Ribot on 10th September.

Thursday 27th [September 1917]:

They really are employing the college students to do a wide variety of jobs. Guess where Goffient is working ? . . . he is a driver at Teathy's. The headmaster is persisting in his requests: he has been given 3 hours per day for his workers then a half-day, but can one be sure that it is in good faith? When, oh when, will we be rid of the Germans? If that could happen soon, we would light fires of joy, we would dance, recover our former energy, but no, we are disheartened and at the same time one continues to hope in France, one hopes in something miraculous: in God.

Tuesday 2nd October 1917

On Sunday, we went for a walk, and we have heard today that the headmaster has been shown the door: all hope is lost!

Saturday 6th [October 1917]:

On Thursday, Pierre and Robert loaded up the Sedan bells[;] they were thrown out from the windows of the bell tower and made a huge hole in the ground: today it is the turn of the bells from the temple.

Sunday 7th [October 1917]:

Robert is 17 years old today! It is icily cold and there is torrential rain. Tomorrow, the 8th, the big ones will be loading up the bells and organs from Balan and Sedan. It really is a shame, regrettable, wretched, infamous, ignominious, I just can't find a strong enough term to describe it: the boches, this race that I hate, but with a fierce and deep hatred, are allowing the civilian prisoners whom they have torn away from their families to die of hunger: go and see the graves in the Sedan cemetery. You can count them in hundreds; no, you can't count them, they are countless; the big ones have seen with their own eyes prisoners foraging in a manure heap onto which the boche bakers had thrown their refuse!

Wednesday 10th [October 1917]:

The big ones are loading up the bells from Torcy. There is also another shameful thing, a disgrace: the town council: it is stealing from its citizens whom it ought to be protecting: when supplies come, it pounces on them and then distributes what is left, if there is any, to the populace.

Thursday 11th [October 1917]:

The big ones are loading up the ornaments of the Don le Mesnil church. In the Reichstag there is a great fuss: the socialists are demanding to know from the emperor, that bandit, why he is making war? They all want peace. Only in peace will they find true life [205]. In the midst of all our concerns we have heard a really sad piece of news: the death of Pierre Mousty, poor young man, who had volunteered and has died gloriously for the fatherland. The headmaster is continuing to submit protests, which are always refused.

205. The reference here is to the socialist representations to the Reichstag on 6-8 October on the pan-Germanic propaganda in the army.

Saturday, 20th October 1917:

Murder of the Lepage maid. This maid, due to an unaccountable choice, had grown fond of a Flemish prisoner; one day this prisoner went to see Mme Lepage and told her what had happened, declaring that the maid had been unfaithful. The latter was in the next room and, taking advantage of the fact that the mistress left the room, the prisoner went into the room next door and plunged a dagger into the maid's back, who fell down uttering loud cries. It is not necessary to say how much fear there is of the Flemish now . . .

21st October – Sunday [1917]:

A photograph of the young people of the parish surrounding the parish priest was taken at 3 pm.

22nd [October 1917]:

The headmaster's complaints have borne some fruit: the students are to have every other afternoon free! It is very little, but it is better than nothing: you should see the college: there are only a few students; the lessons are not very interesting.

Tuesday 23rd [October 1917]:

The big ones are continuing to load up the bells from the region, no other news –

Thursday 25th [October 1917]:

The French have taken the Malmaison fort near Soissons [206] and the booty includes 17,000 prisoners and 25 large-calibre cannons. It is a small victory for which we rejoice.

Saturday 27th [October 1917]:

The French have shot down 4 Zeppelins; otherwise no fresh news either at the front or at the station, nor amongst ourselves: always the same life.

Sunday 28th [October 1917]:

Adoration [of the Blessed Sacrament] in Fond [de Givonne].We are praying for France and the Allies: the boches claim that they have defeated the Italians[207]; it's not true.

---

206. The reference is to the successful attack on La Malmaison, on [the ridge of] Chemin des Dames on 22nd-23rd October, which resulted in the taking of 11,000 prisoners and the capture of 150 cannons.
207. The reference is to the breakthrough of the Italian front by the Austro-German forces at Caporetto on 24th October, which resulted in a withdrawal to the Piave, 140 km to the rear at the beginning of November. The attack of the powerful centre was not overcome until mid-November. 300,000 Italians were taken prisoner.

Tuesday 30th [October 1917]:

A horrible rumour, a stupid report is going round: the boches have taken 100,000 Italian prisoners! It's all a joke!

NOVEMBER

Thursday 1st November 1917:

Today is All Saints Day: the Big Ones ought not to be having a holiday, but they have taken one. The weather, which is superb, makes it possible to go to the cemetery: what a grim spectacle: one can count the Russian, Romanian, Italian and French graves by the hundred! So many prisoners have died of hunger: just think about the last moments of these poor people, victims of the barbarity of a nation which claims to be civilised and of an impious and blood-thirsty emperor! Surrounded by comrades who are moaning, their limbs only skin and bone and calling for bread, the poor prisoner thinks of his home country, he sees once more the corner of the earth where he was born, he reviews his all too short life: his mad escapades in the hills, his running races with his friends, he sees again the time when as a schoolboy he more than once cursed the wise men and their knowledge, then came adolescence, he thinks of his girl friend whose lovely face, in his mind, joins that of his old mother: where are all these dear creatures? Perhaps they too have become the victims of a merciless soldiery! His father may well have been shot and be lying dead in some corner, his girl friend perhaps pursued by the advances of an enemy officer! And he, poor prisoner, no longer hears the moans and groans of his companions, his head is spinning, hunger tortures him, he asks, opens his mouth to speak but cannot do so: something to eat, I am hungry, I am dying, have pity – there is no pity for the weak – call a priest – you'll get over it – some bread – in 3 hours – but in 3 hours I shall be dead – what do I care – broken by these words, the poor prisoner falls back onto his pallet, he shivers with cold, he cries with hunger . . . What can he do: die! Die, yes, die far from his own, abandoned by all on foreign soil. Ah, if his old mother were there, how she would cradle him in her arms and comfort him, but there is no-one, he is alone: he calls out, then falls back . . .He lies there now under this cross of black wood: may he rest in peace.

Friday 2nd [November 1917]

The big ones are paid.

3rd [November]

It amounts to the abuse of young girls: 30 young girls from Hanchecourt [208] and Remilly have been brought to Sedan to work; the girls from Floing are in Bazeilles! It is disgraceful! In general, life is very disagreeable and monotonous, cabbages fill the saucepans and dominate every meal, one has the everlasting sensation of being hungry even though one's stomach is full, the rations are reduced month by month: what will we find ourselves eating: hope!

---

208. i.e. Angecourt, a village to the south of Sedan, close to Remilly.

Tuesday 6th November 1917:

Fear of the Flemish is everywhere, stories are told about them, some of which are undoubtedly the fruit of people's imaginations whereas others describe real attacks on people. But what can one do? These people are dying of hunger. Whose fault is that? The boches, these villains whom I hate. I can't find the words for it, I would crush my pen on the paper in attempting to write it down: I hate this race from the bottom of my heart. So, the Flemish have robbed the Lanceraux bakery and attempted to murder a man returning from work in La Garenne. You can guess the fear they instil into people. Every day after lessons, the young people, with sticks, escort the ladies home. Seemingly we are to receive 3,000 emigrants whom the boches intend to evacuate from Chemin des Dames.

Thursday 8th Nov. [1917]

Seemingly there is to be a departure for France in the near future. What a blessing for these people who will be returning to their Fatherland. The headmaster, who is very depressed on account of the rejection of his demands, intends to emigrate. Mr Gout, H. Goguet, [and] Lombard are also going.

Sunday 11th [November 1917]:

In Fond we produced a little show for M le Curé entitled: 'The judgement of St Peter', the 'talented' composer was my elder brother. We are going to adoration in Balan. It is a very poor tribute. News from 'Chemin des Dames': we have taken 24,000 prisoners there.

Wednesday 14th [November 1917]

The story is that the Crown Prince is going to live in Seville with the Benoîts [???]. It would seem that the Italians have regained the advantage and have advanced 20 km. The boches are spreading the rumour that Painlevé has resigned [209]: it is not true! We have also been told that the headmaster intends to emigrate. He is not to blame for that because he has his pension, moreover he is separated from his family and gets nothing but refusals for the petitions he has submitted. Mr Laroche, the German teacher, will take his place; our first thought is that the college is going to be very easy-going as this man is very lazy.

Friday 16th November 1917:

Grandfather has approached Captain Marthaus, for whom the two older boys are working, in an attempt to secure the afternoons for them, but the Captain's reply was: 'Find substitutes for them; your grandsons will be the first to be released'. It is unacceptable for honourable citizens to report on their fellow citizens. The boches have taken 3 hostages in the town, no-one is quite sure why; some people are saying it is because the forthcoming exodus has something to do with it. The hostages who have been taken are: Courtehoux, Gillet from Fond de Givonne and our cousin Lucien Qinchez who views his situation calmly, looking upon it as a point of honour. At the station, Pierre has got to know a Russian from a military school whose name is Michel Lebedeff. He is a very distinguished young man who speaks French and German, moreover we have noticed that, on the whole, the Russians

209. The Painlevé administration lost its majority on 13th November. Clemenceau succeeded him on 15th [November].

tend to be big and strong and that they have a remarkable gift for 'patching up' their clothes with bits of rag; generally speaking, they are nice people for whom I have a strong liking [210].
The most ridiculous rumours are the result of gossip among other things: the caretakers are telling one another as a great secret that the Avenue is going to be cleared for the Crown Prince whom I have no hesitation in sending to his majesty Pluto to become a shadow in the dark underworld of Tartarus!

Monday 19th [November 1917]:

Winter lessons recommence. The gatherings in the evening are getting longer; each one takes his or her place around the family table, really what a joy it is for us to be together up till then.

Tuesday 20th [November 1917]:

L. Quinchez is expecting to receive his official orders from one day to the next. We are quite anxious as we do not know how long this separation might last. In Germany, Mikaelis has been dismissed and replaced by von Hertling [211]. Their newspapers which made so much of the changes in government in France are casting the cloak of Japheth over this change [in Germany].

Wednesday 21st [November 1917]:

Fortunately, Lucien has not yet gone, provided he remains here. Gillet has found a way of getting himself removed from the list on the pretext that he would be leaving his mother all alone; it is a cowardly trick, it is a desertion in the face of the enemy, and does him little honour. He has been replaced by Mr Picquart the notary. The English, our allies, have managed to advance in the north: near to Cambrai where the boches, our hated enemies, have withdrawn 9 km [212].

Friday 13th November [23rd November 1917]:

The English are advancing everywhere. In Asia Minor they are 19 km from Jerusalem. If they capture that, it will certainly be a good thing because the name [of Jerusalem] is known everywhere and the repercussions of such a seizure would be regarded as a stunning victory [213].

Saturday 24th November 1917 :

Marthaus is refusing the afternoons: the bastard. We have had a visit from Bächtel about whom I have written where and when appropriate. Seemingly the boches have been thoroughly trounced at Lens and St Quentin. We have had a lot of snow in the past few days.

---

210. It should be pointed out that Yves Congar enjoyed the companionship of Russians when he was a prisoner during the Second World War. He even began to learn Russian. Might one be seeing here the beginnings of his interest in Orthodoxy?
211. The Chancellor, Michaelis, resigned on 29th October 1917. He was replaced on 1st November by Count von Hertling, who also had close links with the military.
212. The reference is to the surprise attack by the English in the direction of Cambrai which began on 20th November using tanks and with no preliminary bombardment, which penetrated the Hindenburg line by 8 km and secured 8,000 prisoners.
213. The British forces gained control of the high ground close to Jerusalem on 21 November. They entered the city itself on 11th December.

Wednesday 28th [November 1917]:

Bethlehem has been taken. The English have taken 10,000 prisoners. Seemingly the hostages will not be going: so much the better!

Friday 30th Nov. [November 1917]

Pierre has produced a canticle for the Children of Mary. The boches are saying that Russia is seeking peace [214]; I don't believe it and I regard this silly story as a joke; moreover, Lebedef laughs in the faces of those who mention it to him: 'Russia making peace!! For goodness' sake!'

1st December 1917 – Saturday:

The Flemish are continuing to attack isolated people: hunger brings the wolf out of the wood. The cannon is booming quite loudly. The big ones are still working; today is pay day.

Sunday 2nd [December 1917]:

Today, Sunday, they worked until 10 [pm]. They are very tired and will soon be going to the doctor. Today the soldiers of the great Germany have a succulent meal: the Russian peace! What a story! All the people from the town are coming up to the Fond with children's prams in search of vegetables; it is quite touching, but basically not at all a laughing matter[215].

Monday 3rd December 1917:

Robert went to the doctor and was given 4 days. There is frost and it is very cold. Pierre will soon be following Robert's example. The boches are famished with hunger and are as badly off as we are and that's saying quite something.

Wednesday 5th [December 1917]:

It is very cold, 10° below zero: it is magnificent winter weather; what snow there is makes the branches of the trees white and intermingled like lace. Pierre went to the doctor and has 3 days off work and some medicine to take (a phial) every 3 hours.

Friday 7th Dec. [December 1917]

The boches believe in the Russian peace. They dine on it and are nourished by it! It is freezing! They are searching for copper and are taking everything; at the Laroches, they have taken the lamps and the handles of the piano which they pounced on at once.

---

214. On 26th November, Russia asked Germany to enter into negotiations with a view to an armistice. Germany and Austro-Hungary accepted the Russian proposal on 29th November and the armistice was signed on 5th December in Brest-Litovsk. The peace treaty would not be signed until 3rd March 1918.

215. There were a number of gardens under cultivation in Fond de Givonne.

Saturday 8th Dec. [December 1917]:

We have heard with deep regret of the sudden death of Bernard de Jonge: still quite young and who has been killed by the hard work the boches forced him to do in Glaires; he used to get up at 4 a.m. have his meal down there under the hot sun and return in the evening! Damned race! A suicide in Sedan: Mme Canaux threw herself into the water one does not quite know why, [and] her body was found near the Sedan mill. At the Pouplier in the Fond, people whose house was burned down, 500 kg of potatoes have been stolen! It's a [serious] loss! One can almost tell where that came from, they have 8 German lodgers, which says everything! . . .

Sunday 9th December 1917:

It is today, the Immaculate Conception, that the canticle Pierre composed is to be sung:

> Happy those who can find shelter under your wing . . .
> May our souls on this day be pure in your eyes
> And following your immortal footsteps . . .

The celebrations in the Fond are admirable, we have really made the best use of the small chapel. It is being said that there is an allied conference in Paris [216]; if only it could lead to peace! There is talk of Japan joining in.

Monday 10th Dec. [December 1917]

There is shortly to be a departure for France and another for Germany, this being . . . the departure of the hostages (L Qinchez, Courthoux, Picquart); our best wishes go with the first, our tears accompany these latter.

Tuesday 11th December 1917

It is this morning that the departure for France is scheduled. In addition to the 3 hostages, the boches have arrested some of the town mayors. M De Montaigne, aged 70, was summoned and kept as a hostage without seeing his family again. We have been told that the hostages will not be going; they are at Charles Antoine's and Jardin is cooking for them.
People are saying that the next supplies will include poultry.

Wednesday, 12th [December 1917]:

Jerusalem has been taken! This capture will have great moral effect. Tales are going round the town, started by the boches – the famous Russian peace! What nonsense! The emigrants have gone. Isn't it shameful? They will arrive in France and will there be at their ease and before they left, they were fed like princes! Mlle Hubert, one of the emigrants, will not be going; her case had a double bottom, so she will be in prison for 2 years. One man had gold pieces hidden in his mouth. The boches have taken lead weights in clothes as hidden gold pieces. Idiots!
The Big Ones have seen Lucian out walking in the town with a boche. The boches are uneasy about the Russian peace, they believe in it, yes, but . . .it is not quick in coming!

---

216. The reference is to the inter-allied conference that took place from 29th November to 4th December.

Friday 15th [December 1917]:

The supplies do include poultry. The Big Ones are still working on detestable wagons at the Station. Nasty dirty boches! Things have been re-arranged: formerly, they ate their bread at home and had a biscuit at 10 a.m., but now they have a good bowl of soup in the morning and will eat their bread at 10 am (German time). What a lot of re-arrangements.

Wednesday 19th [December 1917]:

All these days have been very cold, real wintry weather. We are cold and hungry, cold all the time, and hungry both before and after eating. Mr Roup, who is staying with Grandpa, has an officer lodging with him. Flocks of cranes are flying past, dismal messengers of winter, alas!

Friday 21st [December 1917]:

At last! Some butter, flour and chocolate in the house. But don't think in terms of plenty, there are 2 pieces per person. It has been such a long time, it seems like a ray, a dim memory of meals, of feasts even, from before the war! We are living through some very sad times. Maledictus sit qui bellum in Galliam ferre voluit! It is very cold in our country and the cold sharpens the appetite! The Big Ones are going to the Station in sabots to help keep their feet warm! Some thoughts console us: the first is our confidence in France and our hope in God; the second is that it is almost as bad in Germany as it is here with us. The hunger is in the large towns: in Berlin, Dresden and Baviera [217]; upon my word, let them all die!

Sunday 23rd [December 1917]:

Pankok is leaving for Boulzicourt. Mr Gislain having died, and a supply of fine coal being due, Papa volunteered and was authorised to keep the records of the supply; for it has to be done, come what may.

Monday 24th [December 1917]:

It is very cold: 12 degrees! The Meuse is full of blocks of ice and its banks are frozen. It is snowing and it is a real Christmas Day, but unfortunately, since everything is imperfect here below, there will be no midnight Mass and no peal of bells. But in this I am mistaken; there is, if not a peal of bells, a huge quantity of waffles! And cocoa! What a feast ... how good it is. It was an unforgettable evening! We sang until 10 p.m., together as a family, and all the time Tere was reminding us to eat the waffles. It was really good!

Tuesday 25th December 1917

Christmas! . . . another one . . . alas!

---

217. In fact, it was the winter of the previous year which was the most severe in Germany. Supplies had improved somewhat in 1917, prior to a marked return to food shortages from June/July 1918 onwards.

Wednesday 26th [December 1917]

Yesterday we had superb ceremonies, and the Fond crib is magnificent. Every day recently there has been fantastic moonlight! Everything is covered in snow and the moon reflects the whiteness of the earth! The great German hope is for a formidable and early offensive [218], but after that . . . perhaps it will be the earnestly longed-for peace! . . .

Thursday 27th [December 1917]:

They are taking Grandpa's shop. In Remilly, they have harnessed 15 young girls to the stone roller. In Fleigneux, women up to 45 years of age are engaged in ploughing. 'Modern Huns'. Basically, a real-life presentation of a scene in verse by Pierre entitled: 'The wish of the provinces of France (see Pierre's book of poetry).

Friday 28th [December 19

Snow, cold wind! Today the mathematics exam, dead silence in the classroom until, all of a sudden, Mr Laroche, the headmaster, appeared and read to us an order to the effect that the Turenne college, like all the other schools, is required to go and clear the roads of snow. Chaos, noise, laughter, questions!! Not long afterwards, one could observe, on the avenue the improvised sweepers under the kindly supervision of their teachers, having cast far away from them their school and their knowledge, sweeping away, if not with fervour at least cheerfully, the snow which was falling again behind them.

Saturday 29th [December 1917]:

It is very cold. At the station where they are still working, the Big Ones are cold in spite of their sabots. It is 15 degrees below and the Meuse has frozen over.

Monday 31st [December 1917]:

Mme Guichard has died like so many other elderly people just now. Thefts of coal. The college students are still sweeping up the snow. Today is the last day of the year and tonight is the presentation of 'Voeu des Provinces de France' [219].
As a wish, if I may put it into words, I would say: 'that the war be over, the trial come to an end and that in peace of heart, having returned to her God, France may enjoy the taste of victory – Amen.

---

218. This would be the German offensive on the Eastern front made possible by the withdrawal of German troops from the Eastern front following the cessation of hostilities with Russia.
219. See entry for Thursday, 27th December [Trans].

1918

January 1918

1st January 1918:

Yet another year! I don't know what feeling of weariness comes over us, I want to give everything up, my diary and everything and to lie and to sleep for ever, and not to wake up until the war is over! Utopia! Alright then, since it is a utopia, let's do our share and get on with it.

In the morning, we exchanged little gifts, but we are going to lunch in the Avenue. The College is still on duty today but I have taken a holiday. At 4 p.m., as has been the custom during the war, we all assembled in Mr and Mme Qinchez's house: The group included Mr and Mme Cousin, Mr and Mme Auguste Philippo-teaux, Mme Chapsal and the 7 of us[220]. We recited little bits of poetry, ate tasty gingerbread. The conversation turned to the best way to cook the herrings which the supplies (bless them) are sending us and also about the hostages who, it seems, the boches are going to seize, both men and women. Everyone present is afraid of being taken, but it is not very likely that it will be from among ourselves. We are quite at ease about it.

Wednesday 2nd [January 1918]:

It is less cold, there may be some people leaving for France. The boches talk a lot about the Russian peace! Pure nonsense! We have exchanged visits – (less so than in peace time as the circle of friends and relatives has shrunk)

Friday 4th [January 1918]:

It is very cold. I went to sweep in the town but we were sent back in the afternoon. On the way back H. Facquier came up to me and informed me that hostages had been taken [221] from Fond de Givonne: Mr Richard, Mr Facquier and Mr Congar! The excuse being, seemingly, the people from Alsace-Lorraine . . . my pen almost refuses to write the following pages and I beg my readers to forgive me if they do not find all the emotion that I would wish to express. The news was confirmed in the evening by Papa, who gave us the list, 27 men and 33 women. We received it very calmly but not without a certain anxiety although we feel they will not actually be going away. They may take 50 kgs of baggage with them, but Papa will only take a case and a bag.

---

220. The four children, Tere (the mother), Georges (the father) then aged 46, and Taïe, the aunt.

221. Due to France's refusal to release the people from Alsace-Lorraine who had fled to France at the beginning of the war, the Germans rounded up several hundred hostages from the countries they had invaded, all of them well-known people, in order to intern them in the territories captured from Russia. Twenty-two men left on 6th January for the Mileygany camp in Lithuania, in atrocious conditions of transport and internment. They were later transferred to the Roon camp. Eight of those who were deported, including two from Sedan, died in captivity. On 12th January, twelve women were deported as hostages for the same reason to the Holzminden camp west of Brunswick. These women returned to Sedan on 8th July, and the men on 23rd July.

Saturday 5th [January 1918]:

The Big Ones are not working on account of Papa's departure. It is very cold. This is the last day that we will be spending together. Just now, one thinks of all sorts of things which were expected to happen in due time, we have to mention everything, discuss everything all in one day, and make preparations. Our general attitude is calm, I have so little faith in the news that is going around, namely that they will be going to Russia, that this departure does not arouse in me all the feeling of anxiety, of sorrow and depression that one might feel in similar circumstances, or at least, I am not aware of it. Papa is very calm and wishes with all his heart that France should not give up the people from Alsace, moreover what can they do to people who are hostages, that is to say people who are entitled to every respect, who are grown up and honourable? No, they will be treated well, it is probably to put pressure on the future emigrants so that they call for peace in France.

Sunday 6th January 1918:

In the morning supplementary rations were distributed to the hostages: 1 carton of milk, 20 biscuits – butter, cheese – 5 pounds of bread; they have been told to take warm clothes. In the morning, the Big Ones carried the case to a shed close to the Tankstelle[222]. The time was approaching, the last moments, the last meal taken together, wishing for their return before long, then the afternoon which passed fairly uneventfully, and at last it really was time, the time for farewells, embraces, hugs, the last: 'What if's' and then, yes indeed, the feelings of anxiety, of anguish invaded my heart, I wanted to cry. Papa will go to the station accompanied only by his sons; we set off, they were walking a bit ahead and I was lagging a little bit behind, along the wall, I looked at the houses, turned away from the passers-by, because my lips were tightly closed and my eyes all screwed up; from time to time I made an effort, I moved a few steps forward and looked at everyone but this effort could not be kept up. We met a number of people who displayed their sympathy for the hostages as best they could, we made our way through the town and as we passed by everyone turned their head . . .
Opposite the service station there was a crowd of people. We arrived with J. Laroche [223] who had accompanied us; then Papa took us aside and said to us: 'I think I will come back, but it is good to foresee all eventualities. If I do not come back, to you, Pierre, I give the desk that is in Marie's room, to you Robert the chimneypiece, to Mimi the chest of drawers in the office, and to you Vonet, uncle Victor's watch; I embrace you all, farewell, think of me, burn the papers I told you about, goodbye'. Then he hugged us and went into the shed which was stifling. Also the windows had been opened, everyone there was deeply moved and the last farewells were being said at these windows. 'Calling for Mme Lacroix'. 'Here I am'. 'Where have you put my napkin with the food?' 'There it is' – 'Thank you, come, let me kiss you'. – kisses – 'Where is Loulou? Come on, Loulou. In the end, a policeman appeared and put an end to these conversations, everyone moved away, with tears in their eyes, but we 3, Henri and Théatre stayed with Théatre's sledge. We waited for a long time until at last the hostages from the outlying districts arrived, poor people taken by surprise and carrying a little bundle on their shoulders, they went into the shed. Another long wait, night was approaching when we saw a hostage emerge from the shed, Mr Péleraux; we went to him and asked him "What's new, are you being released?' 'Yes, I have been released and some others but I do not know who'. Then a second, a third and in the end 5 hostages were released: Abbé Lanson, Mr Péleraux, Mr Vattieux, Mr Lombart [sic], Mr Bertrand, Mr Massin. We questioned them but they knew nothing. Then a window was opened and Mssrs Facquiers, Congar and Théatre appeared and began to chat to us. 'It is very hot, we have opened the window, conversed in low voices and there we exchanged the last hand-shakes, the last recommendations, the last embraces, the last farewells. Finally, Mr Péleraux came up and said. 'Gentlemen, I swear to you on my word of honour that I am not in the least pleased by my release, I swear it!' Then Mr Lombard came up and gave Papa

222. Service station.
223. Jean Laroche, a friend of the Congar children.

2 bottles of coffee. Then Mr Wattiaux, who offered himself in place of anyone who was ill among the hostages: nobody said a word and yet there were sick people, but they were mostly people of honour who would have regarded any weakness on their part as a stain on their honour. Finally, seeing that it was all useless, we decided to leave and return tomorrow; by now it was a very dark night and we took advantage of it to snatch from the warehouse 8 enormous briquettes which we put on the sledge with myself on top of them and having passed the bridge we found in the Avenue, there in front of us, a cart: a last hitch-up; we hitched ourselves to it; we had just done so when suddenly the cart set off at a trot, we ran, the briquettes fell off, we picked them up. In the end we caught up with the cart and, at last, with a thousand precautions, we returned home, cheered up by this capture. The first impression that I had was a sense of loneliness: there was the kitchen all closed up [and] poorly lit in which, sitting close together and reading, there were two women, Tere and Mimi. Yes, in the future the hearth was going to be very empty, especially to begin with. Finally, what else can I say after all that except that I am tired and will give up my diary which must be of very little interest, but after all forgive me, I have tried to depict for you the things that have happened, to show you what I think and every night I add to my ordinary prayers a prayer for my father and for the hostages.

List of the hostages who were taken in January 1918 [224]

Monday 7th January 1918:

We made enquiries about the departure: it would seem that they left at 5 am, indeed a man confirmed this news to us: Papa had given him on leaving a word for us. The weather is very ugly, a detestable thawing weather. The big ones saw 50 Italian prisoners, small, thin, dark and yellow, under-nourished and treated abominably.

Tuesday 8th [January 1918]:

Departure of émigrés for France. Mme Mousty. Seemingly they will stay for a while in Liège. Another event: a wedding in Fond: Mr Pouteaux (aged 21) and Mlle Thierry (aged 24), fine people who have been going about together for the past year. The wedding feast will be at the Thierry's place, where the couple will be living afterwards.

Wednesday 9th [January 1918]:

It would seem that the hostages are at Cassel; is one to believe this report? I don't know, but seemingly they will be well treated, so much the better. A fine and icy snow is falling continually. In accordance with Papa's advice, today we moved 120 kgs of potatoes from the henhouse[225] to the cellar.

Thursday 10th [January 1918]:

The nastiest day for the big ones. An icy wind, unceasing snow which stings one's face and one's hands, a disgusting thawing weather and on top of that, in addition to the mud up to one's ankles, a wagon containing bottles full of frozen water and covered with unpleasant snow.

---

224. Yves Congar did not, after all, write down any names at this point. The list is given in 'Sedan et le Pays sedanais', annex 23. It comprised 23 men and 17 women. Two hostages died while deported.

225. The hen house was some distance from the dwelling house.

Friday 11 [January 1918]:

Immense black ice. We were ordered to clear everything in front of the railings. The female hostages have been told to get their bags ready. Will they take away the women? How shameful! Barbarians!

Sunday 13th [January 1918]:

Yesterday the women brought their luggage to the station. People are saying that the men are in Poland in Vilna and that the women will be going to Holsminden. The emigrants from the most recent departure have seemingly remained for 4 weeks in Belgium. It's a lot! People are saying that France does not know that she is required to receive them and that they are being held back until she accepts them.

Monday 14th [January 1918]:

We have some bread that is black and heavy. Don't think that I am saying that because I don't like it, but if it is heavy, one gets less and one gets so little!

Thursday 17th [January 1918]:

People are saying that the hostages are in Silesia (?). Foul weather: wind, frost, rain, storm! There is a notice: one must declare the number of rooms, beds and inhabitants of each house, in order to accommodate the civilian prisoners. That would be unpleasant.

Saturday 19th [January 1918] –

Yesterday the lads dealt with a wagon full of rotten and smelly bones of which I have already given you a description; fortunately my stomach is empty and will not give back what it has not got. Seemingly letters can be sent to the hostages on 10th February, it is a long time, but we will wait – still no news. Pierre had his first lesson in Greek with Mr Claudel.

Monday 21 [January 1918]:

The Meuse is rising a lot due to the unceasing rain – Pierre has a holiday – People were saying yesterday that news will be sent to the hostages on the 10th, today that they will be coming back?! When all's said and done, that is possible, but our doubts were settled by a visit from Wolf, an officer's orderly who has lodged with us. Papa had the good idea of writing to this officer and so we have news. Papa writes that he went through Frankfurt, that all are well and he sends us the warmest kisses. We are very happy to receive this news but not pleased that it is being spread all over the town. A wall close to the 2nd hollow collapsed due to the damp [226].

226. The family house being built on an old quarry, there were three enormous cavities carved out below ten metres of rock: these are the 'hollows' referred to here.

Wednesday 23rd [January 1918]:

Grandpa is threatened with an officer, it is quite a nuisance for him, but after all it is the common law. There is an important notice which I will summarise for you: 'Everybody is required to work, including the hostages when they are not 'on duty'; exemptions granted by German doctors do not impede this. To make things easier for those with small families and who are working, the Germans (always concerned for the weak), are setting up war kitchens to provide rations for the above-mentioned people. We have eaten haricots from such supplies, veritable *glajots*, salty, and bitter, stinking the fireplace, horrible. In old Ardennes there used to be a saying, a short prayer: 'Lord, preserve me from the wicked, preserve me from bread from Sapogne and wine from Mouzon', not that I am asking the Lord to deliver me from bread and wine wherever they come from, but one could ask him: 'Lord, deliver me from the boches, from the *bochines* and from the *glajots*[227] included in the rations'

Thursday 24th [January 1918]:

More rain, the level of the Meuse has gone down suddenly; the Italian prisoners are working in the mud on the Avenue Pasteur, it would not only be difficult but above all painful for me to paint a picture of them for you; their uniforms are in tatters, not only on account of the battles [they have been in], but also because of pieces from them that they remove to exchange them for bread, they are thin, yellow, their faces worn out, yellow, dark and bony, their cheeks hollow, their lips white, their eyes dark and languid, their skin wrinkled, they look at us and murmur 'brot' [bread], 'tsigaret' [cigarette]; their hands tremble, they are thin and screwed up, they show you their medals, their leggings and offer them to you in exchange for bread! Poor people, you have to see them to believe that in a civilised century, in the midst of people who call themselves civilised, misery can reach such a point! The college has been requisitioned to go and sweep the mud. This evening, there are bombs and the cannon, there is no gas. Provided it inflicts damage on them!

Saturday 26th [January 1918]:

Warning: Take all weights that are not being used to 'headquarters' in order to remove the copper! They are very low. Robert is having an altercation with Louis over manure which he wanted to put on land that is ours, the rascal!

Sunday 27th [January 1918]

The big ones are working this morning in the midst of the fog. Today is the Wilhelm celebration (Curse him!) The boches are not making much noise. They have erected a platform in Place d'Alsace, there is some singing in the town – there are always flatterers. Today is the anniversary of Papa's and Tere's wedding (20 years). We did not meet together for this family celebration but our unity is still there in our thoughts. Catherine Lenel has come from Givonne; there they have potatoes and vegetables in abundance, lucky things!

227. The words 'glajots', 'bochines' do not appear in current French dictionaries. They may well be either Ardennais terms for items of food, or even Vonet's adaptation of German words, since he speaks here of the **German** food kitchens! (Translator).

Monday 28th [January 1918]:

We have heard details about the Wilhelm celebration: to begin with, a rumour: 'Wilhelm had come to Sedan for his feast!' 2) an astonishing piece of news: The soldiers were all lined up in the Square, then General von Metzch appeared and spoke when all of a sudden a cry went up from the ranks of soldiers: ' Marmelade[228]! Was the general asking for it, talking about it? I don't know. The weather is very foggy. Pierre brought back from the station an Elzévir[229] (?), he looks upon it as a treasure and is very pleased about it. We have news of my Aunt who would very much like to return, she says she is in good health, so much the better! The boches are coming for the electricity at last! But they say that a second pole is needed and that we must wait. Again?!

Wednesday 30th [January 1918]:

Our hen the day before yesterday. The boches are enforcing the evacuation of the Lafuite residence and that of Mary. There has been a frost to freezing point. Mme Jaeger, a tenant on the Avenue (1st floor) has died. There is a revolution in Germany. Principally in Berlin, and also in Vienna. The women are the most enthusiastic: apparently already some 500,000 people, including soldiers, have mutinied. That's all to the good for us! [230]

Thursday 31st January 1918:

We have had further news of my Aunt through Marie Williaime and Tahar ben zaroue!: 'To see you all again is my one desire!', she writes; alas, it is our desire too but not ours alone! 20 emigrants have left to fill a train of evacuees, happy people! (including Mr Colas).

FEBRUARY 1918

1st February 1918 Friday:

Some Belgian prisoners passed over the Torcy bridge – they were dying with hunger and only just able to support one another, the younger supporting the older ones. One word will serve to describe them: they were wearing the red arm-band. [231]. . .

The German revolution has extended beyond Berlin and is affecting all centres. We have news of Papa. We are delighted, it has come from the same source as the first time and is dated the 11th; on this day they were passing through Goudbinnen (on the Polish border) and were making for Kovno or Vilna. They had travelled without stopping for 5 days and 6 nights, and for food they received in the morning a German soup (that says everything: a little dirty water) and in the evening a coffee, that's all! Papa is travelling with 600 companions, one from Vrigne-aux-Bois whom he knows has died! (he is not the only one!), a 75 year-old priest who was taken unexpectedly is with them, they are forced to give him something to eat! This letter which is rather a sad one has left us wondering, and in spite of our joy at having received news, we are sad and uneasy.

---

228. This unidentifiable word could mean 'stewed fruit', but since Vonet himself was puzzled, what is a translator to do, 100 years later?!
229. Probably a Greek New Testament published by Elzevir [or Elzevir] a famous Dutch publishing firm. [Trans]
230. The reference here is to the major strikes of the end of January and beginning of February in the principal towns in Germany and in Berlin, particularly in the war factories. These strikes, clearly pacifist and revolutionary, involved two million people.
231. The reference is to civilians being deported to work in other occupied regions: the red arm-band was the distinguishing mark imposed by the occupying forces. In 1917-1918, the fortified castle in Sedan was the place where as many as four or five hundred French and Belgian civilian prisoners were interned. The conditions of their imprisonment there were atrocious.

Tuesday 5th February [1918]:

For 5 people, we can take 1,800 grs of potatoes per day and no more; the cabbages are rotting and will not last until May! What a lot of calculation about food! Yesterday we heard news of the female hostages, they are at Holsmindel, sleeping 4 per alcove [???] with, seemingly, a servant for 4! There is white frost. The big ones have been given help at the station: 6 lads who do nothing but play about. We today received a devastating piece of news: the death of Mr Laroche! [232] This sudden death has upset the town and people considerably: [that] someone has died is already unfortunate, but death from what? Hunger? Cold? What distress! These are the moments when we would all like to be together. Oh dear! When they left it was being said that each pair would have an orderly An orderly per pair? But what is that when they are given orderlies? One has died . . . and perhaps yet others too, and from all the regions! . . .

Thursday 7th [February 1918]:

The boches want to make the soldiers believe that it was not in Germany that the strike took place, it was all a mistake, and that it is in London and in England that there was a mutiny!

Friday 8th [February 1918]:

Generally speaking, the boches are furious, they speak angrily about the war. Pierre is now swimming in books, he is in his element. The Italian prisoners are still working in the mud, I have already given you a sketch of it, there is no need for me to describe a skeleton. It is frightful, frightful.

Sunday 10th [February 1918]:

Seemingly there has been a conference in Versailles and the result is a decision for all-out war[233]. The big ones are working until 12.20! – film show in the workroom.

Tuesday 12th [February 1918]

The Italians have been given cigarettes! Poor fellows, they have no bread, so the cigarettes stifle their hunger. The boches are talking about a hypothetical peace with the Ukraine! [234] One may write to the hostages, but without knowing where they are.

Wednesday 13th [February 1918]:

What an account you will have to give to God for your crimes, Wilhelm, but call a halt to your crimes! When one sees in the streets the arrival of two prisoners in rags, supporting between them an old man also in rags who has fainted with hunger, in order to lay him down on his bed . . . or, rather, on his board, oh! It is terrible!

---

232. One of the hostages who died in the camp.
233. It was on 1st December that the first conference of the Supreme inter-allied Council was held in Versailles.
234. A peace treaty between the Ukrainian Republic and the central Powers was signed on 8th February.

It is Pierre's 19th birthday, I shall soon be 14! People are saying that the boches are preparing a fierce offensive! The last one, perhaps . . . . Today someone rang at the front door. I went to open it, but Mme Olivier had already done so and a boche appeared, then Tere, who was in the kitchen and who thought it would be a hostage coming for accommodation, asked me: 'Who is it?' 'It's one of the boches' – Then Veinberg (I have learnt since that that was his name, which I fear like the plague) looked at me furiously, asked my name and my age and said: 'I will teach you to respect the Germans!' I'm in a right fix now for it seems that that particular person is like a hedgehog: anyone who touches it gets pricked, and I most certainly touched it! This scoundrel is taking the whole of the 1st floor and the dining room from us, and wanted to take more than this. The visit created a very bad impression on us; we almost thought we would have to move house!

Thursday 14th [February 1918]:

RÖRAS[235]! That is our cat's name! Pancakes. Jacques Gibert and Mme Farnier are very ill.

THE END (not, alas, of the war)[236]

235. Added later in Yves Congar's writing: 'This word (the name of copper mines) means that on that day we had hidden our coppers and other things.' It is not clear quite what this code word in German means.

236. This is the end of the 4th exercise book (1st January 1917 – 14th February 1918) of Yves' war diary, who wrote 'The End' in large letters.

WAR DIARY 1918

Cover
of the fifth and last
exercise book

Y Congar

DIARY

Begun on 15th February 1918 Y. Congar[237]

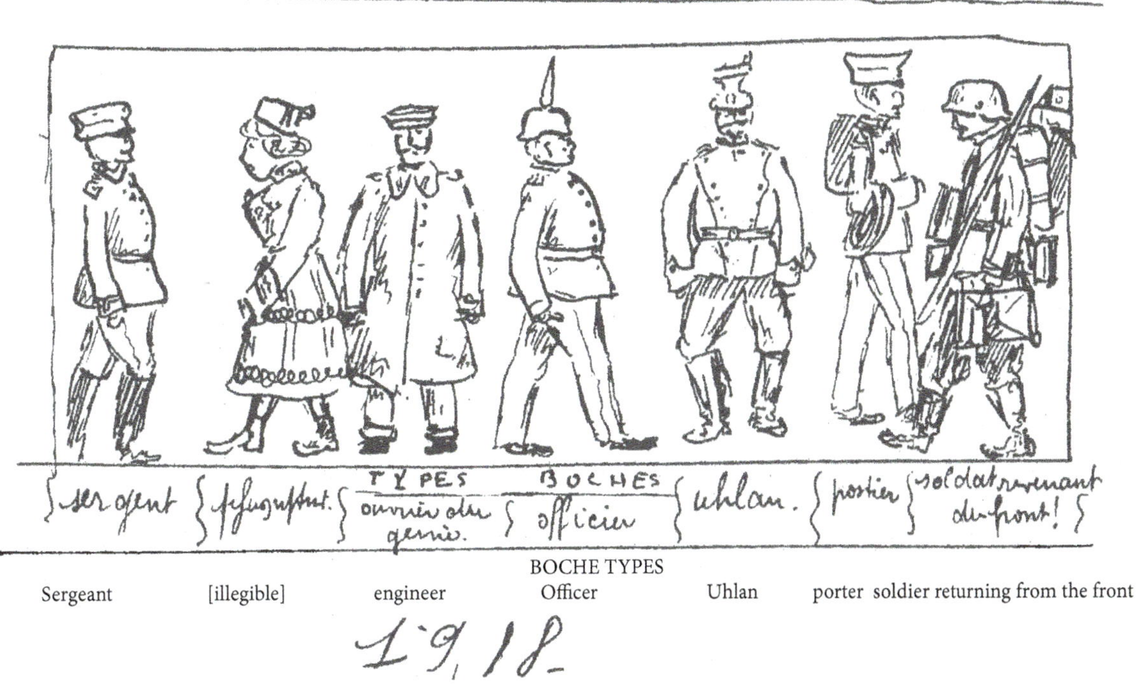

BOCHE TYPES

Sergeant [illegible] engineer Officer Uhlan porter soldier returning from the front

February

Friday 15th February 1918:

The big ones have seen in the town a group of Russian, Romanian and Italian prisoners dying of hunger, exhausted, indescribable! It is very sad to be there helpless at the sight of such wretchedness, and not be able to bring help to these unfortunates! Mme Tromy's bed has been brought to our house, to the dining room for the 'general'. They are coming to instal our electricity, so much the better, it is such a long time since we applied for it that we had almost given up hope. An officer from the Avenue is going to occupy their bedroom.

237. As in the previous exercise books containing his diary, Yves Congar counter-signed, *a posteriori*, the beginning of this fifth and last exercise book.

Sunday 17th [February 1918].

There is news of the female hostages in Holsmindel; they have little to eat and their lodging and sleeping accommodation are very poor. No news of the male hostages, though! It is not even known where they are! Today is the first of the Lenten talks given by the parish priest. Seemingly the Ukraine peace has come to nothing. the boches were counting heavily on it. So much the better for us.

Thursday 21 [February 1918]:

The electricians have come at last! Yesterday, I was complaining that we did not know where the male hostages are: today we do know: they are in the camp at Mileigani [238] between Korno and Vilna. Today I went to look for Robert down there. We were walking along the Avenue when a woman called us: 'Come'. We went over to her. 'Go in there, they are arresting the workers'. We entered the passageway and asked her what was up.'Me, it's got nothing to do with me, it's for your sakes, a little young man has just been arrested'. 'Please tell us what he was like?' 'Not unlike yourselves, a cap and a large haversack on his back' 'Look, go out this way', then she made us go out by the embankment. Well, we have had a narrow escape. Henri, because it was he (H Facquier) is in prison. We are extremely grateful to that woman, for we are deeply indebted to her!

Friday 22nd [February 1918]:

It seems that the boches have been badly beaten at Tahure [239], there is talk of 30,000 men done for!. Pierre went in the hope of being given a holiday, but the doctor was Bendix so Pierre got nothing! What a criminal I am! I am a bandit! A bandit who has been court-martialled. Today, we received a communication: Mr Congar is to appear before the judge of the day on such a day at such a time. Believing that it had something to do with Henri's case, Robert went, but he came back saying that it was I who had been summoned: a word came to my memory: the Veinberg affair! So I went, I went from one office to another, I entered the room. A boche, excuse me, a German (because I am not keen on being a bandit) came up to me, took me by the cape and said: 'What did you do?' 'I don't know, but if . . . ' In the end, after a few more questions, I replied: 'I used the word 'boche' 'Oh! Oh! That is a great insult' 'I didn't intend to insult anyone'. 'But if' . . . 'No' 'It is a serious insult to the German army'. 'Go into the corner'.
In the corner, oh refuge! The early days of my childhood! Shortly afterwards, he called me back: 'It is a serious insult' 'I don't know' 'But if . . .' 'I see that now, but I didn't know anything about it'. 'Where did you learn that word?' 'On the street'. 'Are you going to school?' 'The college' 'You were a scholar. Now you are a bandit'. Yes, me. We went into a small very stuffy room: 'It is a serious insult'. 'I didn't mean any harm by it'. 'But if . . . ' 'You little wretch! If you do it again, you will go to prison for 2 years'. 'Two years!?' 'Yes, 2 years!' 'Oooh!' 'Away with you! You will be sent to prison'. And I made a very quick exit!

Saturday 23rd [February 1918]:

A great many troops are passing by, probably for the offensive. Henri was released today.

238. For 'Milejgany'. Georges Congar later said to his daughter: 'Oh! I would not like your mother ever to know: they admitted 600 of us where you would not have put 60 pigs!' (Diary of Yves Congar's sister, personal archives of Dominique Congar).
239. The reference is to the repulse of a German raid near Tahure, in the Marne on 18th February.

Tuesday 26th [February 1918]

30 women from Sedan have been requisitioned to go to Daigny in order to manage the telephone lines. We hear that a hostage has written; is it true? I don't know.

Thursday 28th [February 1918]:

Nothing. Death of Mme Doin, poor woman, who will not have seen her husband again! Impressions: days that are difficult to live. What calculations in order find food to eat! And the prices are exorbitant. Wretched life.

END of FEBRUARY 1918

March 1918

2nd March [1918]:

It is snowing and very cold. We are thinking all the time of Papa; we are very worried about him, at every moment we think of him: in the morning, he used to do a bit of everything and this everything, we are obliged to do now: it is the wood, the tools, the leaves, the fireplaces, everything, in fact. At mealtimes, we express the wish that he has standard fare as good as ours, all over the place, we think of him.

3rd March [1918]:

We are heading for Lent. Seemingly Mr Doin [240] has written and is asking for money and food. We talk about these requests and conclude that they are hungry! It really is unfortunate.

4th March [1918]:

Seemingly the plan for the German offensive has been found; so much the better, as it is quite possible: the boches see spies everywhere and they are as aggressive as angry dogs. Humbert and Caillaux are in prison,[241] thank goodness, dirty villains, bringing shame on their country! Let them all be put in prison, and severe measures be taken against them as in '93, and for God's sake let the Republic be preserved.

---

240. One of the hostages in Lithuania.

241. The cases of Caillaux and Humbert are part of the context of the repression conducted by the Clemenceau government against 'pacifist' scheming, some of which could in fact be regarded as a betrayal. As leader of the radical party prior to 1914, Caillaux imprudently multiplied contacts during the war with neutral or allied personalities with a view to seeking a way of securing a compromise peace with Germany. He was accused of treason by the nationalist press, arrested on 14th January 1918, and condemned to three years imprisonment by the High Court of the Senate in February 1920.

Charles Humbert, director of 'Le Journal' and a senator, was implicated in the manoeuvres of German agents in relation to the paper which he owned. His parliamentary immunity was rescinded in November 1917 and he was arrested on 18th February 1918.

5th March [1918]:

A rumour is doing the rounds: the boches are in Petrograd! [242] What nonsense! Moreover, if it were true, they would be celebrating it a bit differently from what they are doing! They all have the faces of 8 days' rain! An egg costs 228 sous – a litre of haricots 10 fr, a kilo of onions 3.50 – such prices! It is worse than the siege of Paris.

6th March [1918]:

Today we had a visit from 'Mr Veinberg' a man to be treated with respect.
In accordance with one of Papa's last recommendations, we today fixed the joists. Our cat Rösas is a nuisance, we are going to get rid of it.

7th March [1918]:

Our cupboards are being emptied free of charge (these good Germans help everywhere!). We are probably soon going to have an officer.

8th March [1918]:

This evening we were writing the letter to send to Papa. We tried to put in a few words all our thought; besides, we are playing a trick and in fact sending two: one in the name of Lucie Desoye[243] and the other in the name of Pierre Congar. We are also putting together a parcel in which we are putting our whole heart; there is everything in it, including a little bag of coarse salt like a broomstick! Oh, if only this parcel reaches him, he will be very happy and all the little bags we are sending him will speak more loudly than all the sentences on earth!

9th March [1918]:

There were bombs at one o'clock in the morning; I do not remember having heard them (I am writing this on 13th April, my birthday, on which there was a real bombardment). It is a shame to see the Italians, hunger is driving them. Just imagine the suffering of a man who is refused food. He asks and gets nothing, he begs but in vain, oh just imagine what these prisoners must suffer! And we are there powerless in the presence of such misery! At the station, these poor fellows gnaw at the putrid, green and fetid bones, they scrape out the lids which had the remains of jam! It's pathetic.

We have written to Papa and to my aunt through Tahar ben Zarouel. We have learned of the death of Mr Hullot of Torcy, a hostage in Mileïgani, that's 2 deaths already and perhaps yet others!

242. The Brest-Litovsk Treaty between the Central Powers and Russia was signed on 3rd March, following a last German offensive begun on 18th February, on the expiry of the armistice.
243. Yves Congar's mother.

Saturday 16th [March 1918]:

Guess how much a kilo of coffee costs? 56 fr.
Our whole family has the flu, and I have got it very badly. We shall perhaps be having a doctor. Henri has been sentenced to 3 weeks in prison for his affair, but we don't know when.

Wednesday 20th [March 1918]:

Mimi is in bed. The big ones have planted the first potatoes. To give you an idea of the rumours that are circulating, I will tell you a fact: 'Mimi is sick, that we know.' This morning, Mr Molard came up here in a carriage and also went to call on Mr Douffet; an hour later, you could hear it being said in the bread shop, amongst other rumours: 'The little Congar girl is very ill, they have come to take her to hospital!'.

'canaros facere humanum est'

Thursday 21st March [1918]

The boches have sent back the parcels and the letters to the families of the hostages! Hence, those men who no longer see their families, those men who are far from their homes, will be there without news, hungry and shivering with cold! And here are the civilised people! Barbarity of barbarities, refinement of cruelty, the whole thing is a barbarity!

Friday 22nd [March 1918]!

It is all nothing but barbarity. Yet another hostage has died, Mr Bonneville, the mayor of Balan! [244] So they must be hungry to die like that. 3 from Sedan, in 3 months! What a lot of vengeance to take, so many deaths, so much mourning!

25th March 1918:

A rumour: The boches have bombarded Paris from 120 km! Using an enormous cannon. What a story! And with that they give the particulars, the location of the cannon, its dimension (240), the type of projectile! [245]
There is some news: I was speaking to you about barbarity yesterday, I could speak to you about it yet again today (and every day, alas!). We have heard that the emigrants who left on 8th January are still in Liège, stripped of everything, dying of hunger and asking for money and food. The mayor of Liège would be willing to give them supplies if the mayor of Sedan offers guarantees, there's a barbarity for you if ever there was one!
Seemingly the money does reach the hostages, so much the better. Today is not a happy day, the entire town is downcast as it has never been. The boches have announced the capture of Péronne and Rheims; according to them they are waging all-out war[246]. For myself, I do not believe it and I am perfectly happy not to believe it.

244. Yves Congar has the name wrong. The two hostages who died were M Laroche and M Baudelot from Balan.
245. The first bombardment of Paris with a long range gun which had been set up in the region of Crepy-en-Laonnois took place on 23rd March.
246. The reference is to the major German attack on Amiens which began on 21st March, over a 70 km front, and which routed the British 5th Army. Péronne fell on 23rd March, the date on which the link was broken between the French and British armies. Noyon fell on 25th, Albert and Montdidier on the 27th. The Allies did not recover from this extremely serious situation in which they found themselves until 5th April. The breach in the Allied front achieved by the Germans was at that time almost 70 km. deep.

A common sight in the town is to see, in the evening, returning from work the thin and bony shadow of a group of prisoners with red arm-bands, going back to their living quarters for their evening meal (such as it is).

Tuesday 27th [March 1918]:

The boches are claiming that they are still advancing and the town is more and more downcast; the boches are afraid of the aeroplanes because they are sticking red crosses everywhere. There is talk of the hostages returning shortly, but I don' believe it.

Wednesday 27th [March 1918]:

Seemingly the boches have captured 45,000 British prisoners but on the other hand what they don't say is that the British have stoically put 165,000 of their men out of action. They have taken M Quinchez' 2nd floor, always being a nuisance! We are getting 30 gr. less bread, just when more is needed because of the work in the fields! For everywhere, the land is being tilled, everywhere people are working in order to live.

Friday 29th [March 1918]:

Seven hostages have written: Mme Reignois, Gérard, Auskine. Lallement, Wahart, Gérault and Lacroix. All they have to eat is a soup and twice coffee, and that for months on end! And just look at the way the prisoners are being fed in Germany!

Sunday 31st [March 1918]:

What a very peculiar Easter, or rather how peculiar everything is, it is sad. We have been living abnormal lives for such a long time!
A soldier from the Red Cross brought a letter for Mme G . . . (?) at the request of his officer. But she left for France 2 years ago!

From 1st to 4th April 1918:

Some prices: flour which cost 10 sous before the war now costs 10 fr.; and an egg which was worth 2½ sous has gone up to 45 sous!
In addition to the so-called German advance which I will pass over in silence, I record that mattresses are now being requisitioned, it's delightful! Henri is in prison on account of his thieving escapade: 3 weeks.

5th April [1918]

We have planted the potatoes, and are hoping for a yield of 2,800 plants this year; for God's sake, we do not want to fail, especially if Papa returns.

10th April [1918]:

The boches have returned Mr Laroche's clothes and there was written on a card: Georges Congar came to see M Laroche. We are building a thousand suppositions on that, quite naturally! About twenty healthy French prisoners have arrived in Sedan. What a contrast with the boches, they are at least clean and good looking! The town is still very downcast and demoralised, because the boches continue to maintain, quite wrongly, that they have advanced 50 kms. We are continuing to plant potatoes in so far as we can!
A very amusing incident, relating to the incident of the cannon 120 kms away. It is no longer at a distance of 120 kms but at 150! But no, sir, here is the German newspaper: the cannon was located at a distance of 20 kms, hidden in private property by some spies! All of that is excusable, it's time for the posters relating to the 8th instalment of war-time borrowing.

Thursday 11th [April 1918]:

The boches are requisitioning mattresses. When we are short of nourishment, we could recuperate our worn-out bodies by resting on a nice soft bed, but no, these gentlemen need wool, so they are taking our mattresses! Such wretches! Such villains'! We have had a list of questions from the Hennecarts [which] we are clearly pleased about, but it says so little! Put yourselves in our place, really and truly we have no news, and when we have a hope of receiving some, they conceal themselves from us!

Friday 12th [April 1918]:

We hear the cannon very loudly and a great number of wounded have arrived in Sedan. Their offensive having been checked, they are reforming the front on Rheims[247]. Let them not succeed. Henri has been transferred to Macdonald[248], but unfortunately for him as he will be less well off.

247. The only offensive that occurred on this date was that of the Germans on the Lys which began on 9th April and ended on the 18th.
248. See footnote 166.

Saturday, 13th [April 1918]:

Today is my birthday and it was undoubtedly in my honour that there were a great many bursts of the cannon during the night! Goodness me, what a bombardment, good heavens! I am still blue from it. It is night-time, everyone's asleep, suddenly I am awake: bang-bang-bang. I know it very well, this noise, it is France knocking at my shutter to say: 'keep calm, I am on the watch'. This confused murmur of an engine, it is the voice of the country, the sweet melody of the fatherland and these repeated thuds, it is a little of the breath of the front passing over our towns, it is the image of the country in arms to defend its interests, it is the image of mighty France saying with us: war on the barbarians!
Nevertheless, things are serious, the missiles are whistling over the roof, let's be prudent and go down. And it is thanks to you, the country's envoys, that I get to sleep with Tere on a nice soft bed.

Monday 15th [April 1918]:

Rain, wind. The damage from the bombs, though not very extensive, has had a huge moral effect on the boches, soldiers who above all fear the aeroplanes. The Berlin newspaper [Tageblatt] has been suppressed completely on account of the opposition, and people are saying that the boches will do the same with the Frankfurt one. This proves the kind of mood there is in Germany. Besides they are short everywhere and are paying for disgracefully dear vegetables, clearly we owe them nothing. We are paying 12 fr. for haricots and 5 fr for potatoes, almost as it was during the siege of Paris where a kilo of potatoes was worth 7 frs.

Wednesday 17th [April 1918]:

We have been summoned to a supply of shoes. It is a stroke of luck as I was walking in bare feet! Moreover, Providence has never failed us and we hope in her! With her we will conquer, God of the armies, fill our soldiers with your love so that they may deserve to be victorious, Amen!

Friday 19th [April 1918]:

Not much news: snow, in April, on 20th April! What foul weather. Due to the forward thrust of the French Salonica corps, the Bulgarians have withdrawn and abandoned 12 villages[249]. So much the better, they are rogues! Very serious trouble in Austria. The conduct of the minister, cXernin [250] is truly shady in his secret proposal of peace with France; the boches are very upset and the Emperor of Austria, who is trembling, is in a right mess lest he fall and his country and his allies with him! (19th April 1918).

Saturday 20th April [1918]:

In the schools they are asking the pupils whether they want to continue their studies, then registering their name and their age, why? Is it for a good purpose? Opinions are sharply divided. For myself, I have not been registered. I have only just turned 14;

249. On 16th April, the Allies in fact managed to advance a short distance on the Struma.
250. For 'Czernin'. Count Czernin became Minister of Foreign Affairs immediately after the accession of the Emperor in Austria-Hungary, whom the latter urged to seek a general peace without annexations or indemnities with the Allies. He was forced to resign on 14th April 1918 when the secret negotiations entered into with France were made public by Prince Sixtus of Bourbon-Parma.

if it is not for a good purpose, that's all the same to me, if it is for good purpose (which would be really surprising) I would say that I am 14.

Monday 22nd [April 1918]:

A female hostage from Vendresse [251] has returned from Holsminden! Mme Anonet de la Grange. The Spanish Consul went to see them in Holminden and finding them in a very poor state, he insisted on the repatriation of those who were least well. So there are 15 from this region. While this lady was in captivity, her title deeds, her property, everything, were taken from her. She is in the hospital in Sedan and has asked to be allowed to go to France, but she has been told that she would have to spend a preliminary period of 3 months in Belgium! How disgraceful.

In Holsminden they are neither well housed nor well fed: they are given two soups per day and one coffee, all of it German, enough said! They are in fact being robbed! Taking advantage of their being stripped of everything, they are sold a spoon, for example, for 1 mark!

It is a real shame, something indescribable! When will the turn of our own people come?

Tuesday 23rd [April 1918]

Our own people's turn has come. Today is the feast of St George[252]. Not being able to be united except in thought, we went to Mass in the morning, and on emerging what did we see: the Facquiers on their doorstep. 'Papa is there: here are his cases, he is in Sedan, he'll be coming any minute, the man who brought his case has seen him and spoken to him![‘] What a piece of news! What a thunderbolt! I am still all over the place and cannot believe it. It was precisely today that Henri is to end his 3 weeks' [imprisonment]. I could do nothing this morning, nothing.

I am going to tell you here everything that I learnt during the next few days both from M. Facquier and from Mr Doin who came with him and M. Merieux. I won't go into great detail, but you will see for yourself the barbarity with which the boches have treated the French hostages.

When they left, as we have already said, they were given a broth. After journeying for 5 days and 6 nights, being given a soup and a coffee per day, they arrived in Mileighani in the middle of a fierce snowstorm. Just imagine a long line of exiles with empty stomachs crossing the snow-covered fields exposed to the elements, a long black line turned to grey by the abundant snowflakes that were falling under an icy north wind. At last they arrived, covered in snow, their feet frozen, hungry and thirsty in a huge barn which could have housed 80 but 4000! No air, no light no beds, no meal, groans everywhere! And to remain there for weeks [253]. And those who died, they had no doctor, there were 4 civilian doctors, one of whom died without medication[;] they tried to help those who were dying. Mr Laroche remained in Mileghaini without assistance until the very last moment, then arrived in Vilna where he died! If that is not disgraceful. For lunch they had a coffee, a soup, a little bread and in the evening coffee! There were jobs to be done and those who did not want to do them had to pay 4 marks to those who did them in their place. Then, while they were working, they managed to scrounge a little. Papa used to do the chores for the others, and this enabled him to cover his expenses. In a word, they were treated as slaves would have been treated in antiquity! I will tell you more when Papa returns, which I hope, and pray to God, will not be too long now.

251. A village about 15 kilometres from Sedan.
252. Yves Congar's father's name day.
253. The word 'months' crossed out.

Friday 26th [April 1918]:

Mr Rouy has also returned but in a much worse state than the others; he had left on a stretcher!
The boches are taking advantage of us, they are making use of the fact that we lack everything in order to make us return ill-gotten gains. They have sold seeds to the hospice:

1 kilo of cabbage seeds	200 marks!
1 kilo of onion seeds	400 marks

1918    1918

The boche loan, the 8th, is not working at all, it is a great defeat. At last, the German socialists are publishing news-sheets addressed to the German people, informing them in black and white 'We are broke. England has defeated us commercially, they have achieved their aim. Without colonies, without money, with no outlets, no raw materials, what will Germany do?' That is beginning to become clear, and we are hoping for a speedy and happy ending.
Today, 6th May, brings us to the day before we will be sleeping on kelp! Tomorrow is the day they are coming to take our mattresses (9 in the whole house). We have had more reliable news through Mr Doin, who had not spent some time in hospital as M Facquier had done. He was the bearer of a note from Papa making some useful suggestions and asking for clothes and some bacon. Papa is well, seemingly, and we are hoping to see him soon. Amen.

7th May [1918]:

There is a lot of talk about the return of the hostages. According to one German newspaper, they would seem to be on the way home; it is being said that they will be here on Sunday. Reason would tell one not to believe it, but I do not know what is urging me to believe it, I have something that tells me that they will be coming back, if only it could be true.

The boches have behaved towards the hostages 'in a Prussian fashion', but the way they are treating the military and civilian prisoners is much worse. Go to the cemetery, my God! Rows and rows of black crosses! What slaughter! Where are the Romanians? In the earth. The Russians? In the earth. The Italians, they are on the way . . .
Just lately, the boches have killed a French prisoner. And the English and the Scots from Dijonval . . . they are dying of hunger and the guards amuse themselves by making things worse and depriving them of their meagre soup!
Miserere, Jesus! Miserere nostri!! . . .

Thursday 9th [May 1918]:

Today is the Feast of the Ascension. All the talk is of the return of the hostages.

Saturday 11th [May 1918]:

A lady asked us in all seriousness whether they were back yet or not. They are expected tomorrow. It's marvellous.

Impression

Difficult, painful period, no vegetables, the prospect of real famine. We are making a dish of nettles once a week, that helps a little. When you look around you, not very far away, you always find others worse off than yourself, alas!

Sunday 12th May [1918]:

But the days follow one another without resembling one another. Our hopes were dashed: we may now write again and send a parcel. We are trying to put our whole heart in a letter and preparing a parcel into which we are putting as much as possible of the things that Papa asked for through M Doin: bacon and summer clothing. But we also believe that that does not mean a great deal, it is perhaps only to make us despair. Today is the feast day of Joan of Arc who is celebrated magnificently in the Fond and it is with all our hearts that we say with the people of Fond de Givonne: 'Blessed Joan of Arc, save France!'

Monday 13th [May 1918]:

Once again, the days follow one another without resembling one another: there has been a counter-order: we may neither write nor send a parcel, only money. What antics! Our hopes of seeing them return being greater than ever, when we hear someone coming up the hill [254] we go out to see if it might be Papa.

Friday 17th [May 1918]:

No fresh news. Dull weather. Mimi has whooping cough. Last night there were bombs, seemingly dropped quite a long way off because near here there was little more than a few cannon rounds. Clearly it is on all my birthdays that there is shooting!

Monday, 20th [May 1918].

Yesterday was the feast of St Yves, my patron saint. We have some news which confirms our hope that the hostages will be returning soon: we are no longer allowed to send money! This [must mean] that they are on their way because we have always been able to send money. Moreover, seemingly the money that was recently deposited at the army headquarters is to be returned to us. This is a very good sign; at last this separation will come to an end and we shall all always be together again and, I hope, for a long time to come. Thus we are hoping they will be back by the end of the month in time for the procession which will be on 2nd June.

Tuesday 21st [May 1918]:

The Big Ones are earthing up the potatoes in the lower plot; today they did half of them; these potatoes are very fine. There is to be an exodus shortly, including a halt in Belgium; this will probably take place on 1st June. The workshop and the boys are coming to prepare the paths for the procession; it is quite a difficult task as it is very hot. We have made an early start, which promises a superb procession at which, I hope, Papa will be present.

The children from the workshop and the catechism class are preparing the paths for the procession. The spirit is wonderful. I heard one of them say: 'As for me, I am sure that when baby Jesus comes this way he will know that it was me who prepared the path'. What a spirit!

---

254. Path leading to the house from the entrance to the property.

Friday 24th [May 1918]:

Yesterday, it was real July weather, close and stormy. Our potatoes are growing well. Today we learned that the French have carried out an air raid on Cologne in broad daylight: there's cheek for you! What's more, the boches are scared stiff of French aeroplanes.

Sunday 26th [May1918]:

The big ones have been sent home from the station as there is no work. In the evening, they went to Evening Vespers in Balan. The priest was pleased because he is having difficulty in his parish which does not give him what it ought. In the evening, we went to cut up and bring down a tree in Mack; they had cut it down and were planning to take it away, but we arrived in time. Already on Wednesday we had to do the same thing.

Monday, 27th May [1918]

M. Laroche, the village policeman, came on account of the Mack business. The rest of the potatoes down in the lower plot have been earthed up. A lovely preparation: we are hoping for an excellent harvest.
The hostages' parcels have arrived in Sedan. The contents are excellent. See Tere's papers...
It means that they will soon be here. We are hoping they will get here in time for the procession which promises to be splendid.

Thursday 30th May [1918]:

M. Notté has mowed the grassland. The hay is good and we will gather it in before the procession. We are all the time thinking of the hostages who ought to be here soon. Tere has received a summons to the Arbeiteramt [255]. She has been told that she will be working in the afternoon, but it is more a tiresome threat than a reality. People are required to declare sheets and pieces of material at the town hall. They are very low [in supplies].

Saturday, 1st June [1918]:

Yesterday the big ones earthed up the potatoes under the cherry tree, they are lovely. People are saying that the women will be arriving this evening. There are even people saying that their beds and their supper are ready. I don't know how much truth there is in it, but what is certain is that they will be at the procession.

We have learned of the death of M Charles Wotte, a volunteer soldier, who died gloriously for his country!

255. For 'Arbeitsamt' = employment office

1st June 1918 (Saturday):

Preparations for the procession seemingly involving less activity than in previous years because everything is ready beforehand. The procession will probably be lovely because we have brought in all our hay, since we have had such fine weather.

The boches [claim to] have reached Rheims and Soissons [256] [and to] have taken 35,000 prisoners: what lies!

Sunday 2nd June 1918 – Procession

Unfortunately, Tere cannot be there: she has been summoned, together with Mme Misset, and will have to work, probably haymaking. It's unfortunate, she has a lot to do with her classes and she will perhaps be working all day long – superb weather – bright sunshine but not scorching hot – all the preparations for the procession are complete.

5th procession

All the hay is in, the weather is superb – all the preparations well done. I will go straight to the afternoon. The last few hours were filled with a terrific hustle-bustle, but in the end everything was ready. There was a huge crowd (700 to 800 people[257]). From all the parishes: Balan (with the parish priest), Torcy (with Abbé Langon), Sedan (Abbé Lallement and the seminary). A lot of young girls with veils, boys and men. The altars are lovely (see photos[258]). Here is more or less the sequence of people: First the children from the choir, then the other children (a great many) followed by the little girls strewing flowers before the Blessed Sacrament carried by M. l'Abbé Drouart (Balan). The Blessed Sacrament was escorted by the young people: young France, believing France, Catholic France whose loveliest motto is 'Catholic and French always'; the France of the future! Then came the young girls wearing veils, not only those from the Fond but also from all the parishes, they were singing hymns and were directed by the parish priest; then the seminary with Abbé Lallement, the children from Torcy with Abbé Langon and finally the people in immense numbers, recollected and devout. 'O Lord, how many prayers are being offered to You, how many petitions concerning relatives, friends, special intentions for our France, or rather for Your France! Hear us, O my God.' Hear the people of France, the people of the Sacred Heart, and do not let it fall under the yoke of sacrilegious barbarians, O ever-living God, good God, just God!'

The procession as a whole is superb, it is the first that has been quite so lovely. The parish priest was delighted, and we were only sorry about one thing, namely that Papa was not with us, for even if he was united with us in thought, we would have preferred to have him here with us.

---

256. The reference is to the battle of the Aisne between 27th May and 6th June, which, to begin with, proved an astonishing success. Soissons was lost on 28th May but Rheims remained in French hands.
257. Yves Congar wrote the word 'more' above the bracket.
258. In fact, these photos which were perhaps inserted into the diary originally are no longer there.

Procession in the Congar family property in Fond de Givonne in 1917 or 1918.

8 juillet

Par ordre de la Commandanture

M. Congar Yves
88 F. de Givonne

Devra se présenter sans faute le
à 4 heures (temps allemand), place
Turenne, No 2, Bureau de l'Arbeiteramt.

Sedan, le 1918.

By Order of the Commandantur
M. Congar, Yves
88 F. de Givonne
is to present himself without fail
at 4 pm (German time) on 5th June 1918, in
Place Turenne, nº 2, Arbeiteramt Office.
Sedan, 5th June, 1918.

Monday, 3rd June [1918]:

We are receiving all sorts of expressions of appreciation for the beauty and success of the procession. May it be of benefit to the France that I love so much that I cannot put it into words here. Our potatoes are superb and I will confess that though I asked God during the procession for some spiritual graces, I also asked Him to make our vegetables flourish! Tere summed up our sentiments by quoting for us some words from the Gospel. Jesus saying to Zacchaeus to whose house he went: 'Indeed and indeed I tell you, salvation has come to this house today'. In fact, what could be lovelier? Me, a nothing, a poor wretch who lives by the goodness of God, me, I was escorting Jesus Christ, God Almighty! Oh! What a miracle! What goodness, what example!

Our potatoes have all been earthed up and are in flower. We have finished bringing in the hay; for this reason, the Big Ones did not go to the Station today.

It is today that Taïe[259] did her first day of work: it is disgusting, she returned home very late!

Thursday 6th June 1918:

During the night of Tuesday to Wednesday, there was a fire in the Fond, in the Leclaire's house. The house was burnt down completely, but all the furniture was saved; just to give one example. Pierre had lent the son 2 books, but they were saved.

A German offensive has been foiled, so much the better!

259. See footnote 7.

Sunday 9th [June 1918]:

We are allowed to send letters to the hostages in the same way as to prisoners, but we did not have the paper, thank goodness we knew about it! Will the letter actually go?

Monday 10th [June 1918]:

Taïe had her day yesterday. The big ones brought a letter from the hostages.

Thief! The thefts committed by the French against the Churches have been imitated by the boches. How disgraceful! In all there are now in the Fond only 6 candlesticks in copper! Not even the number required by the liturgy! It's disgraceful! However, if we have the grace of God, they will not take them from us, and with his grace we can conquer! Long live France!

Friday 14th [June 1918]:

There is a very senior officer visiting the station. There is talk of the big ones and their team being replaced by the English (?)

Today is the first day of the retreat for the First Communicants. The children are coming to play.

Sunday 16th June [1918]:

Uncertain weather – will it rain or will it not? – no-one quite knows. The children are making their 1st Communion today, not solemn, but very moving, very impressive.

1,500 French prisoners have arrived in Sedan, some who are black and some who are English, I would love to see them They have been installed in the Castle where the boches have set up some huts, in Fabert where there are some Englishmen, in Manège, and perhaps also in Macdonald[260].

Thursday 20th June 1918:

I have seen the Frenchmen, they look very good, their uniform is superb [261]. On seeing them, one could repeat Marot's epigram:

Lorsque Maillard juge d'enfer menait	When Maillard, hellish judge, was leading
A Montfaucon Semblecay l'âme rendre,	Semblecay to give up his soul at Montfaucon
A votre avis, lequel des deux tenait	Which of the two, think you,
Meilleur maintien? Pour vous le faire entendre,	Bore himself best? To help you understand,
Maillard semblait qui mort va prendre	Maillaird it was who seemed heading for death
Et Semblecay fut si ferme vieillard	and Semblecay was such a sturdy old man
Qu'on le cuidait pour vrai qu'il menât pendre	that one would have thought that he was on his way
À Montfaucon le conseiller Maillard.	to hang the Councillor Maillard at Montfaucon.[262]

260. See note 166.
261. Until then, Yves Congar had seen only the pre-1914 French soldiers' uniform. The horizon-blue uniforms introduced in 1915 had hitherto been unknown to him.
262. In 1527, Jacques de Beaune, baron of Semblançay, was hanged on the gallows of Montfaucon for alleged peculation. [Trans]

Today, the Colars have pulled up their patch of carrots. They have sold them at the rate of one bunch per household. It is really sad to see the people jostling one another to get them! It's a real famine. How many people never have a main meal, if you can call a plate of 'soup' followed by a salad a main meal! It's sad.
Sometimes I no longer want to continue writing this diary, but now I am not sorry about it. May the feelings I am trying to express in these lines enter into the hearts of all French people. May France know from these pages, brought together from day to day, what the invaded parts of the country have suffered, what the prisoners, the refugees, the poor people of the Ardennes have suffered. May they realise to the full the barbarity of the boches and may these feelings root them firmly and always in love for their Fatherland!

Saturday 22nd [June 1918]:

Most of the French [prisoners] have left today for Carignan. Some Saxons have arrived at the station.

Sunday, 23rd [June 1918]:

We are sending a packet to Papa and trying to put into it the things he has asked for. It does nothing but rain. An Austrian offensive has been aborted in Italy [263]. Things are bad in Austria, they are dying of hunger, both in the Army and in the towns.

Tuesday, 25th June [1918]:

Freezing mist. It is cold. The packet for Papa was handed over yesterday. May it actually go! Taïe has been released. So much the better, that was becoming boring and wearisome. Always standing, to be released at 8 p. m!

There is famine in Austria-Hungary. That gets to you!

From Tuesday 25th June [1918] to Sunday 30th-

Boom! Boom! 5 days of bombs. Bombs every night! Long live France!
Yes, long live France, but long live also the occupied countries, in the true sense of the word, in the sense of truly living because [264]:

> Macies et nora febium
> Terris incubuit cohors.
>
> Horace[265].

What can we do? The potatoes are lying under the heat, they are not great! What can we do?

Let us hope in Providence!

We are going to the baths. Very dry weather. Sad times of famine. To live! What a problem!

---

263. The reference is to the second battle of the Piave, begun by the Austro-Hungarians on 15th June. It encountered an Italian counter-offensive from 20th onwards, which forced them to retreat between 22nd and 24th June. At the end of June and beginning of July, the Italians, in their turn, advanced along the Piave delta.
264. At this point, the words 'la famine' have been crossed out.
265. 'Wasting diseases, fresh cohorts/Of fevers fell on land and sea'. From *The Odes of Horace*, Book I. [English translation by James Michie].

July

2nd July [1918] - Tuesday:

Two more days of bombs! Always the bombs! [E]very night – The saw mill in Bazeilles has been burnt down. The Austrians have suffered a fierce defeat in Italy. A great many of them are dead. There continues to be famine in Austro-Hungary. No rain: it is a public calamity! What misfortune!

Sunday 7th [July 1918]:

Robert is preparing for his exam which is to be in 8 days' time. He goes to Mr Thynet in Balan every day after his day's work at the station. It is a heavy work-load that one could not endure for a long time on the amount of food we are getting. But he is pleased at the prospect of offering the second part of his baccalaureate to Papa on his return which, we hope, will not be too far away now. It would seem that there are 90,000 Americans in France[266]; it's a great many.

Thursday 11th July [1918]:

Robert is preparing for his exam with commendable ardour. At last a little bit of rain! After such a dry period, what joy! We have learnt of the death of the Great Turk and that Mehmed VI is to succeed him[267], which is a matter of complete indifference to us.

Friday 12th [July 1918]:

We have today read an article in a German newspaper according to which, since the people from Alsace-Lorraine are already at the frontier, it is possible that the hostages will be returning – we hope so. Robert is continuing to study for his exam.

Saturday 13th July [1918]:

At last, some news of Papa! Recent? (no, from 15th June, but nonetheless we are delighted). Not news only, [but] in his own handwriting, and a photograph of his section. It is Taïe who brought it back from the workplace to which she had been summoned. It is a great joy for us, I am going to show it in the Avenue: Papa is not changed, or very little, his hands are a bit thinner. Mr Ninnin, Guérin, Benoit, Peignais have become very thin. Mr Theâtre, Gérault, Gérard, Auskine, Richard, Derule,

266. It was in fact from July onwards that the effects of American aid in men began to be felt. After a first local success by the Americans in Cantigny on 28th May, they participated, from 18th July onwards, in the battle of Soissonnais and l'Ourcq which recaptured Château- Thierry, then in the general allied counter-attack decided on by Foch which began on 25th July 1918.

267. Sultan Mehmed V died on 3rd July [1918] and was succeeded by Mehmed VI.

l'Abbé Lallement (who has a beard like a Cossack) have got thin but they have since recovered (see Papa's letter). Papa is looking forward to returning, he is missing us, but is strong and full of energy. Good for him.

Sunday 14th July [1918]:

The 4th national feast day spent with them, what a shame, abandoned, downcast, worn out, weary, we contemplate with bitterness these pieces of ruin and corpses which separate us from the former years of peace and joy! The fourth . . .

The cannon is relentless and horrible. The Austrians continue to be driven back in Italy and in Albania.

Monday 15th [July 1918]:

Robert's exam (Logic and physics). He is pleased with his written work. If only he can succeed! What a joy for Papa when he returns. There are 2 doctors lodging with us.

Tuesday 16th July [1918]:

2nd and last day of written exams (maths). Tomorrow at midday we will know whether or not Robert has passed.

Wednesday 17th July [1918]:

Two bells sounded as I woke up. One light, and fresh, a bell of the future, then a funereal knell. Robert is eligible, and then has passed! (The only one in his section). We are all delighted, for him, for us and for Papa.

List of those who passed:

Maths: Congar (Paul failed the oral)
Phil: Hénon – Dock
1st Balteau Failed
Lebris Facquier
Aurlier Louvel-Pelérane
Hélène Goquelle (Suzanne failed)
(Someone who had come from Montmédy)
Girulet

2nd piece of news, a sad one: It is a questionnaire[268] from 13th April (my birthday) from Berthe: the death of Aunt Pauline [269], due to pneumonia! . . . So far away, after such a long absence, so much suffering, without a single kiss, to receive the news like that, and not even recent, to hear like that of her death, it is heart-breaking! . . .

She loved us so much, and we loved her so much! The farewells in 1914 had been so upsetting! It is heart-rending . . .

Requiescat in pace [D]omini in secula saculorum Amen![270]

268. Cf footnote 157.
269. Pauline Desoye, Tere's aunt, who was born in 1838.
270. 'May she rest in the peace of the Lord for ever and ever. Amen!'

Thursday 18th [July 1918]:

Yesterday's news has knocked a hole in the joy over the exam result but we are really pleased about it. What cowardly and brutal people are the Germans. (In the Rue des [F]ours), a guard has recently murdered a Belgian civilian prisoner with blows from the butt of his gun. What cowardice! It is not the first time that has happened; they have already killed others by cracking their skulls!
On the other hand, a [German] soldier has been found in the toilets with his skull cracked. Well done!

Monday 22nd [July 1918]:

We heard yesterday that the hostages have arrived in Montmédy [271]. Mlle Béchet, Mmes Devin and Cousin are already in Sedan. At last we are going to see them again after a six months' absence. We are all delighted and are planning what we are going to give him [sic!] when he comes (Pierre his poetry, Robert his exam, Mimi her sonata, me my vocation, Tere a good meal). What joy in the house! It will cease to be so empty. The garden is lovely, he will find everything in good order. We are all agog!
Preparations are being made for our counter-attack. The boches made an unsuccessful one, so they have had to cross back over the Marne, leaving us 18,000 prisoners [272].The immense effort they put into their most recent attack has come to nothing!

Tuesday 23 July 1918 (6-1-18 + 23.7.18) –

Return of the hostages, both men and women! They have all reached Fabert [273]. I do not know how to express my joy! We are watching out the window for Papa. It is in fact quite rare for us to look out at the road but they are on their way back! They, everyone knows what that means, after 6 months, one only speaks of Them: we watch from the window but he is not coming quickly. Mme Triquelin has indeed gone by, but he? . . . He? He is in France! [274] Precisely, in France. In that marvellous fatherland 'where milk and honey flows!' He is in France, that is great, when one thinks about it, but there and then one feels a bit disappointed, but it is only a feeling that one experiences because, materially speaking, it will be better there for him and that, moreover, is what he is aiming at, he will find a good job, It is the time to act, and those who can are taking advantage of it! Nevertheless, what a welcome he would have received, how I could tenderly open my heart to him!

A huge downpour!

From 23rd July to 15th August [1918]:

I have decided not to continue writing up my diary day by day; this is not because there is nothing happening, quite the contrary, but it is because times have changed and with time one's outlook. One is far from being as cheerful as formerly: the disappointments, the daily bereavements alter one's spirit. The attentive reader will perceive in this diary from the way things are written the different ways of thinking; all that I can say, and it is a lot, is that, thanks to the hardships, the sacrifice of one's

271. Forty kilometres east of Sedan.
272. The allied attack forced the Germans back over the Marne on 21 and 22nd July.
273. A district of Sedan.
274. Georges Congar, who was released on 23rd July, had chosen to return to unoccupied France rather than to Sedan, in order to seek a new job in Paris. He did not return to Sedan until December 1918.

own will, we have come to the point of expressing our needs to God and expecting mercy and justice only from Him, to receive everything from his hands and to link our least actions to his will. This spirit is rare in the world, and from this point of view, the war is a difficult but important school.

15th August [1918]:

Procession [commemorating] Louis XIII's vow, in our garden[275].

O [blessed] Virgin, you are our mother, I rest on your breast, pray to Jesus for me, I beseech you; pray above all for France and obtain for us from the Father of Mercy victory and peace in the love of God!

I will not describe this year's procession as I have already given two descriptions, but I will pause here for a while: I am writing about all this on 20th September 1918, when things are serious and I am thinking just now of the things which, then, had not come into my head – a month is a long time and full of happenings. A month ago, I was saying: 'what a lovely day, it can only be compared to a spring day', in a word, it is Our Lady's feast day; but now, I can see further: it is perhaps the last of those blessed hours during which God's ray shone down on us – what am I saying, it will perhaps soon be [a question] of separation and death; but, after all, 'jacta cogitatum tuum coram Domino et ipse enutriet te'[276], yes, let us trust in God, He alone will not fail us, in Him alone is eternity, he is our Father.

From 15th August to 29th September [1918]:

A great many things have happened since I closed this notebook: I will only write a small part of it and will give a general picture.

In France, materially, things are fine: the factories, agriculture, business are more flourishing than they have ever been; the Allies, apart from the Russians, are as well provided for as ourselves. As for morale, things have improved: the imprisonment of people like Caiaux, Mr Cochin's deputation to Rome [277], the muzzled press and a number of other measures, the good moral state of the country all speak in favour of the Fatherland.

In Germany, the quality of goods is deplorable; the only raw material that is still available is paper! Everything is made of paper ('iron' trellis), (braces, clothes, footwear, dressings, etc . . .) and what's more they are not available when one puts in a request for them. Their morale is as shaky as their material: no colonies, no trade, they see that they are ruined and are more and more given to despair; their allies, the Austrians and Bulgarians are also very low; today, the Bulgarians are demanding an armistice, yesterday it was the Austrians; the Turks [278] are under more and more pressure; they are retreating everywhere and soon, left utterly alone, having lost everything, the Germans will be writhing in the convulsions of their last agony, convulsions that will be terrible for them, but equally terrible for Ourselves. Oh us, we are very sick, we people of the Ardennes, we people of Sedan; as I write this, separated from Papa, seeing our friends (the Claudels who have just left) fading away around us, faced

---

275. This procession was instituted in memory of the vow whereby Louis XIII dedicated his person, his kingdom, his crown, and his people to the Blessed Virgin on 10th February 1638.

276. Cf Psalm 55, 22.

277. The Catholic deputy from the right, Denys Cochin, minister from November 1915 to July 1917, visited Rome at the end of June/beginning of July 1918, as the unofficial intermediary between Clemenceau and the Holy See. In particular he pleaded for the rebirth of Poland.

278. Following the successful allied offensive which began on 15th September, the Bulgarians requested an armistice on 25th September and it was signed on 29th September. The Austro-Hungarian proposals of a conference between the belligerents, turned down by the United States two days later, began on 14th September. In Palestine, Allenby drove back and overwhelmed the Turkish forces from 20th September onwards and entered Syria on 22nd and thereafter (Damascus was taken on the 30th). The Turkish government sought an armistice on 14th October,

The Congar family:
The father is missing
due to his deportation.

with the prospect of evacuation, whether forced or not, separated from the two big ones, the misery of the bombardment, there is only one thing left for us to do, place ourselves in the hands of the Lord.

To go back a little in time, let us go back to Friday, 13th September. That was the day on which M and Mme Claudel left for France, for this much loved Fatherland, but when will they get there? One doesn't know. On their departure they left us some potatoes. And yet, we had a laugh in reflecting that we would have none, that we would be feeding ourselves throughout the winter on Greek books that they were giving us to keep for them. The Gorons have sold their linen, in the hope that the Claudels would give them potatoes; how we laughed in thinking that the Gorons would have everything! After all, all that one can wish for them now, these travellers emigrating to a more merciful sky, is that they have a good journey. They will be sorely missed here, because they were friends, in the full sense of the word, we shall be quite lost without them, above all Pierre, who will no longer have his Friday lessons, all of us their advice, me my future teacher. In the hope of seeing them again in France, bon voyage!

Today is the 29th, feast of St Michael patron of France. It is quite likely that our prayers have found an echo on the other side of the front, because the Lord has listened to them. They are producing good fruit because the cannon is getting closer with the speed of lightning. All the talk here is about evacuation[279]. All the young people have prepared their bag in order to leave because they can in fact do so. It is a delight, a joy! We are no longer the same people. We are hoping the French will soon be here, from one moment to the next. So here it is, this much longed-for moment, longed for for 4 years! It is approaching with

279. The offensive by the IV French Army and the 1st American Army, the former aiming for the Meuse between Sedan and Mezière, and the latter for the Meuse between Sedan and Stenay, began at the end of September 1918. In October, the people of Sedan realised that the area would become a battle zone.

giant footsteps; and yet one cannot but see it arriving without dreading the bombardment, the evacuation, the gases, the fire, perhaps even death, all that, for people who have only lived during the past four years for this one moment; it is a bit tough! It results in irritation, an indescribable fever.

The news has something miraculous about it. The [troops] are advancing 10 kms at a time, giant footsteps are not enough for us. We have reached the outskirts of Vouziers and soon we shall be driving them out of the Ardennes.

1ST OCTOBER 1917

Day marking the start of the new school year. It is a sad one. The lessons are not organised. It is deplorable and discouraging, being the first day; it is not [just] anti-social, it is truly deplorable.

2nd October 1918:

Great news! The Bulgarians have signed a treaty, the allies have taken over the railways, everything is fine! At last, here it comes, the much longed-for end of this loathsome war; the Bulgarians have been defeated, it will be the Turks' turn next, then the Austrians! The allies have reached Sophia, everything is wonderful! Long live France! The consequences of these events will be enormous; if it is not quite the end of the war, I believe that it is at least the beginning [of the end].

There are some English prisoners in Sedan, about 100 of them; there may also be some Americans but I'm not sure about that.

3rd October 1918:

The French are at St Quentin, others say they have even reached Douai and Cambrai, but that is not certain [280]. At last they are advancing and one can say that France is beginning to move and to get up! We have taken 50,000 Turkish prisoners. We are heaping victory on victory! Unfortunately we have here in the town a sad picture of what we ourselves may become: refugees passing by, men, young people, women and children on carts and wagons.

According to the conclusions we have come to, the boches are demoralised and down-hearted, they are uneasy although acknowledging very easily the loss of their country! It is a people that we will never be able to understand. The town is in quite an upheaval, everyone is making preparations; the vegetables have come down in price, we are no longer receiving orders. One senses everywhere that something is going to happen. The only thing to do is to trust in God.

280. On 27th September, a new attack had been launched on the Saint-Quentin front but, from Flanders to the Argonne, it was the entire German line that gave way at the end of September. Saint-Quentin and Armentières were recaptured on 2nd October, Lens on the 3rd, Douai on the 5th, Cambrai on the 9th, Le Cateau on the 10th, Laon on the 13th, Lille and Douai on the 17th, Roubaix and Tourcoing on the 18th.

Friday 4th – [October 1918]

Lens, Cambrai, Armentières are in French hands!
When will it be possible to say the same about Sedan? Vouziers is on the front line and will soon be recaptured. What a victory! It is impressive; they will soon be obliged to make peace, making pointless so much shedding of blood. People are saying that there is a list at the town hall of the young people who will have to leave, and that we will know on Sunday. Everyone is ready and the two big ones [281] have put together everything necessary for such a departure. We shall see . . .

Saturday 5th [October 1918]:

There continue to be refugees passing by. There are also some captured French soldiers, and on the other hand, there are some Americans in Sedan. The German government has changed! There is a new chancellor, Max de Bade with Scheimann as his secretary[282]. This democratic government, universal suffrage, may perhaps make it possible for the will of the German people to prevail and lead to peace. Now, in fact, it is no longer victory the soldiers are asking for it is peace.

Sunday 6th [October 1918]:

The famous list of young people has not appeared. It is an appalling joke. Moreover, people are saying that there is no such list; it is ridiculous the state certain people get into. Damascus has been taken with a great number of Turkish prisoners. Seemingly Wilhelm is offering peace. He must be at the end of his tether to take such a step. We have already taken 350,000 prisoners in the course of this offensive. The Crown Prince is at the Goldnisch's in Balan. They will be coming to live here on Tuesday.

Monday 7th [October 1918]:

The Turks have withdrawn to the north of Damascus in disorder, with our bayonets behind them. People are saying that the Austrians have accepted the 14 points as a basis for peace [283], but that is not true, they are simply asking Wilson to summon a congress to discuss the 14 points as a basis for peace. They say hypocritically that there is no need to connect this request with current events, it is simply being done with the humanitarian aim of stopping the already excessive flow of blood. But let the Entente realise that once again it is the entity responsible for delaying the peace! In the meantime, the headquarters and its services are heading for Belgium. Lorries and cars keep passing along the road; let them go! They are being replaced everywhere by the Vouziers headquarters.

Tuesday 8th [October 1918]:

Last night, we heard the cannon booming very loudly, especially towards morning. The doors were shaking, and we were delighted; what will be said about it this morning. Grandma and Grandpa have a captain and a general lodging with them; they

---

281. Pierre is now 19 years of age and Robert 18.
282. For 'Scheidemann'. This leader of the majority SPD party, who had supported the Imperial government during the war, became secretary of state in the Government of Max de Bade, who was appointed chancellor on 3rd October 1918. During the night of 3rd–4th, he sent a memorandum to the United States asking for peace on the basis of [President] Wilson's 'fourteen points'.
283. It was in fact on 7th October that the Swedish ambassador delivered to Washington an Austro-Hungarian memorandum asking for an immediate armistice.

have dogs and are followed by a pile of junk. For us, we have 3 officers and 3 orderlies, who also bring a whole household-full with them. The big ones continue to be ready to leave, and they have dug a hole in the cellar to hide precious things if necessary. It is the prudent thing to do.

Wednesday 9th [October 1918]:

Night of bombs, cannon, an infernal din. At the station, the big ones are overloaded with work, they returned at 7.30 pm, there were so many wagons of munitions and other material returning from the Front; the square in front of the station is unrecognisable, it is so full of stuff: it is the departure, it is the end.

There are two departures from Fond de Givonne: Bergogne and Delcaupe (?): the former has just had an illness from which he has not yet quite recovered and which had him at death's door; so he's leaving, with the cattle sleeping under the open sky, perhaps in the middle of winter. When one thinks that it might soon be our own turn!

Thursday 10th [October 1918]:

The bombs which made such a noise last night were aimed at the police station where they killed a score of boches. They were so well aimed that they killed the sentinel guarding the French prisoners, without touching any of the prisoners themselves, who got off with a fright. It may well soon be the turn of the infernal Kriegsbeute[284] If only that could happen! On the Avenue and Rue des Fosse-haies, they have driven out the inhabitants, including Mousset, Lapierre, Sermone, Franquin and M l'Abbé who is moving house for the second time. For the moment, all the furniture is in the road; as if they had been rescued from a fire! The rout continues. The trains are coming back continually, torn to pieces, badly loaded, real burglaries! On the platform there is indescribable confusion: the banks of the Meuse, normally so peaceful, are more cluttered and filled with confusion than they have ever been! Transport by boat is in fact helping them quite a bit in this need to retreat.

Friday 11th [October 1918]:

The boches have retreated as far as Cateau.

Saturday, 12th [October 1918]:

The Fahrad-depot is moving out [285]. Wilson has sent a reply to Germany [to say] what wisdom told him to say, namely that there will be no peace talks until France and Belgium have been set free [286]. There is a rumour going round the town that Wilhelm has abdicated [287], but nothing is certain, as always.

---

284. War booty store, cf. entry for 12.8.1917 (Trans.).
285. For 'Fahrrad Depot': bicycle garage.
286. On 8th October, in reply to the German note of 3rd October demanding the opening of peace negotiations, Wilson wanted to know whether or not Germany accepted the '14 points' and agreed to the immediate evacuation of the territories occupied by its troops. On 11th October, the German government accepted the afore-mentioned American conditions but, on 14th October, the Americans deemed an immediate armistice impossible.
287. The German government did not announce the Emperor's abdication until 9th November.

Sunday, 13th [October 1918]:

The two older ones have been working all day! On a Sunday, if that is not disgraceful! And baskets of disgusting shells coming from the front! What a filthy place this war booty place is, apart altogether from the fact that it is useful to them. Oh, if only the French could favour it with one or 2 plums, we would dance a jig! The town and the Fond are a sad and deplorable picture of upheaval. The lorries, loaded to excess, dragging behind them other vehicles, the artillery, the horses, the loaded fodder carriers drawn by oxen, the soldiers covered in mud, and the dispatch riders dragging themselves along with tired and dirty faces, the whole in an atmosphere of extreme excitement; then the prisoners, the refugees, pulling their own carts, the women and the children; all that, it is a very strange time.

People are saying that Germany has accepted the peace terms! If that were true, it would be marvellous!

Monday 14th [October 1918]:

(Major Seminary wood). The big ones have pulled up the last of the potatoes (the reds). To say that we are provided for, and we will not be needing them! Taïe is working from today onwards. She is at the Cousins tidying and cleaning the apartments: If that is not a shame, at her age, and in her condition, and her sex! Washing windows! Dirty boche brutes!

Tuesday 15th [October 1918]:

Just now we are very well fed and, when liberation comes, people will not want to believe what we have suffered, and to what extent, because they will see us with rosy cheeks; in fact, counting on being liberated, we are eating the potatoes without counting them. Long live France!

Wednesday 16th [October 1918]:

At the war booty depot, everything is being packed up because all the soldiers are expecting to leave from one moment to the next. The gazette gives Germany's reply to Wilson: Germany accepts everything. One can scarcely believe it; so there will soon be peace, the French will be returning! We heard this evening that the peace had been refused: the boches were continuing to demand restrictions, so the answer was 'no'. The right answer[;] we will be going to Germany!

Thursday 17th [October 1918]

The entente's reply to the boches stated that they would only negotiate when France had been liberated and that, for the moment, their behaviour in France was disgraceful: in fact, it is incredible and unheard-of what they are taking to Germany as booty, they will have the wherewithal to re-furnish their villas! But we will soon be after them and then it will be terrible; stealing, burning, ransacking! Let them watch out! We have recaptured Laon. The boches are extremely demoralised, the big ones see this at the war booty depot to which were brought the clothes of the soldiers who were killed by the bomb in Torcy: there were a lot of them.

Friday 18th [October 1918]:

Victory! Lille, Roubaix Tourcoing and Ostend etc. have all been re-taken. These names and the extent of the recapture say far more than I could put into words!

Saturday 19th [October 1918]:

Our poor streets are having a tough time! So many convoys coming and going! The town itself is unrecognisable: the boches are sleeping in the streets, the convoys stop on the road in order to sleep; in Fond, 2 horses died of fatigue on the same day! It is the retreat

Sunday 20th August [288] [October 1918]:

We have recaptured Bruges and Zeebrugge[289], as far as Ghent and Holland! In Belgium we are advancing very rapidly, and Belgian civilians are taking up arms against the invader and the barbarian! There is an uprising in Berlin (some deaths). Wilhelm is at this moment making a religious retreat with the Crown Prince, I don't know where! What a comedy!
There is a continuous flow of convoys and the town is all topsy-turvy with the arrival of troops. Unceasing rain.

Monday 21st [October 1918]:

More and more convoys! [Also] evacuees: they pass by dragging carts loaded with their luggage: it is sad from many points of view, above all for us who may soon be sharing the same fate.

288. This is clearly a mistake on the part of the author. The date is undoubtedly October.
289. Bruges, Zeebrugge and the Flemish coast were liberated on 19th October.

Tuesday 22nd [October 1918]:

It is dreadful to hear the cannon as we heard it last night! It is really dreadful . . .
There was some bombing last night, a terrific sound as of thunder . . .
The moment is coming and we have begun to make ready the 3rd hollow [290] in case of bombardment; we have to take every precaution and if Papa were here, that is what he would do. We frequently ask ourselves what Papa must be saying; he must be very worried about us; when will we be able to see him again!

Wednesday 23rd [October 1918]:

The cannon continues to thunder enormously, and the evacuees continue to pass by.
The boches from the war booty depot will be leaving, probably on Friday, and the big ones may be going with them (?). People are saying that the men will be leaving on Friday, Saturday and Sunday. How much truth there is in all this I really do not know.

Thursday 24th [October 1918]:

The boches from the war booty depot are tidying up all their things. The big ones, too, are making ready, they packed their bag today, everything is ready. People are saying that some men in Sedan have their document for tomorrow!

Friday 25th [October 1918]:

We still know nothing about the departure. The boches have put 2 cannons on the dyke, probably for the aeroplanes. Here is a truly amazing story: Grandma arrived here yesterday afternoon: 'The armistice has been signed, we will no longer hear the cannon from 4 o'clock tomorrow. It was an officer who said it; today the entire town knew and repeated that a general (Grandpa has a General Awbet lodging with him) had told M Desoye that we would [no longer] be hearing the cannon after 4 o'clock, that the general armistice had been signed, that it was true, very true! What a tall story!

Saturday 26th [October 1918]:

We have more or less finished the preparations for departure: people are saying that Wilson has refused to negotiate with the Hohenzollerns, that he will only negotiate with the German people [291]. What a fine man this Wilson is; let him come to Sedan, we will erect a statue in his honour.

Wednesday 30th [October 1918]:

Seemingly the entente would agree to an armistice, but on very harsh conditions for the boches, the evacuation of Belgium and of France and the occupation by the Allies of Metz, Strasbourg and Coblentz. Seemingly also Wilhelm no longer commands his army and the troops are being controlled by the Reichstag.

290. Cf footnote 226.
291. On 23rd October, the American reply to the third German note stipulated that the conditions of the armistice must make any resumption of hostilities impossible for Germany and that the conditions for peace could not be discussed with the current German government.

In view of the possible evacuation of the population of Sedan, those who wish to travel by train in the direction of Holland must be registered before Friday.

Nobody in Sedan wants to leave, we will perish beneath our own ruins rather than die somewhere on the road.

We feel we have good reason to hope, this notice is a good sign, all the more so in that Turkey and Austria have laid down their arms like Bulgaria [292] and that the boches, left to themselves, will be unable to do anything against our allies and ourselves.

Thursday 31st [October 1918]:

The town is full of excitement and discussion on account of the notice; at home all is calm and the big ones have rounded off their last day of work by pinching the first and last boche bread that they managed to wangle. So it is true that the young people will not be leaving and if we have to endure long hours of anguish, we will do so together. Nothing but this happening makes our souls rejoice [293], and it is with a light heart that we are about to enter into the furnace of the front which is getting closer and closer to us.

1st November 1918:

The boches are preparing trenches in the municipal gardens [294].

2nd November 1918:

Today is the day of the dead, and tomorrow, for us, may well also be a day of the dead; how many bereavements to weep over, and how many more bereavements to be wept over are yet to come! Seemingly, the entire town is due to be evacuated tomorrow at

---

292. Turkey signed the armistice on 30th October. Austro-Hungary accepted all Wilson's conditions and asked for an armistice on 29th October. Bulgaria had already signed the armistice on 29th September.
293. He had written 'our hearts' to begin with.
294. By the end of October, it thus became clear to the population of Sedan that the town would become a combat zone, and on 2nd November an order for evacuation was posted up, to be carried out on the following day. Sedan was at the meeting point between the IV French army and the American 1st army. From 7th to 10th November, the cannonade over Sedan was continuous, between German batteries set up on the right bank of the Meuse, and French batteries situated on the left bank. It was during the night of 10th to 11th November that, between Vrigne-Meuse and Donchery, the French crossed the Meuse, the Americans for their part crossing at Mouzon. But the 120th line regiment did not enter Sedan until the morning of 17th November.

11 a.m. Evacuation is the worst aspect of the war for the civilians, leaving their place of shelter, dragging themselves laboriously along muddy roads, waiting in driving rain the passage of convoys, without food, pushed around from one town to the next, they literally die of hunger, the men are separated from the women, the women from the children and the sick. This apotheosis of inhumanity which consists in causing the deaths of civilians in greater numbers by extraordinarily refined methods is very much part of the German Kultur. They excel in calming down a population in order to make it evacuate its village in a few hours, and see what they are proposing to us today, look at the alternative we have before our eyes: perish underneath our own ruins or perish on the roads! Really, the people of Sedan who have always given proof of their mettle, will today display their courage, for to the order of the German commandant the people of Sedan offer today the most resolute refusal. This afternoon, the leading citizens went to see the commandant to explain to him the attitude of the population. If you remain here, the commandant said, we can guarantee nothing. 'Then are you guaranteeing our evacuation to the French lines[?]' said M Mollart. No reply! What can they say? In this way, their [real] plan was made plain. They wanted to make us all leave and then pillage or destroy the town. But we will stay put, firm and unshakeable in our duty and if we are to die, we shall die. Clearly it is not without anxiety that we are approaching this period of bombardment, but we have already been through fire, and we will go through it a second time, the baptism will be fiercer, but we are strong. Long live France!

Today we have collected the last distribution of rations and have formed, I hope, the last queue.

This distribution of rations is free of charge and quite good and speaks of good-heartedness Down in the hollows, we will not be short of food, milk, sugar, chocolate, biscuits, flower, tobacco, matches, candles, jams, everything, we have everything. We are making ready for the attack and the bombardment which is likely to begin quite soon. What a week we are going to live, what a month perhaps!

Sunday 3rd November 1918:

This day was spent in making preparations, principally in burying things (in the cellar and the hollows). We buried as much as possible and as well as possible all that was most precious in our possession: (jewels, silverware, souvenirs, newspapers, papers, gifts, things of value – linen), then the rest, my word, we left it all to its fate; if we recover it, well and good, but on the other hand if we do not recover it, too bad. We are now beginning a terrible week, I am writing these things after the armistice, (3rd November 1 month ago) and from there I see with terror, almost without believing in this nightmare of the battle at our doors. At about 4 p.m. we had a superb spectacle, rejoicing, the first one for 4 years; in the air right above us a vast number of French aeroplanes, all mixed up in the air with the bursting of German shells whistling through the air in squadrons, here was the prophetic sign of the forthcoming battle, it is infallible and we acknowledge in it the forthcoming victory and deliverance. We jump with joy, we make fun, now, of the boches and their orders, these aeroplanes have put back into our hearts an intense joy and I cannot but end this day with an enthusiastic 'Long live France'.

Monday 4th November [1918]:

We hear the cannon continually, quite clearly, although a terrible and unceasing rumble; they leave us tired but at the same time the preparations we are making are filling our hearts with joy because, when they are finished and after a few days of bombardment, we shall be French, we will be alive, not as slaves, but as free citizens! And nevertheless, while the battle rages things will probably be grim, we may even not see some of our own again, many will be killed and the entire town may possibly be destroyed. The great hope is for an Armistice: apparently the conditions for an armistice have been sent to Germany [295] but

295. It was in fact on 5th November that Wilson sent to Germany a memorandum from the allied governments specifying the conditions of the armistice

either they will be too harsh and they will refuse them, or not harsh enough, and that would be unfortunate; when all's said and done, we must wait. In the chapel, we have put away in the cellar the most precious ornaments, everyone is taking their precautions, everyone is preparing for the great event.

Today a laughable notice was posted up in the town: ordering civilians working for the German army to present themselves to the 'Arbeiteramt' in order to resume work; most of the workers will not go, beginning with the Big Ones who will not be presenting themselves.

We continue to make preparations, to hide and to bury as much as possible, so that those runaways will find nothing valuable if they decide to put the house to the sack.

Tuesday 5-11. 18:

Last night we had, in the middle of the cannonade from the front, a cannonade here in Sedan; we also had the pleasant visit of aeroplanes, it is a little prelude which does us no harm, as it is getting our ears accustomed to the great din.

We learnt during the day that the bombs dropped by the planes fell on the priests' garden; they may have been aiming at the castle; damage: 3 boches killed (sentinel, 2 boches from the field post); one mail van with letters, 2 horses, 1 house destroyed (workshops). No civilians. Undoubtedly, not a single bomb blast has hit a civilian in all these 4 years, it is a very remarkable protection, may it continue during the big moment [to come]!

Moreover, the convoys continue to pass up and down, they were moving all through the night and still now there are lorries, dismantled cars, coaches are all going by! It is a real rout, a complete defeat, however we are getting impatient, and would like it all to have come to an end; who would have said, four months ago, when they were still attacking, that by November, they would be in retreat, fleeing towards Belgium? (Sic transit gloria mundi)[296]. At about 4 pm, the rout became a rush, groups of infantrymen, covered with dust and mud, discarding their equipment, without helmets or rifles, are strung out alongside the convoys; whole groups of them pass by, thus telling us that the front is approaching, one would say that the cannon fire is coming from La Marfée or Wadlincourt [297]; I ask myself which it is; really and truly, we will have seen everything, from the defeat to the victory! What a nightmare these past 4 years have been; when will it be over? And on the road, under an unceasing driving rain, heading for the depths of Germany are the German cohorts who are on the run, laden with booty, with a bayonet in their kidneys.

Wednesday 6.11.18.

The night was relatively calm, give or take a few booms of the cannon. But on the road, there continue to be convoys, people fleeing; official vehicles, covered in mud [and] heavily laden, caissons, supply and forage trucks. On the pavements, splashing through the mud, dirty, in rags and tatters, panting under the weight of their kitbag, stragglers, deserters, people fleeing, infantrymen, horsemen, artillerymen, combat engineers, all on the run; on the vehicles, no semblance of order, a convoy of artillery drawn by Russian prisoners and infantrymen, chaos everywhere. In the town, the police force set up to arrest deserters is quite inadequate; there are no dispatches, no newspapers, no gas, no electricity; but soon the front, the French front and release from captivity. All the time we hear the booms, and louder and louder, and more frequent, as if there were a battery installed along the Meuse, what indeed can these booms be? We don't know, but people are expecting a battle, and defence on

---

and inviting the German government to send a delegation authorised to sign the armistice.

296. Thus passes the glory of the world.

297. Wadelincourt and La Marfée are on the left bank of the Meuse.

the Meuse, and yet there are not really any trenches, the boches have very little in the way of defence works, at least in Sedan. This booming is tiring, all the more so since we do not know what it is, it is thought that it is the front or the German long-range artillery, we are continuing to make a few preparations, but in fact all the preparations have been more or less completed. Throughout the day, always those convoys, convoys going in both directions, but very few troops, only groups of infantry. After 4 p.m., we were told that the station had been blown up, as well as the wooden bridge and the Stackler factory close to the Meuse. There you have a much-tried family because, if the factories have been destroyed, and the house with them, if all their souvenirs have been burnt [298], a lot of furniture and wood destroyed, what is that as compared with the loss of Mr Stackler? So much mourning, so much destruction, and all that by one man, one bandit!

Just now the French are approaching, they are at Chemery [299]. It is quite close. Long live France, here at last is the battle so much longed for for the past 4 years, here is what we have been praying for with all our hearts. Long live France!

Long live France, yes, but in the evening, above the trees, from Mon Repos, there was a great red glow, an immense glow. In the direction of Pont Maugis [300] [hence] in the direction of France! Towards the front – in a day or perhaps two, the same glow will be seen above Sedan, then we will not flinch and towards heaven will arise even more insistently and unanimously the cry: Long live France!

It is sad to see in the distance the glow which we already saw in 1914, and to realise that, over there, there are many families without a roof over their heads, without any means of shelter in the midst of shells, in the midst of the battle, that many cries of distress are being uttered, and that over there, in the midst of the flames and the Front, a lot of mothers will not be able to find their children, and many children will be left orphans! And this is war, this is the work of Germany and its leaders, and as they retreat, laden with booty, we shall be suffering here, through their fault! It is atrocious, it is unjust! Oh, history and France will not know what we have suffered here, we and the prisoners, tomorrow we will be right in the centre of the Front, exposed to the same dangers as the troops but without weapons and without shelter. However, once again today we shall sleep in our own home, though not on the second floor which could be exposed, but in the dining room [301]. During the day, some cannons have been installed, they are located at Maltournée and La Rapaille [302] and throughout the night, they are shooting in the direction of the Front which cannot be far away. They are shooting continually at more or less regular intervals, from the picture window we can see the flashes which throw a very vivid glow on the hills all around. We see the glow, we hear the booming, then a long whistling and over there, at the front, the shell arrives, and perhaps kills one of the soldiers! The noise is terrific, but it is only a prelude as compared with the great onslaught which is to come. We are behind the lines and tomorrow will be in the front line: while we await tomorrow, let us sleep!

Thursday 7-11-18:

I slept well, as did everyone else in the house! It may well be the last night that we spend at home, but it wasn't wasted! The Maltournée cannons and the La Rapaille batteries are continuing to thunder with great violence; we hear distinctly both the thuds and the whistling.

Convoys continue to pass by on the road, they are the last to go, the horses are exhausted, done for; some of them fall on either side of the road. A convoy of sick horses passed by towed along in a vehicle! It is pitiful. The men, too, are in a pitiable state, they throw their helmets and their rifles onto a railing or a wall or an embankment, they pull out of their pocket a morsel

298. The words 'all their goods' have been crossed out.
299. Fourteen kilometres from Sedan.
300. This, too, is on the left bank of the Meuse.
301. The dining room was in fact on the ground floor.
302. Both these locations were nearby, above the Fond de Givonne and about 800 metres from the family house.

of bread which they eat hungrily. It is an utter defeat, all the more so in that they are not very numerous and, as we have seen later on, barely enough of them to put up any kind of resistance. The French are getting nearer day by day, they are [now] at Chéhéry [303]. This evening or tonight they will be attacking the Marfée, tomorrow Sedan will be bombarded, the day after tomorrow we shall be French! For we are very close to the front, the shells whistle continuously all day long, the cannons booming vigorously above the town. In the afternoon we went out, Mimi and Pierre and I, to say goodbye to [them all in the] Avenue. The town is dead and sad. Everyone is getting ready; we see people carrying things to their neighbour's cellar where they will have to live through the bombardment.

In the Raffi house, where the cellars are large, there will be 200 people. Pierre went to the Peignois funeral. It was Mme Peignois who died yesterday, but she is being buried today in case it might not be possible to bury her tomorrow. The town is full of patrols and sentinels of all kinds, wearing helmets and boots, as at the front; all that's missing is their masks; we are all in a state of siege, as in those grim days of 1914. The Avenue is completely empty, our steps ring out on the pavement, all you can hear is ourselves, you might say the town was dead. There are pipes poking out from some cellars which are already emitting smoke, because everything is being done in the cellar, and one has to set things up. We reached Grandpa's; they are very calm, and full of confidence; they too have made their preparations, very peacefully, their cellar has been arranged like a hotel, they would be very comfortable there if there were several ways out and if there were 2 m. of concrete, but the hollows are made of brick and there is only one door! Above all, they will be cut off on the Avenue, which will become a kind of suburb. All along the Meuse and the meadow land, trenches have been dug, there will be machine guns at the Benoit's and the Lamotte's; all things considered, they are very badly off, and it occurs to me at this moment that perhaps I may not see them again; and yet they are so full of confidence and such a natural confidence!

It is really sad to say to oneself that perhaps I am embracing my grandparents for the last time! They will really be fully exposed to machine gun fire, and I ask God to take care of them! Because it is God and only God who is in charge of everything that happens, of all circumstances: the entire town of Sedan, since 1914 has been dedicated to the Sacred Heart by Mr Aclozane (?), it is our last resource as well as our only help and support. For the moment, the town is going through a very painful period of transition, we are no longer part of the hinterland and we are not yet the Front; [and] the people of the 'under class' are taking advantage of it by looting the German depots and ambulances. Today they are at Nassau and the Harbour [304], that will go quickly for it is only for that people are moving about in Sedan, in order to filch things!

The boches have again installed new armaments in La Garonne, in front of the Goulden castle. They will probably be beginning the dance either tonight or tomorrow morning: little by little, everything falls into place, and soon we will become the front line. For the moment there is not even a cat on the road, a sudden calm has replaced all the activity of earlier in the day, it is like after a storm before anyone has yet emerged from shelter. Everyone is making ready at home, arranging a shelter that is as 'invulnerable' as possible. This impression of calm is even more tiring, because one's nerves are on edge, in spite of the calm surrounding us.

After 4 pm, the Facquiers arrived with their organisation, their trunks and their cases, followed by Mme Tuot! What an idea to come so soon; Pauline is very strung up, she cannot keep still and she is fantastically afraid. They are going to establish themselves in the hollow, which means that they will be trying it out before we ourselves go there. They will make it feel lived in, which will be no bad thing. As for ourselves, we are continuing to sleep downstairs, all of us, and we are not planning to move into the hollow until it becomes necessary, in the meantime, let us sleep.

303. Approximately 11 kilometres from Fond de Givonne.

304. The Sedan river port, close to the Fabert Bridge.

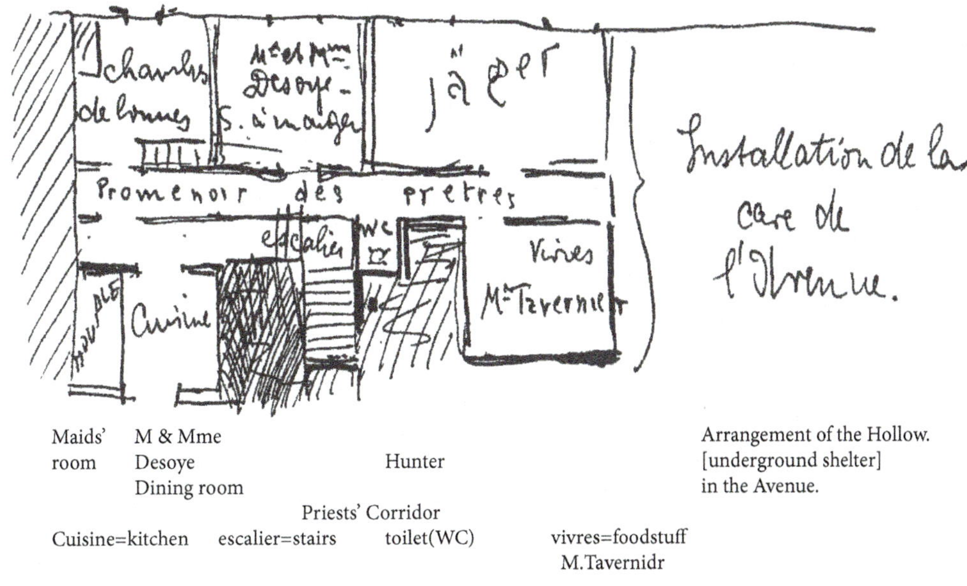

Maids' room

M & Mme Desoye Dining room

Hunter

Arrangement of the Hollow. [underground shelter] in the Avenue.

Priests' Corridor

Cuisine=kitchen escalier=stairs toilet(WC) vivres=foodstuff M.Tavernidr

Friday 8-11-18 .:

We slept very well, the sleep of the just. The night was absolutely calm. I would like to give here some details of the 'battle Masses'. Before the Mass, which was at no set time, M le Curé, with the help of his two satellites (Legée and myself)[305], went to the cellar to bring up the precious things for Mass. We go with one candle, in an air of mystery, and very proud, after all, to be carrying the Mass things and return in the same way by the light of three candles, for there is no electricity. M le Curé says the Mass. There is no longer anything in the tabernacle, for the host in the monstrance has been broken into 4 pieces and consumed; the hosts are consecrated as needed and once, not having consecrated enough hosts, M le Curé did not give Communion to everyone, in short we have gone back to the days of the catacombs! When Mass is over, we take the things back to the cellar and each day we ask ourselves whether tomorrow, buried in the cellars, we will not hear the bullets whistling above us in all directions.

The Facquiers slept badly in the hollow, or rather, they did not sleep. They drank black coffee and talked, but that will have to change when we go there too, or else we will put them out underneath the shells, all the more so in that they have really settled down in the hollow! There will not be any room either for us or for our own baggage! Because we may well soon be going there[;] in addition to the cannon we can now clearly hear the machine guns and the rifle fire coming seemingly from the [M]arfée [306]. For we are soon going to be part of the front line, and then of France; yes, that is about to happen. That seems to us something extraordinary, something marvellous, and in spite of the fact that it is what we are asking for, and that we are so near, one can scarcely believe it will happen so quickly.

305. In other words, two future seminarians.
306. Cf note 34.

Sedan, 1918. Boys' choir.
Yves Congar is the youngest,
standing, on the far right.

Note written on 17th July 1923.

There the diary stops. I could continue it, and so get to October 1919, which is when I left for the Junior Seminary [307], and from then onwards letters written regularly and preserved record my memories! But after all, I prefer not to bring it to an end. Even now, my memories are quite clear: moreover, the notes or diaries of my brothers and my sister are sufficient[308].

What would be interesting would be to record some dates and some specific facts: that is more difficult.

However, here are some indications, taken from the diaries of Pierre and Mimi, from a notebook in which Robert noted down events (a little green notebook with a soft cover entitled 'medical notebook'), and from the correspondence entered into with Papa until he finally returned to Sedan; in fact, based on the memories which all of us have faithfully kept.

I shall put into double brackets [(...)] the thoughts or details which I myself add to the texts I am copying.

A Taken from Robert's notebook:

==========================

(I begin with the night of Wednesday 6th to Thursday 7th Nov. '18)

During the night of Wednesday to Thursday, 2 guns, one between l'Arche and Givonne and the other between l'Arche and Daigny, were firing towards the front at the rate of one round per minute [(at that time we were sleeping in the dining room, with our heads turned towards the bay: we could see the horizon full of streaks and then lit up as each round was fired; during the day we counted the time that elapsed between the firing of the shot and its impact: that is, 15 to 18 seconds)].

In the morning (Thursday 7th) [November 1918], they continued to shoot, but less frequently, one could hear the 77 at the front and the machine guns

No convoys

During the night, relative calm; a few loud explosions.

307. In Rheims, where Yves Congar spent two years.

308. Robert's diary was found by his daughter, Françoise, in June 1997. Pierre's diary was also found by his son François. Mimi's diary was probably destroyed by Mimi herself.

Friday 8th [November1918]

Absolute calm in the morning . . .
(Mass, Communion) – A rifle shot
Some soldiers dragging carts with no rifle
Tere went to see Grandpa and Grandma. Taïe visited the Quinchez'
The Facquiers and M. Tuot spent the night in the hollow.
Noon: an allied plane (white cross) came to fly over Givonne
4 p.m.: 4 planes as at midday.
1 wretched convoy on the Fond de Givonne road
I soldier in the convoy wounded.
At about 6.30 pm French reply towards Fleigneux St Menges (?) from 1 to 10 k. (15 to 20)
We slept in the hollow; night of exchange of artillery, nothing more
boches reduced to silence

Saturday 9th [November 1918]

Morning calm: back ache
Soldiers living in Fond de Givonne.
Observer plane at 8.45 am, then throughout the day round after round.
Cannons silent; clear night forecast;
Calm night; we slept in the house;
1 plane in the evening – amazing calm.
[(This absolute silence lasted for several days: it was very wearisome; we had no news and no contacts. We were cut off and on the alert)]

Sunday [10th November 1918]

Two low Masses.
Frightening calm. Talk of an armistice: a few aeroplanes
Not a single cannon shot.
Afternoon: 4 officers to lodge; they begin to prowl around – altercation –
raid.
4 p.m. shooting at a plane.
punch 18 officers – cooking in the house
a few rounds fired in the distance
in the evening, attack on Floing and on Douzy; becoming fiercer at about 10.45 pm, then decreasing towards morning.
journey by night;
The 18 officers were only 9; they sang for an hour and that's all; they were quiet for the rest of the night.

Monday 11th Nov. [1918] – Our boches keep telling us that the armistice begins at 11am.

In fact, we hear only a few rounds of cannon fire. The rumour is confirmed; the news was made public in the afternoon.
Then we cleared everything out of the hollows
Boches calm during the night.

Tuesday 12th [November 1918] – unsavourycharacters passing by

Our boches . . .
Mass – Com [309] of the armistice
in 30 days 10 km beyond the Rhine
150,000 wagons; 10,000 engines; 500,000 men still here
Surrender of the navy, submarines, French prisoners at once.

Wednesday [13th November 1918]

This morning, Mass of thanksgiving to the Lord for the victory He has given to France –
Departure of Lili Briand – TB
Tidying up to right and to left
Prisoners returning from Belgium all the time

The town decked in bunting: no more Boches

Thursday morning: [14th November 1918]

bringing out the things that had been hidden
In the afternoon. To Wadlincourt
Long live our soldiers!
Our officers are amazing
A little Parisian
Crushing armistice – chapel bedecked with flags
4 French soldiers to lodge (prisoners)

Friday 15th [November 1918] – in the morning, 4 French soldiers as lodgers,

they take chocolate with us
They are very light-hearted.
There is one from the south and one from Paris
1 from Valenciennes; 1 from Upper Saxony.
We went down [into the town]. Mme Quinchez met us; she has seen M' Manet, Fernand

309. Probably 'Announcement'.

At midday: 'blow-out' with Grandpa and Grandma – cabbage, rabbit, potatoes, salad, wine, cake, champagne, coffee, brandy, tobacco! . . . Very good!
4.30 p.m. Met up with Laroche and Vauché in order to go to Olly.
On the way: an Algerian, (misery in Germany), cannons, shells, etc . . .
Illy deserted; cannons
Nobody lodging with us this evening.

This is the end of the information taken from Robert's little notebook; on the basis of this correct and precise information, I can fill out some memories.

My diary comes to an end on Friday 8th [November]: The letter to Papa [310] dated 16th December [1918] describes the night we spent in the hollow, I fully recall the memory of the sand, of the drops of rain which were falling! The Saturday was calm; as on all those days there were aeroplanes. On the afternoon of Friday, one of the French planes seemed to us to be quite red (the sun was setting at about 4 p.m.) and it was pointing downwards; we thought it had been hit and was on fire, but in fact it was machine-gunning a convoy on the road; a boche had been hit in the ditch; that made a terrifying impression on everyone. The outstanding feature of those last two days (the night of Sunday to Monday excepted), was the terrifying and wearisome calm from all points of view, the total lack of news, the emptiness and lack of something to do.

But during the night of Sunday to Monday, at 10.45 p.m. things were quite different: immense cannonade to right and left of the town.
on Mouzon-Remilly and on Don le Mesnil-Donchery. So then we got ready to go to the hollows; in order to make ready for this exodus, it was decided to send the two of us [myself and Mimi] with Taïe, in order to be ready for everything. I can still see that exodus in the night, each of us clutching a bundle and with our bedclothes over our shoulders; we know the garden well, but at night everything is different; I walked into a bush; Mimi followed me; we reached the road at the end of this 'fairy path' as we used to call it, full of the forks [311] used to support the fruit trees and which seemed to me to be longer than usual.

End of the fifth and last exercise book of Yves Congar's war diary

310. See ANNEXES, Document 2.
311. Yves Congar's father used to support the low hanging branches of the fruit trees with Y-shaped props.

ANNEXES

Preliminary Note

Yves Congar's war diary actually ends on 8th November 1918, then continues until 15th November thanks to the notes copied from Robert's diary in 1923.

Nevertheless, in order to complete this text, we deemed it useful to reproduce also the following four documents:

1. The rough notes for Yves Congar's diary for the period from 3rd to 15th November. In fact, from Sunday 3rd November until Tuesday 12th, Yves Congar's diary is duplicated by three rough sheets (one of which had first been used for a Latin translation dated 4th December 1918, which is strange as the text of the actual notes appears to have been written up day by day a month earlier) with a brief description of events.

2. Yves Congar's letter to his father, dated 16th December 1918. (Yves had not seen his father for several months, and the deportation of his father to Lithuania had upset him considerably. Though released in July 1918, Yves' father had remained in Paris for professional reasons. On 16th December 1918, although the armistice had been signed a month earlier, he had not yet returned to the Ardennes).

3. A text written by Yves Congar in 1924, a kind of post-face (or preface as he himself calls it), which perfectly expresses the author's attitude towards the war, the German occupation, as well as towards his own diary, six years after the armistice. Yves Congar had put this text with the five exercise books containing his diary of the war.

4. A text published by Yves Congar in 1978 in *Le Pays sedanais* (nº 5) and entitled: 'Enfance sedanaise [312] (1904–1909)'. This text had been written at the request of his brother Pierre when the latter was chairman of the Société d'histoire et d'archéologie du Sedanais [313].

Stéphane AUDOIN-ROUZEAU
Dominique CONGAR

312. 'A Sedanese Childhood'.
313. 'Sedan Historical and Archeological Society'

Document nº 1

(Rough Draft of part of Yves Congar's Diary)

Sunday 3rd: The fleet of aeroplanes. Unfaithful friends.
Monday 4th: Cannon continually and close. Notice summoning people to work. Armistice conditions sent to Germany.
Tuesday 5th: bombs in the priests' garden[,] convoys passing all night, defeat, rout. Nobody went to the war booty depot.
In the evening, chaos, quick defeat, enormous explosions, unceasing rain which ...[word missing]
Wednesday 6th: Calm night. Line of convoys; loud explosions in the morning, people on the run, deserters in rags
Evening
The station, the Stackler factory blown up. It's said tonight [that] the French [are] at Chémery, no newspapers, no dispatches, no electricity.
In the evening an immense glow in the sky in the direction of Pont Maugis.
Thursday 7th: The boys slept in the dining room. Terrific cannon fire at Rapaille and at Maltournée. Last convoys, men and animals exhausted, they throw away their rifles. The French said to be at Chéréy. Every day after Mass we tidy the things away in the cellar. Cannon fire whistling all day long. In the evening, Peignois funeral. Farewell to Grandpa and Grandma. Machine guns at Benoît and Lamotte. The boches are leaving Sedan. Town on edge. Looting in Nassau and the harbour.
New artillery pieces set up at the reserve fishing area. The Facquiers and Mme Tuot came to the hollows. Sudden calm. Strange silence, no-one on the road.
Friday 8th: Slept very well. The Facquiers didn't. We went to possibly the last Mass. We can hear the machine guns and the shooting at the Marfée.

(on a separate sheet)

1918 Friday 8th: Calm night for us. The Facquiers in the hollow did not sleep. Machine guns and shooting (Marfée). Mass in the catacombs. [T]ere went to the Avenue (8 o'clock). All calm on the road. 1 o'clock attack (aeroplanes) –
Evening: French reply precise and very clear. Went to the hollows to sleep. Calm but nerves on edge. Facquiers fairly calm (except for G and P, and sometimes F.). Not a good night. M F snored – Too hot.
Sat. 9th: wearisome day. Not a sound except for the planes constantly overhead: thudding all the time. No sign of an attack; the silence is tiring and frightening. We slept in the house. Tere has a headache.
Sun. 10th: good night. Seemingly the French have reached the Marfée. Boches to lodge, detestable – trying to loot the attic – to rape Tere – they are going to prepare a punch to celebrate the armistice which, they say, is to come into force at midday tomorrow. One cannot believe this. That is not going to make it Sunday. We will be on the watch. –boches cooking – extraordinary! Night bombardment Floing and Douzy – we were forced to sleep in the hollow; it is disgusting.

Mon. 11th: chapel like a catacomb. armistice? **...** Yes. Fr[ench] seen at Wadlincourt! Trenches in the middle of the town – We are all on edge . . . Fr[ench] here tomorrow.
Tues. 12th: morning, the boches leaving! Joy!
Armistice conditions: total evacuation in 30 days as far as 10 km. beyond the Rhine; surrender of the submarines, torpedo boats, etc.

Surrender of 10,000 engines
150,000 wagons

[release] of the French prisoners immediately; we retain the German prisoners until the peace (we are keeping the boches prisoners) + 500,000 afterwards for reparations.

Document nº 2.

(Letter from Yves to his father,
found in the Dominican Archives.)

16.12.18 –

My dear Papa.

I have lots to tell you, but a letter would be too short and I will be patient for yet another week; for now I will give you some details of the hollow and of the way we lived there. It was on the evening of Friday 8th that we went there; we could distinctly hear the French response in the middle of all the shells that were whistling through the air, and prudence suggested that we should seek a place of safety, so we arrived in the hollow in the middle of the Facquiers' arrangements, and there we camped as best we could, or rather as worst we could, because there is not much space and there are 12 of us. Outside, a fierce storm, the blast of the shells, the explosions; the noise was like that of the wind in a forest, the missiles whistled through the air; it is the front line. In the hollow, the noise is not deadened, but we did not hear it as M Facquier and Mme Tuot set up a chorus as to which of them could snore loudest!

We sleep little, the sand trickles into our neck and our hair and from time to time a merciless drop of water came to cool our hand or our forehead, but when all is said and done, war is war, and the hollow is an excellent shelter, because it would take a very malign missile to find its way to us. Moreover, it is Mr Facquier rather than the booming of the cannon who prevents us from sleeping; in his sleep, he sings the Marseillaise, then snores and then, all of a sudden, he cries out 'get out, all of you, and at once', he thinks he's there . . . oh, what memories . . .

Now it is all over, and it is difficult to believe it, we are all full of joy at our deliverance. For myself, I took advantage of my freedom to go by bike to Donchéry two weeks ago on Sunday. Since then I have had flu, but now I am better and filled with joy at the prospect of your arrival.

Before I end, I must tell you that we are having a torchlight procession every Saturday evening, and on Sunday a concert and in the evening, at supper, coffee with milk and bread; also that the Claudels returned on Monday morning. They had tried to get back to France 3 months ago on an emigrants' train but got stuck in Belgian Luxembourg. They have had lunch and supper with us, the 2 ladies even slept in our large bed, their house is somewhat damaged. And so, before embracing you in fact, I embrace you from a distance and with a full heart, signing myself

Your little Yvonet

Kisses to Maguit, Berthe and all the family. [314]

314. The reference is to the members of the family living in Paris.

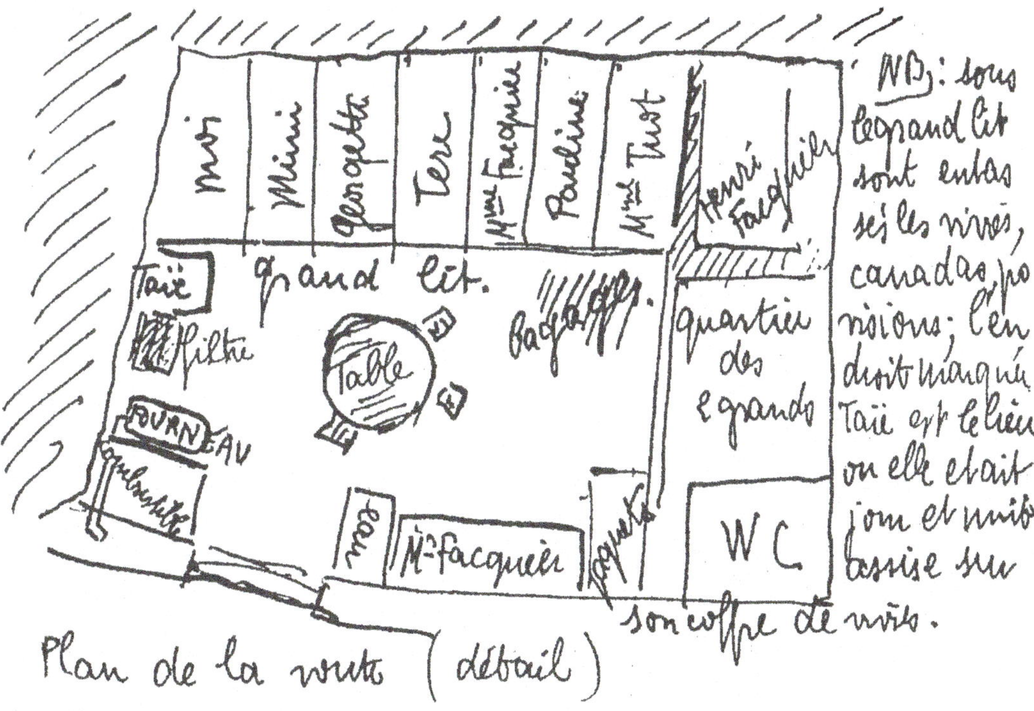

Plan of the Hollow (detail).

moi=myself
filter=filter
fourneau=oven
combustible=fuel

grand lit=large bed
bagages=luggage
table
eau=water

quartier des grands=
the Big Ones' room

NB: the foodstuff, potatoes and provisions were piled up under the big bed; the place marked 'Tere' is the place where she sat day and night on her walnut chest.

Document no 3

Note re
the invasions and the war
and
France's vocation
(unfinished)

As preface to my Diary of the War
(1924, I think) [315]

Before beginning the account of the battle of 1914 and of the four years of occupation that ensued, the little 10 year old boy that I then was wrote the following:

'25th August 1914: Here begins a tragic story; it is a sad and sombre tale written by a child who has ever in his heart love and respect for his country and a great and righteous hatred for a cruel and unjust people.' It was with these sentiments that we, the invaded, fought the war: for we too fought the war. Only a very small number had the honour of performing amazing feats for France, or of carrying out a war mission; but we all did what our bearded [316] brothers were doing: holding out[317].

I have frequently dreamt of doing great things during the war: like Louise de Bettignies, I would have liked to act as a spy for our soldiers; like the heroine of a novel by L Dumur (Le Boucher de Verdun), I dreamt of killing the Emperor; I saw myself haranguing the people of France and, prior to victory, dragging all of them to Sacré Coeur on their knees. I did not accomplish any of these dreams; you will find nothing out of the ordinary in this diary; I just fought the war, with my little boy's heart: I played a lot at being a soldier, seriously, lovingly: I played a few tricks on the boches; I prayed a lot, every day, for the soldiers and even, later, when I learned of the appalling conditions endured by the prisoners, I talked to them sometimes and, when I met a group of them, under my cape, I would make the Sign of the Cross as the priest does when he gives a blessing, and I prayed with all my heart for them.

I did nothing extraordinary; but with all the French who had been invaded, I suffered; we all suffered and endured to the end: that was how we fought the war, that is also how we won the war; because it was a question of suffering and sacrifice: 'to fight is no longer a question of beating oneself, it is to wear a hair shirt; it is to harden one's soul against one's body, to force oneself to seek, in weariness, being stripped naked, the distress of the flesh['].

315. Seemingly the author was 20 years of age when he wrote this preface, which he only dated later on. The year 1924 seems likely: none of the references in the text are later than 1923. We have respected the original formatting of this text.

316. Before writing the expression 'our bearded brothers' Yves Congar had written 'the soldiers', before crossing out these last two words.

317. Note by Yves Congar: 'While I am writing this to you, the Dead Man [Mort Homme] is on fire; it is terrifying and, under this hail of fire, men are holding out. Many have been killed; but those who are still alive will never give in.'
Abbé Cheveleau (?): letter from Verdun, Holy Saturday, 1916, cited in E. Beaumann: *L'Abbé Cheveleau,* Perrin, p. 83-84.

Yes, indeed! Later on, when we are asked what this war was like, we will reply that it was the battle that takes the monk to the depths of his withdrawal. It was a war of sacrifice, a campaign of renunciation, a battle between two sorrows and two self-denials: and the one who managed to endure the longest will be the one who conquered [318].

Thus we too have fought the war by enduring; we too have won the victory by our suffering: 'Victory belongs to the one who can suffer for a quarter of an hour longer than anyone else' was what was taught to our soldiers [319] – 'those who suffer well always conquer[320]'!

By uniting our sacrifice with the holocaust of our soldiers, we did more than just fight and win: with them we redeemed!: 'It would indeed seem that our mission is to save the world simply by the power of suffering'[321] – 'If we believe in the power of the blood shed on Calvary, how should we not also believe, analogically, in the power of the blood shed for the Fatherland? The power of this blood is as certain in the natural order as the power of that other blood in the supernatural order. Yes, we know that the blood of the hosts offered for the fatherland purifies us. We know that it purifies France, that all power comes from it, that all virtue comes from it, that its power is infinite – that no fatherland can live without its power.

Sine sanguine non fit remissio. [Cf Hebrews 9,7] But there is no need for the witness of the Bible. We know well, all of us, that our mission on earth is to redeem France by [our] blood[322]'.

318. Note by Yves Congar: Fr Martial Leken [?]: *Mes cloîtres dans la tempête* – Plon, 1923, pp 205-206.
319. Note by Yves Congar: *Manuel du chef de section d'infanterie,* Paris, Imprimerie nationale, 1917, p 15.
320. Note by Yves Congar: quoted by L. Madelin: *La Bataille de France*, Plon, 1920, p 362.
321. Yves Congar once again quotes the reference to: Fr Martial Leken : *Mes cloîtres dans la tempête* – Plon, 1923, pp 205-206.
322. Note by Yves Congar: Ernest Psichari: *Les voix qui crient dans le désert*, chap. IX, Ed. Conart, 1920, p 189.

Document nº 4

A Sedanese Childhood (1914-1918)
Yves Congar
of the Order of Friars Preachers

'I would like to live once again in this country where my reason was formed, where my imagination became what it is, where I first became aware of both good and evil', wrote Proudhon in exile. It is a long time since I left my own Sedan to which I return so rarely and for such brief visits. But everything that I have lived away from the little town where I was born and grew up, I have lived with the sensibility, the convictions [and] the temperament that my childhood and adolescence in the Ardennes formed in me. All my sap came from my roots: they are embedded in Sedanese soil.

I was born on 13th April 1904, fifty metres from the Meuse. I entered the 11th grade in Turenne College in October 1909. I have very clear memories of those years. I can see the College as if it were yesterday. At the entrance, Turenne asleep on a gun carriage; the concierge, Zéphyr, who used to sell croissants and liquorice sweets and swept up the dead leaves in the autumn; Fay the Principal, who used to impress us with his 85 metre height and his great black frock coat. I see once more the series of mistresses we had: Mme Pacot, Mlle Charlier. The fashion then was to make the waist as small as possible and to increase the roundness of the rump. Mlle C made me think of the map of America that hung on the wall, with the curve of San Francisco, the isthmus of Panama, [and] the rounded shape of Brazil on the Atlantic coast. In 8th grade, we had M Tuot. I can still see him changing the nibs in our pens with a huge pair of pincers and [in doing so], making his temporal and lower jaw muscles dance as if making a great effort. In September, I had fallen under the influence of a young teacher, M Schmitt, who occasionally played ball with us. Having experienced only the monotonous repetition of our lessons, I had been enchanted by a scene in the Misanthrope which he had recited with living intonations. He was, of course, called up in 1914, but I met him once more at the distribution of prizes in the large hall at the Town Hall in 1919 and he recognised me!

1914! I was ten years old. It was thought that the war would not last more than a few months. Towards the end of July, my mother said to my brothers, my sister and myself: 'Keep a diary'. I still have mine, kept up regularly until the Armistice in 1918, which left the French on the left bank of the Meuse and of the Torcy canal. The Germans [had] entered Sedan on Tuesday 25th August, 1914. On that day, I felt the need to draw a long line across the page and to write below it: 'Here begins a tragic story; it is a sad and sombre tale written by a child who has ever in his heart love and respect for his country and a great and righteous hatred for a cruel and unjust people.' The years 1914–1918 marked me deeply. I know very well that no-one is particularly interested in me, but if anyone **is** interested, they should know that they cannot understand me if they do not take into account what I experienced during those years.

As far as the Germans were concerned, it was a case of organised plunder. Being themselves seriously deprived, they took everything: crops, copper and metal (everything was taken including the bells and organs from the churches), wool (mattresses, which were replaced by kelp); requisition of accommodation. The town lived only in slow motion. Leaving it was forbidden. We were hungry. Without a monthly distribution that came from the United States, grocery supplies would have been reduced to zero. We, the lads, put up a limited resistance as best we could. If a German asked us the way to Bazeilles, we would direct him to Floing. We used to cut the straps of the carriages stationed in the Quai de la Régente. My brothers having been conscripted for work at the station (at the 'Kriegsbeutesammelstelle'), took what they could, in spite of the searches. One evening, in the winter of 1917-1918, we had gone to steal some coal briquettes from the station: my brothers were trailing the sledge because it had snowed and it was freezing; I was sitting on top of the heap of briquettes with my cloak covering them, and so we were able to pass under the noses of the guards.

Some people were worse off than we ourselves, [namely] the prisoners who began to appear as their countries entered the war. The Russians, for whom we used to sing their national anthem; Flemish civilian conscripts who were lodged in the castle and who we saw returning from work in a half-starved line and supporting one another; Italians who shivered in the winter but above all wanted cigarettes; the English, pretty miserable. The Germans kept pinning up notices: 'Gotte strafft England! May God punish England'. The extremity of wretchedness was endured by the Romanians who arrived on 1st January 1917 dying of hunger, not in the normal sense of the word but literally: several of them died there in the street. Many of these poor men are lying in our cemetery, beyond the [18]70 monument. We saw no French until after the major German offensives in the spring of 1918. They were cooped up in the great depression that separates the castle from La Rochette. We used to talk to them, in spite of the guards, when they went to look for water at the fountain at the entrance to the Faubourg du Ménil. They were quite a good colour and their necks pink, in contrast to the quite macabre faces of their guardians. Up to then, we had never seen the horizon blue uniforms. It was the dawn of renewal for a hope that had never in fact left us.

Our morale had in fact remained quite high. France had entered into the war in 1914 with a credit balance of patriotism of which no-one today can have any idea. In Sedan we had one infantry regiment, two of dragoons and three generals. When the cavalry trumpets used to sound in the Avenue, our German teacher, who was in any case a poor disciplinarian, could barely keep us in our seats. The moral unanimity of the nation was complete. It has never been recovered since except perhaps in the summer of 1944. Must there be war for the people to dance to the same tune? Or, rather, great hopes of liberation.

The entire college was occupied [and] transformed into a quarantine area; it smelt of ether when one walked along the walls. For premises, we had Mme Devin's house; for playground Pillas Street, all on a slope. The boys used it in the morning and the girls in the afternoon. Very few of the pre-war teachers were left; such supply teachers as were available were used. What I learnt of French and Latin I owe above all to M. Balteau, who normally taught English, was a really gifted teacher, and whom I had for two years. The rest, my God, were no more than so-so.

I belonged to the Fond de Givonne parish where, with my sister, I had made my fervent first Communion on 24th May, 1914. Three months later, our church had been burnt down by the Uhlans who had also taken the parish priest, Abbé Tonnel, to the cemetery and threatened to shoot him. For several weeks, our celebrations were held in the chapel of the Brothers' school at the bottom of Avenue Philippoteaux. Then Pastor Cosson offered Father Tonnel the little chapel next door to the protestant Orphanage, which has since been pulled down. This was our chapel for six years. I am convinced that this detail is not unconnected with the ecumenical vocation that I became aware of in 1928. Besides this, we had some protestant friends, the children of friends of our parents, and even some Jewish friends (Marguerite Auscher, her brother Léon who died when he was deported, and one of whose daughters was a friend of my nieces. Hence, three generations of friendship). Our protestant friends were the Bacots, the Goguels, Pastor Cosson's children, the Brégi family (and when we had lunch with them on a Friday, they were careful not to serve meat!).

Parish life was intense during those anguished years. Fr R Tonnel was an educated man, familiar with his Bossuet. At Saint Charles, Fr Daniel Lallement had organised a boys' choir, several of whose members subsequently entered the seminary. I too followed this path in 1919.

The war had confined us to Sedan. After the winter of 1918–1919, was the time for cycle rides and for the discovery of the Ardennes. I had already been to Bouillon, Frahan, Corbion, where we had spent a holiday. At the time, there was no hotel there and we stayed in a baker's house. We already loved the woods and the Semois, but it was only after the war that we really got to know and, as it were, gain possession of the country. The Semois had not [yet] been invaded, as it has been nowadays, by a vulgar tourism; it was virgin and wild and, at the same time, quiet and familiar. We shared a little of its mystique. And how to describe the woods, the silence in the heart of the forest, the play of light and shade in the tall trees? I love trees, they are for me as it were friends. Their silence does not stand in the way of their presence. What nobility there is in the outward thrust of their branches from a powerful trunk. And when, in Holly, in the early morning or in the evening, one could see the does at liberty without disturbing them: what grace, what an evocation of innocence and of wide-open spaces! . . . Ah! That sequence of bluish horizons, shrouded in a light mist by the fine summer days! It was indeed there that my imagination was fed and formed. 'One does not carry one's fatherland on the soles of one's shoes.' But one carries everywhere what has become flesh in us.

My conscience and attitude owe something to the somewhat Jansenistic outlook in Sedan during my childhood. In my faith and my prayer all those from whom I received their germs in my parish and my family continue to live. I have hardly spoken about the family, but my mother [323] . . . Such fidelity as there is in me comes from my roots and from the oak trees of my country. My ecumenical vocation has a prelude in the relationships of my childhood and the chapel in the Fond de Givonne. When I was working at the Council, in the international theological Commission, the Latin that I had learnt from M Balteau and M Lacroix served me well. My anti-Nazi attitude, my eighteen months in Colditz and my two years in a high security prison camp are all in line with my mini-resistance as a boy in Sedan. But many visits to Germany, and friendships made there, above all in the world of the University, have entirely annihilated the 'great and righteous hatred' that I wrote about on 25th August 1914: nothing is left of it except the memory.

I hope I have omitted the uncertain and the questionable from the experiences that I have described, but have retained what is of value. I pay homage to our town, to all those men and women who have nurtured in me the life of a man.

Le Pays Sédanais, 1978, no 5, pp 27-30.

323. Yves Congar loved his mother dearly. His diary of the 1914-1918 war bears sufficient witness to that. 'My uncle had planned to write a long essay about Tere in conjunction with his sister, but he never managed to do so.' (Note by Dominique Congar).

YVES CONGAR
A WARTIME CHILD

On Monday 27th July, a ten year old boy began to write his diary. He did not finish it until four and half years later, at the age of fourteen. Behind this simple statement there lies a sort of miracle: 'The writings of childhood are fragile and soon destroyed. Or else they remain hidden', a specialist has written [1]. Yves Congar's diary did in fact remain hidden until his death. Although it was known to exist (the author himself referred to it during his adult life, at times even going so far as quoting from his early writings), all trace of the five exercise books that had been written during the war had been lost. Fragile as they were, that was undoubtedly also due, if one thinks about it, to some of the upheavals he experienced later in his life[2]. But the mania for classifying which had been his since childhood undoubtedly contributed considerably to the process which made it possible for such a document to be kept, then brought to light after the author's death[3].

We are talking about a document which is absolutely exceptional for a number of reasons. In fact, there are very few personal diaries written by children as young as Yves Congar was in 1914; still less, clearly, such diaries that have been *edited.* The very great value of such a text is due to the fact that the writing of a child, always rare and precarious, even in cultured circles which are more inclined to encourage children to write such as that to which our diarist belonged[4], it is more characteristic of girls than of boys[5]. Even more frequently, a diary or a journal is the prerogative of what we call nowadays 'adolescents'. Moreover, journals written by children are often disappointing: even in wartime they mostly tend to record the petty details of everyday life, repetitive events of the strictly material order, which are of no interest in the eyes of the adult world. They may well be of interest to childhood specialists, but they have little value for other readers [6].

This is not the case for Yves Congar's diary. Of course, the details which in our eyes are the most insignificant of his daily life are there, above all when Yves was still quite young; they then become mixed in with wider reflections on the war, such as this entry for 29th July 1914: 'I am not at all reassured. I can only think about war. I would like to be a soldier and fight. I believe in today's declaration[.] [W]e are going to gather pectoral flowers to make herb tea no news of Pierre. I have colic[7].' Yves will never

1. Philipe Lejeune, in: *Le Récit d'enfance,* under the direction of Denise Escarpit and Bernadette Poulou, Paris, Éditions du Sorbier, 1993, 312 pages, p 18. On childhood, an extremely important work, even though it does not cover the writings of children, cf. Marie-Josef Chombart de Lauwe, *Un monde autre, l'enfance,* Paris, Payot, 1917.
2. One thinks, in particular, of the second removal of the Saulchoir (then located close to Tournai) by barge, from Belgium to France on 2nd September 1939. One thinks also of the author's captivity between 1940 and 1945.
3. I thank Étienne Fouilloux, Dominique Congar and Fr André Duval for having pointed me towards this document, for allowing me to analyse it, and to benefit from their comments on this text. On this last point, my thanks go also to Annette Becker and Laurence Bertrand Dorléac.
4. Étienne Fouilloux has defined Yves Congar's social milieu as follows: 'A family well known in the town, though of limited means' ('Frère Yves, Cardinal Congar, dominicain. Itinéraire d'un théologien', *Revue des sciences philosophiques et théologiques*, vol. 79, n° 3, July 1995, pp 379-404, p 381.) In 1975, Yves Congar described his own family circle as follows: his maternal grandfather was a 'dealer in wool', whereas his paternal grandfather had established in Sedan 'a small local bank': 'He had made quite a success of it, better than my father, who was not very good at business… My mother worked very hard to ensure that shortage of money did not affect our life as a family.' *(Une vie pour la vérité. Jean Puyo interroge le Père Congar,* Paris, Le Centurion, 1975, 239 pages, p. 8). With reference to the Congar family I have also consulted: *Histoire généalogique familiale Bridier-Congar-Desoye*, undated. 46 pages, (Document kindly lent by Dominique Congar).
5. Philippe Lejeune, *Le Moi des Demoiselles. Enquête sur le journal de jeune fille,* Paris, Éd. du Seuil, 1993, 454 pages. *Journal d'enfance*, 1993, 454 pages.
6. On the other hand, the childhood diary of Anaïs Nin is of exceptional quality. It is true that the child was twelve and a half years old in 1914, and that she was close to adolescence when she began in 1914 and afterwards in New York a journal that she continued to write for the rest of her life (Anaïs Nin, *Journal d'enfance, 1914-1919,* Paris, Stock, 1979, 421 pages).
   For a commentary on this document, cf 'Une enfant catholique dans la Grande Guerre. Le 'Journal d'enfance' d'Anaïs Nin' in *Chrétiens dans la Première Guerre mondiale* (under the editorship of Nadine-Josette Chaline), Éd du Cerf, 1993, 201 pages, pp 35-46.
7. I have respected Yves Congar's original in all quotations included in this monograph.

move very far from the little everyday concerns. But the acuteness of the young boy's view of the war and of the adult world, the precocious maturity to which his diary bears witness, even the quality of his writing make of his diaries of the war what may well be a unique document. Of course, it remains the writing of a child. But Yves is an unusual child[8]. One cannot read, understand and endeavour to interpret such a text if one forgets this vital point.

Why write a diary?

It was on the advice of their mother that each of the Congar children[9] took up a pen in the summer of 1914. Was it a question of a record of the events that were about to take place, or are we to regard this motherly suggestion as mere coincidence? In fact, we have proof that the 'Journal of the Holidays 1914' was not the youthful Congar's very first diary: earlier, during a journey to Paris in the summer of 1913, Yves had kept a diary in a small black notebook. The existence of a first attempt at a diary prior to that of the diary of the war may well provide evidence of a custom that was at the time fairly common in Catholic circles, where to keep a diary was often regarded as a means of education on the intellectual and above all on the spiritual level. From this point of view, it may well be that their mother's suggestion was no more than a repetition of one that had been made on the occasion of the previous year's holiday. In any case, one is struck by the fact that the first entry in Yves' diary is dated 27th July 1914. By this date, in fact, following a month of widespread lack of concern among the public in general in the face of international events, people were becoming aware, in France in particular, of the gravity of the situation in Europe as a whole. The fact that, on 27th July, Yves' diary begins with the international situation: ('today rumours of war were already in the air'), clearly indicates that the rush of events and Yves' recording of them fully coincided. Hence, one cannot exclude the hypothesis that the diary was begun merely in order to describe the war that was clearly on its way. Moreover, the whole of the first entry in the diary is written in the imperfect tense, and it was only on the following day, the 28th, that the diarist used the present tense. This was, in fact, the day on which Austria-Hungary declared war on Serbia, thereby setting in motion the process that led to general war. Thus, everything happens as if the journal had in fact only been begun on that date, 28th July, when the war was already imminent. All this thus tends to confirm the hypothesis of a genuine 'war diary' and not a simple 'journal of the holidays' overwhelmed by the international situation.

Even so, the document we are discussing is undoubtedly the result of a complex writing process. In fact, and this comment is decisive for understanding the effort made by the writer between 1914 and 1918, it seems clear that the diary is not the fruit of the direct recording of events. When one compares the 1914 diary with that describing the visit to Paris the previous year, which was written down there and then and day by day, one is struck by the great difference between the two documents. Undoubtedly, in the space of a year, the diarist had acquired greater skill in writing, in syntax and the overall presentation of a text. There is, however, a gulf between the 1913 diary and the one begun in 1914. It therefore seems reasonable to suppose that Yves' war journal was written slightly after the events on the basis of an earlier and less developed text which made it possible for him to 'rearrange' things to some extent in the definitive exercise book. Moreover, it so happens that there exists one of these 'rough copies', written at the very end of the war, between 3rd and 12th November, 1918. By this time, however, Yves' handwriting was much steadier than in 1914: but he still felt the need to make a quick note of the main events, without undue concern about editing them. Hence, everything seems to indicate that his journal was preceded by a preliminary editing of documents of this type. Indeed, a detailed analysis of the diary itself fully confirms this: the reference to loose sheets inserted between its pages

8. Yves seems to have had, already at this age, a very strong character: 'Apparently I had quite a dreadful character when I was a child. (...). Quick-tempered, pig-headed.' *(Une vie pour la vérité, op.cit.*, p 26.)

9. This was certainly true of Robert, part of whose diary Yves copied in order to complete his own, in which there were some gaps during the last days of the war. It was also true of Marie Louise, who also kept a diary and who almost certainly destroyed it at a later date. Pierre, then aged fifteen, was away visiting a German friend, but he, too, kept a diary between the years of 1914 and 1918.

and sometimes lost, as well as some confusion in dating, reinforce the hypothesis of a text that was written some time later than day-to-day events as they occurred. The regrouping of increasingly lengthy entries to which the diarist had recourse as the war dragged on and as he grew weary of writing up his diary from day to day, point in the same direction. The author makes use of this method for the first time at the beginning of 1915, when he re-arranges his account of the days between 24th and 28th January. Two years later, it was a case of several weeks, or even of several months being regrouped in the same way.

Hence, the very skilful arrangement of the diary scarcely indicates that it was composed 'on the spot'. Yves' text is frequently broken into in order to insert carefully constructed 'Impressions' of the war (the first of these follows the entry for 15th October 1914, the second at the end of December), 'personal thoughts', or even poems (some isolated, others in series), all of which required from the diarist great skill in the overall arrangement. The diary thus becomes a place of synthesis for texts that had been worked on separately. The same is true of the very detailed drawings that the author multiplies in the course of the first two exercise books[10]: it is clear that these, all produced in relation to the text, were inserted, prior to any editing, as part of a sophisticated arrangement of the text which leaves little or no room for spontaneity. To sum up: Yves Congar's text is indeed a diary, but a diary that is the result of a process of writing that has been edited in advance in a number of different ways, at the cost of a fairly long gap between the events as experienced and the definitive recording of them. Such a method of operation undoubtedly involved an immense effort of syntax, orthography, arrangement on the page and graphic research. In the course of such a procedure, can one exclude the idea that one or more members of the family saw him at work and may even have helped him?

It does not really matter. There can be no doubting the effort he made, and it was considerable. Moreover, it extended over a very long period of time for a child who was only ten years of age when he began to write. And herein lies the kernel of the matter: for, when all is said and done, Yves Congar did not write a diary in the ordinary sense of a word. From the beginning, what he wanted to write, what he wrote, was a *book*.

Everything in his five exercise books bears witness to this literary concern. Hence the title he gave to the first of these exercise books, based on those of the 'real books' of his childhood: *'Diary of the Franco-German War 1914-1915, by Y Congar. Illustrated with 42 drawings and 2 maps, from the declaration on 4th August* and even from *27th July 1914 to 27th January 1915'*. The expression 'for publication' which follows immediately and states categorically that the work is understood to be dependent on the time scale of the war further stresses the young boy's desire to attain an editorial perspective. His diary is thought of as a published, or publishable, book, a book consisting of several parts carefully integrated with one another ('continued from n° 1' is written on the cover of the second exercise book), a manuscript book modelled on his own childrens' books (one only has to look at the careful way the cover of each of the exercise books is arranged to be convinced of this). Naturally, the title given to each of the parts changes with the continuation of the conflict: the *'Diary of the Franco-German War 1914-1915*, is followed by the 'Diary of the World War' and this by the 'Diary of the 1914 – 1915 war, then 1914-1919 . . . ', and finally 'War Diary 1918'. But these variations are of little importance, because it is always a question of one and the same book in spite of the diversity of titles and the multiplicity of exercise books. A book about the war begun when the war began and completed, give or take a few days, when it ended[11]. A book that the author had no intention of interrupting before the end of the conflict, as is clear from the 'to be continued' on the covers or on the first pages. A book on which Yves Congar always intended to leave his mark: in addition to the repeated use of his own name as author (sometimes accompanied by his date of birth and a question mark for

10. Twenty-five in the first (27th July 1914-21st January 1915), thirty-three in the second (22nd January 1915-24th September 1915). Thereafter the number of drawings decreased as Yves grew older: the third exercise book (25th September 1915-25th December 1916) contains only thirteen drawings, the fourth (1st January 1917-14th February 1918) no more than three, and the fifth exercise book (15th February-8th November 1918) only four.
11. It is striking to note that having written consistently for more than four years, Yves Congar 'omitted' the armistice and had to describe the last hours of the conflict after the event thanks to his brother Robert's exercise book and his own *a posteriori* memories.

that of his death at some future date[12], or even the mention of copyright fees to be paid to him should the book be reproduced in some form[13]!), he went so far as to add his [adult] signature (sometimes twice over) on the covers of each exercise book, on their first or last page, and also at the end of his poems. A book, decidedly. And also an author.

A book, then, clearly by an outstanding author, but a book which is also frequently quite conventional. In fact, the originality of the project, the growing maturity of judgement and style, the keenness of the outlook are accompanied by a great many platitudes which are frequently linked specifically with this reaching for 'good style' which torments this child who is writing only for others and for the future. There can be no doubt that at times he felt overwhelmed by the mission he had undertaken, as is suggested by these lines written in December 1915:

'Oh, my childhood pen
You could never write
all that I feel
and all that I would like to write.'

This child by means of his diary, this author by means of his book, seeks above all to *bear witness*. This aim seems never to have altered in any way between the beginning and the end of the war [14]. It is to his post-war readers that he addresses himself and in particular those who will never have experienced the German occupation during those four years. After all, does not the fourth exercise book bear the admittedly crossed-out title 'Dedicated to lukewarm French people', which speaks for itself? These lukewarm French people are clearly not the Sedanese whom Yves nevertheless observes mercilessly at times. They are much more likely to be the French people of 'free' France who were unaware of the sufferings of those who had been invaded and were in danger of never knowing anything about them. At least to persist in bearing witness, to go on bearing witness, to bear witness always. This is the meaning of the many passages in the diary that are addressed to those who had been cut off by the front-line and who perhaps had adapted themselves rather too facilely to the trials endured by their compatriots who had been invaded. In the 'thoughts' recorded on 22nd February 1915, these lines of poetry express, for the first time in the diary, this reproach and this source of anguish:

'Oh France! You Queen of the earth,
You leave your children enduring brutal force
Succumbing to need! You see what they have suffered
And what they are still suffering under hands of metal.'

At other times, as in January 1917, Yves Congar seeks to reply directly to the accusation by the 'Boches of the North' which may well have been levelled at the occupied peoples or the refugees, if only by applying their reproaches to themselves:
'Yes, we work against the French! Yes, we are forced to do it! Oh, you French, do not come and say to us after the war: 'It is

12. Cf the poems on 20th February 1915.
13. Poem on a loose sheet inserted into the first exercise book.
14. And undoubtedly continued after the war was over, as is clear from the fact that, after 1918, the three Congar brothers organised a family war museum in the family house, of which, according to Dominique Congar, there were still traces after 1945.

shameful, you semi-boches, who are working for them' because we will reply: 'Why were you so cowardly as to abandon the soil of the fatherland, you who had sworn to defend it until death?'

From beginning to end of the diary, this witness to the suffering of the people who had been invaded constitutes one of the main threads of the constraint endured by the young diarist. 'Still no fresh news', he wrote on 2nd April 1915, 'it is annoying and this diary must make very dull reading but it describes 'life in the occupied countries' and if it is disagreeable to read, life 'in the occupied countries' was disagreeable to live.' Is not the use of the imperfect tense a clear indication of the perspective from which Yves viewed things? He is working for the future and, quite suddenly he is worried by the monotony of his diary, realising that this might prejudice it's being read at a later date, and hence the mission of bearing witness which he has undertaken: My diary of the war is too long – it is becoming monotonous and the war too', he wrote on 14th January 1916. However, he kept going, and without sparing any detail for his future reader. This concern for accuracy caused him to leave blank spaces where he did not know the details, as in the 'list of the things taken by the boches' on [27th] June 1915, or again the list giving the names of the hostages who were taken in January 1918: he waited until he knew the full facts *a posteriori*. The same concern led him to compile boring tables showing the way prices had increased since the beginning of the war, and to draw up the most accurate descriptions possible of the material sufferings endured. His desire to bear witness is at times so pressing that Yves Congar sometimes goes so far as to address directly his future reader, as in January 1917: 'There is no longer any point in recording day by day, event by event, the things that are happening under my eyes, it would be too boring and moreover, I won't do it; it is sufficient for you to read these lines to give you an idea of how we are managing to live.'

This same desire to bear witness prompts him to break into his description of day to day events in order to devote space to long compositions, clearly written on the basis of the most traditional scholastic style, and designed to stigmatise even more forcefully the enemy's brutality: the text on the atrocities perpetrated during the invasion of 1914 written in February 1915 and entitled: 'German atrocities'; the text on the passing of the Romanian prisoners through [Sedan] in January 1917; the text on the deaths of some of the captives in November of the same year; the text on the departure of the hostages in January 1918. For one must not deceive oneself: the extended account of the sufferings endured by those who had been invaded between 1914 and 1918 is in no way a disembodied complaint. It is above all an accusation, and an extremely violent one, of the *enemy*. It is of this enemy and his atrocities that Yves is anxious to leave a record, it is of the suffering inflicted [by that enemy] that he wishes to help preserve the memory. There is no easing off of denunciation in this work which never wearies: at the end of the diary, the anti-German stance is even more pronounced than ever, at the risk of pomposity. Moreover, from then on, it is to France that Yves addresses himself, it is to the people of France that he speaks, in adopting the posture of a privileged if not unique witness of the horrors of the occupation. 'Sometimes I no longer want to continue writing this diary,' he wrote on 20th June 1918, 'but now I am not sorry about it. May the feelings I am trying to express in these lines enter into the hearts of all French people. May France know from these pages, brought together from day to day, what the invaded parts of the country have suffered, what the prisoners, the refugees, the poor people of the Ardennes have suffered. May they realise to the full the barbarity of the boches and may these feelings root them firmly and always in love for their Fatherland!'

'Diary of the 1914-19.. War, by Y Congar, born on 13th April, 1904, who witnessed the war.' This heading to Yves' fourth exercise book summarises perfectly the young writer's chief aim. He is above all 'the one who witnessed the war.' This experience and the memory of it never left Yves Congar. Moreover, it was to the need to *record* this suffering during the war that Congar, as a grown man, referred in the extraordinary 'postface' which he added on a separate sheet in 1924: 'I did nothing extraordinary but, with all the French people who had been invaded, I suffered.'

Things turned out, in fact, as if Yves Congar, like so many of the inhabitants of those regions, had known in advance that what took place in the parts of the country that had been invaded, would have continued not to be fully recognised once the war was over. He was not wrong. Whereas the civilian population in the occupied territories endured the terrible experience of a veritable mutation due to the war in those early years of the 20th century, this was later largely ignored or repressed, including by journalists[15]. It is thanks to Yves Congar's Diary that we are able to perceive more clearly some of the unknown rigours of the occupation and that it conveys the attitudes and protests of those who had to endure it. From the strictly historiographic point of view, this in one of the chief contributions of his text.

The countries that were invaded

First level reading: Yves Congar's diary can be seen as a simple document concerning the countries that had been invaded and occupied during the First World War. From this point of view, its content is a reminder of a reality that has too often been forgotten since the 1930's and even more so since 1945: namely the extraordinary duration of the German occupation in 1914-1918. Unless this fact is borne in mind, it is impossible to understand, for example, the exodus that took place in May-June 1940, which was irrational only in the eyes of those who had not experienced the ordeal of the invasion during the earlier war. From this point of view, the micro-historic scale of this child's diary must not lead one astray, for such a document represents much more than itself. As we have seen, Yves Congar was fully aware of this when he was writing his diary, which in fact bears witness to one of the great historical phenomena of the 20th century, namely the wholesale capture of the enemy's civilian populations by the belligerents.

For a start, one is struck by the extremely restricting framework imposed on the inhabitants of the town, affecting the structure of their daily lives, their movements, their timetables, their social relationships, and also, of course, their material and cultural life. Almost certainly, Yves was only to some extent aware of the administrative organisation which from then onwards governed the lives of the people of Sedan, via the *Kommandantur* and those of its officers who were most clearly visible. On the other hand, he recognised very clearly the consequences of this stranglehold, such as the countless notices with which the people of Sedan were deluged, and the text of which he sometimes went to the trouble of copying. From 1914 to 1918, these notices never ceased to announce new restrictions: limitations on journeys to or from the town, censuses of people and of supplies, the requisitioning of labour and of material goods, all under the threat of fines, imprisonment, or even, at times, of capital punishment. In doing so, Yves Congar inadvertently recognised local variations in the German occupation: that in Sedan itself seems to have been much harsher than in other towns in the Ardennes[16].

This population is a population that is held prisoner, a fact which, as will be seen, determined the young diarist's entire relationship with space and time throughout the war. Shut in physically, as it was not possible for him to leave Sedan, or to write letters to unoccupied France. Shut in and constantly watched, as censuses were taken of the inhabitants and their names written on the front wall of each house. Each one was also obliged to be photographed and to carry an *Ausweiss* from the end of the year 1916 onwards: Yves' own pass has moreover been preserved. Shut in and exploited, for the Germans, there as elsewhere, very quickly made use of the enforced labour of the local population, labour from which not even children aged 14 and over were exempt after October 1916. Moreover, Yves' older brothers were requisitioned for particularly harsh and insalubrious work against which he protests. A population deprived of information, as Yves records from the beginning of the occupation, a factor which represented one of the worst psychological sufferings inflicted on the people in the occupied territories, and one which

15. Concerning the situation of the occupied countries in general and of the North in particular, the most recent works are those of Annette Becker. While awaiting the publication of her work on the humanitarian policies and those cut off by the culture of war by the publisher Noësis, the following articles are relevant: 'Mémoires et commémoration. Les 'atrocités' allemandes de la Première Guerre mondiale dans le Nord de la France', *Revue du Nord,* June 1992, pp 339-354. 'D'une guerre à l'autre: mémoire de l'occupation et de la résistance: 1914-1940', *Revue du Nord, July-September 1994, pp 453-465. 'Lille-Roubaix-Tourcoing, 1914-1918.* L'expérience d'une occupation', *Tourcoing et le Pays de Ferrain, n° 22, 1996, pp. 565-63.* In this connection, whatever the length of the occupation in the Ardennes as a whole, nothing seems to have equalled the fate endured by the people of Lille.
16. On the other hand, we would point out that the occupation in the larger towns was harsher than in the smaller ones and that this, in turn was harsher than in the smaller villages and hamlets.

contributed greatly to their sense of isolation: the wildest rumours circulating in the town and recorded by young Congar, whether he believed them or not, are the most characteristic symptom of a generalised 'hunger for news'.

All this with, just below the surface, sheer boredom. It is one of the greatest figures featured in Yves Congar's Diary, as is clear from this brief entry for 3rd April 1915: 'Absolutely nothing, nothing, nothing. The same for Sunday'. Morale often seems to be very low, as in mid-July, 1915: 'we go about like souls in purgatory, like dishwater. Oh, what a life one lives in occupied countries.' Of this boredom too, however, it is necessary to bear witness, as accurately as possible. This is what Yves does, for example, in describing in detail 'a day under German occupation' such as 1st December 1915.

Two years later, at the beginning of 1917, further complaints about the deadly monotony of the occupation with a very pertinent description of the physical and moral weakening, and of the profound effects of the day-to-day pressure: 'A monotonous life, repeated day after day, constant humiliations, not enough to eat, deprived of real news for 3 years, fed up of constantly hearing the same noise, the boom of the cannon. Seeing only boches, always boches, a state of moral exhaustion, a bodily lassitude made all the worse on account of being unable to leave the town, always on the qui-vive and under an unjust regime, here you have quite a rosy picture of life in the occupied countries.' In April of the same year, for the first time he established a link between his own existence and that of the prisoners: 'All this is not designed to make one love this atrocious, monotonous, inexorable life! . . . I would never get to the end if I wanted to describe all the humiliations of which we are the victims – the worst of all is still the monotony, to be without news for 3 [whole] years. Being locked in, it is dreadful, indescribable, it causes a moral lassitude, a lack of drive, of energy which gnaws at one's spirit and prevents one from thinking!' Without saying it explicitly, Yves Congar here clearly perceives the essence of the matter: the occupation is primarily humiliation, an attack on one's dignity.

This narrowing of the field of everyday life makes it possible to understand a phenomenon to which Yves' diary bears very clear witness, even though he himself was not directly conscious of the changes taking place under his eyes, namely the strengthening and the increased richness of family ties. His mother, Tere, is shown to be the pivot of this family life, which was in fact enriched rather than impoverished by the occupation and by the weakening of [normal] social life. Was it not she who organised schooling from the very first year of the war, as we learn from the cover of the second exercise book, which began in January 1915 ('War School directed by Mme Congar'[17])? Was it not also she who organised the reading of the great works of French literature during the winter evenings? Moreover, the Congar family occupied a central place in the organisation of some of the religious festivals of the parish. Almost certainly it was because all public meetings were forbidden that it was on the Congar family's land that the procession of the Sacred Heart took place, a treasured collective feast in which Yves took part each year from 1915 to 1918 [18]. Similarly, he never fails to mention the trivial happenings in the lives of his two older brothers and of his sister, happenings which took on great importance in this existence centred on the family circle. Undoubtedly, the bond between the children was further strengthened by their experience of the war. The maternal grandparents[19], too, were very much in evidence, as were some friends with whom one perceives the existence of close links, made even closer by adversity. This is borne out by those late afternoon meetings that took place once a fortnight from the summer of 1916 onwards, and possibly even more frequently throughout the year 1918 during which the Congar brothers put on theatrical and musical shows. The deportation of the father during that year, though dramatic in itself, seems not to have interfered in any way with the deep springs of family sociability.

17. Yves Congar was due to enter sixth grade in October 1914. But there were no longer either premises or teachers, other than any who could be found. A private house was used as a school which was attended by boys in the morning and girls in the afternoon; so that each had only half a day's schooling (*Une vie pour la vérité, op cit,* p. 13).
18. Devotion to the Sacred Heart occupied a central place in the wartime devotions. On this subject, cf: Annette Becker, *La Guerre et la Foi. De la mort à la mémoire, 1914-1930,* Paris, A Clin, 1994, 141 pages.
19. The paternal grandparents had died in 1909 and 1910.

All in all, on reading what Yves wrote, the overall picture of the occupation and its hardships is presented in semi-tones: the weakening of social life under constraints of all sorts produced a perceptible increase in people's appreciation of the family circle and also of the bonds of friendship. From this point of view, such a diary throws an interesting light on the complex effects, on the affective level, of the 1914-1918 occupation. This imprisoned population was also a hungry one: hunger was equally one of the principal figures featured in Yves' diary. From the beginning to the end of the war, he never ceases to comment on the effects of the lack of food. In reading the diary, moreover, such a term seems far from appropriate, such is the extent to which what he wrote enables one to understand quite what the lack of nourishment meant for the peoples in the occupied territories. A lack of nourishment which became real shortage, even though Yves' family was able to make use of the produce from their property to give them additional nourishment.

Very soon, as early as the autumn of 1914, white bread and milk disappeared from the town, followed by meat, then by most vegetables, all against a background of inflation and of continual demands for food from the Germans which further complicated the supply of food to an already much deprived population. The two last years of the war seem to have been [quite] dramatic. In 1917, cabbages came to constitute one of the basic foods and, in the spring of 1918, we learn that a dish of nettles was served once a week in the Congar family. Admittedly, the foodstuffs provided by the neutral countries, Spain and America to begin with, then Spain and Holland from 1917 onwards, eased some of the shortages, but far too intermittently. The shortage of food, which Yves interprets less as deliberate bullying on the part of the Germans but rather as unavoidable for an occupying army whose own food situation was equally precarious, produced from the diarist some of his best descriptions of 'life in the occupied countries'. These include his portrayal of the Sedanese, conceivably from the upper echelons of society, making their way, with a wide assortment of vehicles, towards the rare areas available for cultivation from the spring of 1917 onwards; of others, during the summer of the same year, besieging those few market gardeners who still had produce to sell (the Congar property, in fact, was surrounded by their establishments); others, again, jostling one another at the doorway to shops [in the hope of] meagre supplies, as at the beginning of the month of August in the year 1915: 'The supplies have come. Well, you go to the grocer's shop with your bread card; there [you find] a hundred or so people milling round the door and shoving baskets at one another in order to be the first. More and more people keep coming, and you join them; you are punched 6 times, pushed at 4 times with a basket, then all of a sudden a great big man arrives: 'eh im' faud la plasse moi' ['Make room for me'] accompanied by a punch, a thrust with his elbow, a thrust with his basket, another with his knees, and there he is in front by the door, you are squeezed into this mass of executioners and you are lucky to escape with your life.'

On the other hand, the times when food supplies improved were among the great joys described by the little fellow in his diary. When the supplies from abroad arrived in December 1917, at a time when the food situation was becoming critical in Sedan, Yves explodes with joy on account of the feast prepared (one wonders how!) by his mother: 'A huge quantity of waffles! And cocoa! What a feast . . . how good it is. It was an unforgettable evening! We sang until 10 pm, together as a family, and all the time Tere was reminding us to eat the waffles. It was really good . . .'

Other aspects of the constraints of the occupation included such things as the collective fines imposed on the town as a form of reprisal for one or other misdeed on the part of the local population, as well as the requisitions which were clearly presented, and perceived, as downright robbery or gratuitous bullying. It was one of the areas concerning which Yves Congar most clearly reveals his fury, as we see from his protest written in large letters against the fine imposed in July 1915 ('It's disgraceful!!'). The list of requisitions is a long one: metals at the beginning of 1917 (including the bells at the end of the year), foodstuffs (potatoes, fruit, eggs), furniture in January 1916,, and even bedclothes at the end of 1916, followed by mattresses in 1918: here too what Yves Congar writes is invaluable. Thanks to him, behind the term 'requisitions', this banal wartime phenomenon, we see more clearly the gratuitous brutality, the petty bureaucracy, the humiliating compulsion that accompanied each confiscation imposed by the occupying power. On the other hand, his testimony makes it possible to understand the difficulty in maintaining full control of the entire population of Sedan, in spite of the harsh measures imposed on them. From the beginning to the end of the conflict, one perceives a day-by-day resistance to the demands of the occupying forces. The young diarist's mockery of them constitutes in fact one of the aspects of this. However, this resistance does not seem to have become really serious until the very last days of the occupation when, at the beginning of November 1918, the occupying power began to relax its hold. Up to then, they had done nothing but tighten their hold on the population from one day to the next. However, young Congar's diary never gives the impression of a 'normalised' cohabitation between the occupied and the occupiers, but rather that of a steadily increased oppression which was more and more resisted, as a counterpart to the steadily increased radicalisation of the German demands.

The population was also physically threatened by the practice of taking hostages, the systematic nature of which was a characteristic feature of the 1914-1918 war. This practice, to which Yves Congar shows himself to be particularly sensitive – the names of his own father, and even of his grandfather having been included in the list of potential hostages as early as 29th August 1914 – renewed, at the beginning of the war, a tradition dating back to 1870 which consisted in taking captive prominent people known to all as a means of forestalling any hidden desire for resistance, any attempt at sabotage, any attempt at armed opposition. It was, moreover, the same purpose behind the deliberate arson and assassination of civilians that took place during the first phase of the invasion, which were duly reported by young Yves: at this point, the aim was to paralyse civilian resistance, of which, in fact, there was none, but which the invaders believed to be entirely conceivable in the psychological climate of the invasion [20]. Hence, from the very beginning of the invasion the taking of hostages formed part of a double continuity. It prolonged the physical violence committed against civilians at the time of the actual '1914 invasion', but this in turn formed part of the string of other less recent acts of violence perpetrated at the time of the 1870 invasion.

It is true that this procedure quickly fell into abeyance from January 1915 onwards. Once German order had been firmly established and all danger to the occupying German troops eliminated, the taking of hostages ceased. On the other hand, the deportation of Yves Congar's father and of other Sedanese men and women to concentration camps in Germany and in the Baltic was the fruit of a different strategy. At this stage, the taking of hostages was no longer connected with any need to secure the safety of the local occupying troops. In 1918, the deportees were 'national' hostages, taken in the trial of strength between France and Germany on account of the civilians from Alsace-Lorraine who had been taken to France at the beginning of the war, once French troops had entered Alsace. From then onwards, the taking of hostages consisted in the deportation, in less than humane and frequently atrocious conditions from the point of view of both food and hygiene, which resulted in a very high death rate among the deportees. In reading Yves's diary, one realises the extent to which the author, as also undoubtedly a great many of the Sedanese, failed to perceive the real significance of this deportation which affected all the occupied territories in the same way [21]. Clearly the possibility of death in the camps is borne in mind, as we see from Yves' father's verbal 'will' a few moments before his departure, but everything points to the fact that young Yves had difficulty in understanding the meaning of such a wrench, with all the risks attached to it. He, always so suspicious in relation to the occupying forces, reassured himself as best he could on this occasion. How could he have realised that these deportations were a sign, among others, of a growing brutality in the course of the war, which placed civilians at the epicentre of the conflict. How could he understand that the fate of the invaded territories and of their inhabitants were an indication of the terrifying birth pangs of 'total war'?

The most striking feature in this diary of a child is undoubtedly the degree to which Yves Congar held onto his intellectual independence, his independence of judgement. In contact with the adult world, he picked up the news, whether true or false,

20. In this connection, see John Horne, 'Les mains coupées': 'atrocités allemandes' et opinion française en 1914', *Guerres mondiales et conflits contemporains*, n° 171, July 1993, pp 29-45. Alan Kramer, 'Les 'atrocités allemandes': mythologie populaire, propaganda et manipulations dans l'armée allemande', *Guerres mondiales et conflits contemporains*, n° 171, July 1993, pp. 47-67. John Horne and Alan Kramer, 'German 'Atrocities' and Franco-German Opinion, 1914: The Evidence of German Soldiers' Diaries', *Journal of Modern History*, n° 66, March 1994, pp 1-33.

21. *La Gazette des Ardennes*: this German newspaper published by the people in the occupied territories, referred on this occasion to 'necessary reprisals', on 10th January 1918, p 1. It further revealed that the measure affected, in all, 600 men and 400 women 'of the upper classes' from all the occupied areas.

that he heard from it. He recorded honestly what happened to the people around him. But he kept himself aloof. And he formed judgements.

Thanks to the judgements he makes, we realise that this occupied population was not homogeneous. Yves highlights some heroes, whether anonymous or not. There were people whose patriotism never failed, those who knew how to resist in word or in deed, even at the risk of their lives. One such was the Abbé Toussaint who refused to give up his bicycle in January 1915: another was the manager of the gas works who was shot in July 1916; such, too, were the men and women who were arrested in January 1917 for having given food to the starving Romanian prisoners. On the other hand, he talks harshly of the weak, those who denounced others, those who co-operated with the occupying forces,, those who gave in too easily to their demands such as those 'cowards' and 'deserters' who succeeded in securing alterations in the lists of those leaving for unoccupied France. Or, worse still, those who voluntarily placed themselves at the service of the Germans such as those five 'so-called French women who work in the sewing rooms against their country'. Even the fact of showing oneself to be too easily impressionable was enough to earn a diatribe from young Congar, as in the case of the municipality ('those imbeciles who have paid the 15,000 marks', and of those who steal from the people) or of one or other of the neighbours, male or female, who get too worked up. On the whole he has very little sympathy for the adult world around him which is emphatically too emotional, too cast down, too easily convinced by the bad news spread abroad by the occupying forces: 'Since there is something going on,' he complained on 20th April 1915, 'the crowds gather, thereby increasing people's unhappiness instead of waiting resolutely and calmly, but it is excusable: after what we have seen, one can always expect worse to come from them.'

He himself always sought to keep a cool head and his diary represents to some extent the opposite of the normal adult/child relationship: by setting a world of 'grown-ups' who are too often unreasonable against the child who always knows how to keep calm; he does not hesitate to cast himself in this role. As early as 29th August, 1914, he declared that he wanted to be a solder and to fight. Later on, he describes how he had spat at a German soldier he had met in the street, or else stealing what he could from the occupying forces, as well as having been summoned to the *Kommandantur* for having insulted an officer and then making fun of his interlocutor. Moreover, did he not belong to a juvenile secret society for resistance against the enemy (with its numbered membership cards, false names, code words etc)? In 1975, he wrote about this as follows: 'We had undertaken a small war, such as is possible for children. We inflicted all sorts of little torments on the enemy [22] . . .' . If one is to believe this retrospective testimony, Yves Congar was decidedly not merely the author of a book in which he intended to bear witness. The 'autobiographical pact' [23] established between 1914 and 1918 led him, like so many other children during the Great War, whether in occupied territories or not, to live the war on the heroic plane. Yves Congar, child hero [24].

A time and a space

To begin with, the young boy's relationship with the 'time' of the war was always a short-term and even a very short-term one. The end of the conflict, which for him consisted in the proximate arrival of French troops, was always envisaged as being destined to happen quite soon, while the effective prolongation of the war in no way contradicted the hopes he placed in a speedy liberation. As early as 16th September 1914, when he was told of a group of Uhlan troops passing through in a pitiful condition, he at once envisaged an imminent German retreat. A month later, he again spoke of the possibility of their coming on the basis of the loud booming of the canon and unusual activity among the German officers. His disappointment about this, which he recorded at once [25], did not prevent him from expressing his hope once again the following week in terms

22. *Une vie pour la vérité, op cit,* p 22.
23. Expression borrowed from Philippe Lejeune, *Le Pacte autobiographique,* Paris, Ed. du Seuil, 1975.
24. On this point, cf. Stéphane Audoin-Rouzeau, *La Guerre des enfants (1914-1918),* Paris, A. Colin, 1993, 187 pages.
25. Cf Entry for 15th October 1914.

characteristic of the way Yves viewed the time of the war: 'The cannon is booming very loudly. It is coming closer. Oh! If only the French could return'[26]. On December 1st, once again alerted by the passing through of exhausted German troops, he began once more to hope for the 'great day'. On 17th March, 1915, he began yet again to think that 'the French are almost certainly advancing' and on the 26th he was even more convinced of this: 'So we shall be seeing these dear Frenchmen again, so much the better'. Things became even more certain on 31st March, thanks to the assurance of a prophecy by a neighbour to the effect that Sedan would be liberated on 29th April. Hope quickly shown to be false? No matter: on 31st May, he was still hoping that the occupation would not last for more than another month, while at the same time being exasperated at having to wait so long. It is true that on 26th September 1915, he somewhat lengthened the periods of time he usually envisaged: he made a bet with one of his friends that the French would be there for Christmas. More than three months to wait.

In fact, like a great many others, Yves needed quite an extended experience of the war and the occupation before he could give up his short-term view of things and make up his mind to envisage a long drawn-out war. To begin with, this awareness was retrospective, but is clearly perceptible in the entry for 25th August 1915 in which Yves was able to interiorise to some extent, though as yet still only partially, the reality of a long drawn-out war:

1. 'already a year of occupation
for 365 days
we have heard the cannon
always, always, always.

2. yes already, already, already
for a year
we have not glimpsed a soldier
belonging to the good French nation

3. already already a year of horror
already a year of suffering
a year since our poor heart
has not seen its beloved France

4. already a year since the barbarians
have soiled French soil
they will be leaving soon,
because they can no longer remain here.

Henceforward, it was above all the yearly anniversaries that structured his personal chronology of the conflict: anniversary of the beginning of the German occupation ('It's disgraceful: two anniversaries with them: 1st September 1914 and 1st September 1915!'). The wartime Christmases provided another opportunity for measuring the passage of time and for formulating wishes that the next Christmas would be different: 'Christmas Eve! Once again with them this Feast, the next will be in Germany, I hope[,] because, after all, I have had enough of these boches. The second Christmas once again with them! Oh, no, it is too much, and I have had enough.' The following year, in 1916, the date of Christmas played the same commemorative role, and the same effect of predicting a development envisaged in the coming year: 'Sad, sad day. Last Christmas, I had hoped that this Christmas would have been spent with the French, this time, I am convinced of it.' From this point onwards, it is in fact on a yearly scale and no longer that of a month or, indeed, of a week as at the beginning of the conflict, that young Congar envisages the foreseeable duration of his sufferings.

In the spring of 1917, Yves again declares that he is convinced that they will not have to endure yet another winter of war. However, from the very beginning of this year, a new element, apparent just below the surface, in turn subverted this review of the war on a yearly basis. As the result of a steadily increasing lassitude, everything came to be looked upon as if the war was never going to end. The duration of the war had begun to escape, so to speak, the 'control' that the little fellow had tried to maintain over the occupation by means of the time limits – always further extended, always renewed – that he imposed on it as a way of ensuring that it did come to an end. What he wrote at the beginning of January 1917 clearly conveys this impression

26. Cf Entry for 22nd October 1914 .

of an unforeseeable, immeasurable limit to the time of *waiting*: 'I really have nothing special to tell you because, when I began this diary, I thought I would be doing it for 3 or 4 months, and, lo and behold, this horror called war has been going on for nearly 3 years. From then onwards, in fact, the duration of the war escaped all control. All one can do is to endure, to endure interminably. In this sense, Yves would seem to represent the French people as a whole, including those in non-occupied France, who only came to terms with the prospect of a 'never-ending war' after the conflict had gone on for several years[27]. In September 1917, Yves expressed himself willing from now on to 'hope', but without venturing to suggest any possible time limit: 'When, oh when, will we be rid of the Germans? If that could happen soon, we would light fires of joy, we would dance, recover our former energy, but no, we are disheartened and at the same time one continues to hope in France, one hopes in something miraculous: in God!' Similarly, at Christmas, he contents himself with a single sober comment, avoiding any forecast of the future: 'Christmas! . . . another one . . . alas!'

It would take Yves Congar some time before he proved capable of once again envisaging a favourable outcome of the interminable conflict: on 14th July 1918, he contented himself with recording the continual prolongation of the conflict without manifesting the least sign of hope ('The 4th national feast day spent with them, what a shame, abandoned, downcast, worn out, weary, we contemplate with bitterness these pieces of ruin and corpses which separate us from the former years of peace and joy! The fourth . . . .'). In fact, one has to wait until the very last weeks of the war in order to see Yves once again envisaging a positive outcome. This is borne out by the entry for 15th August–29th September, where he records that 'the news has something miraculous about it' and that 'soon we shall be driving them out of the Ardennes'. On 2nd October, he is categorical: 'At last, here it comes, the much longed-for end of this loathsome war'. Even so, the last words of his diary, on 8th November, bear witness to the weariness provoked by the war in recognising that it can at last come to an end: 'For we are soon going to be part of the front line, and then of France, yes, that really is about to happen. That seems to us something extraordinary, something marvellous, and in spite of the fact that it is what we are asking for, and that we are so near, one can scarcely believe it will happen so quickly.' Only three days before the armistice, the negotiations for which Yves knew to be well advanced amongst the belligerents, it did not seem to him possible that the war could be over so quickly. Was it for this reason that he did not write up his diary during the last three days which preceded the cessation of hostilities?

This imaginative outlook on time during the war which, as we have seen, developed between the beginning and the end of the war was counterbalanced by a corresponding outlook on the space taken up by the conflict, which also affected the way in which he described it. A complex space, which could be described as a series of concentric circles. To begin with, there is the geography of the battles that took place quite close to Sedan, by means of which young Congar was able to have an immediate perception of what was taking place close to the town where he lived; further away, the whole of the western front of which Yves could not but have indirect knowledge. Further away still were the other theatres of war. Three different spaces which constitute the 'war map' imagined by the author, itself closely connected with the chronology of the immense event in which he was immersed.

Only seemingly paradoxically, it was the space closest to him that was the subject of the greatest illusions. From Sedan, Yves perceived to some extent the noisiness of the conflict, thanks to the distance over which the sound of the artillery bombardment, chiefly that of Verdun, was carried. But the conclusions that he came to bore no relation to the artillery duels of the Salient: the sound of fire, depending on whether it sounded nearby or further off, provided Yves with the day-to-day mental picture he formed of the front line, and hence of the hoped-for arrival of French troops in the town. He repeatedly describes hypothetical battles of French advances close to nearby localities in the Ardennes. The entry for 1st October 1914 is typical of this imaginative picture of events: 'The cannon is booming very loudly, the Boches themselves are quite disturbed by it, it is being said that we have reached Rimogne and Vendresse; if only it were true'. This representation of the space of the war, which directly links the

27. On this point, cf. Jean-Jacques Becker, *Les Français dans la Grande Guerre,* Paris, Lafont, 1980, 317 pages.

sound of the cannon to the proximity or otherwise of the liberating troops is reinforced by the relationship Yves conceived between German defeats in the nearby area and new rumours inflicted on the Sedanese. The entry for 26th December 1914 is symptomatic of this guided reading of local events: 'They must have been defeated because there is a notice: 'Men from 18 to 48 are to report to the town hall: they are prisoners [28], and also because one can hear the cannon booming very loudly from the direction of Noyer.' Throughout the year 1915, the world of sound marked by the cannon, accompanied by the rhythm of the German demands, helped to feed the young diarist's conjectures concerning the forthcoming evacuation of the town by its occupants. Sometimes, even the most insignificant details (an increase in the number of officers to be quartered in the town, for example), are interpreted through the prism of a localised defeat of the enemy. Flights of French aircraft over the town and their bombing raids are similarly treated with the same exaggerated interpretations: 'We are swimming in hope!' he wrote on 23rd September after two French planes had flown over the town. It was not, in fact, until 1916 that we see him disentangling himself from this 'first circle' of the war and placing his hopes on events taking place considerably further off. A widening of his vision denoting a more realistic picture of the conflict, but also of a growing maturity in the diarist himself, who by now has become a twelve-year-old.

The information that Yves was receiving concerning the major confrontations in the various theatres of the war in which he was becoming increasingly interested seems to have come to him from a variety of sources: the chief such source seems to have been the *Gazette des Ardennes*, perhaps complemented by some of the German newspapers[29]. The often quite crazy rumours circulating in the town, whether endorsed or not by the official newspapers licensed by the occupying forces, also had a role to play, as also the family circle which was another source of 'picked up' information as can be seen by the role played by the two older brothers. Although it is difficult to determine quite what weight to attach to these various sources of information, the filtering process that we see at work in Yves Congar is nonetheless instructive in this context of 'hunger for news' of which he never ceases to complain and which constitutes the framework in which he wrote his diary.

Hence, the western front constitutes the 'second circle' in Yves Congar's war. It is striking to note how disparate is the nature of the data he records about this, as well as the widely diverging time scales in which this information seems to have reached him. Thus, he does not seem to have heard anything at all about the German defeat on the Marne at the beginning of September 1914, and even less about the 'retreat to the sea' in the following months. On the other hand, in 1915, thanks to German sources of information, he knew as early as 26th September of the major French Champagne offensive which had been launched the previous day. At the beginning of 1916 he learnt, again from the same sources, of the beginning of the battle of Verdun and the fall of Douaumont, but he seems to have been extremely badly informed about the way things went from then onwards. In July he seems to have known nothing about the Franco-British attack on the Somme, which moreover gets no mention in the following months. In 1917, he was totally unaware of the entire German strategic withdrawal in Picardie in February-March, and he made no mention of the French attack on the Chemin des Dames during the month of April. On the other hand, the French attack on both banks of the river Meuse that began on 20th August does seem to have been mentioned, as well as that on Malmaison which was launched on 23rd October, and about which Yves already had news on the 25th. Similarly, in November he referred to the British attack on Cambrai only a day after it actually took place.

It would seem, then, that up to the autumn of 1917, the information available to the teenage Congar was very patchy, with no mention of many events of primary importance. However, things changed towards the end of 1917 and throughout the last

28. Throughout the district, men from the age of 18 upwards had been requisitionable since 10th November. In January 1915, men aged between 17 and 48 were deemed to be civilian prisoners. In October 1916, in Sedan, children from 11 to 16 years were also called up and required to work, from April 1917 onwards, under the supervision of the occupying forces. In November 1916, [this applied to] the entire population.

29. One occasionally comes across some of the expressions used in the *Gazette des Ardennes* in Yves' diary. The expression 'all-out war' used, for example, in March 1918, with reference to the German offensive, is derived from a phrase taken from the editorial in the *Gazette* for 31st March 1918 referring to 'a war conducted on a massive scale'.

year of the war. Does this indicate that news had become more widely available in Sedan as a whole, or that a young boy who by now was 13-14 years of age was acquiring a wider vision of things? There is no way of knowing for certain, all the more so since it may well be that both factors may have produced a cumulative effect. In any case, the information available to Yves Congar about the way the conflict was going increased enormously in quantity, in quality and in accuracy of timing. The lengths of time it took for the information to reach him also became much shorter. As early as December 1917, he referred to the possibility of a German offensive on the western front, linked to the weakening of the eastern front. On 25th March, 1918, he wrote at length about the great German offensive in Picardie which had begun four days earlier, then of that in Aisne, which had begun on 27th May, of which he gave details on 1st June. In July, immediately prior to the switch-over in the strategic balance of forces, he was fully aware of the importance of the American support of the allied cause. He mentioned, without the slightest delay, the beginning of the counter-offensive on the Marne in July. On the other hand, he seems to have known nothing about the general assault at the end of the month, which he did not mention until the 29th of September. In October 1918, however, his geography of events on the western front becomes particularly precise. At the end of the month this 'second circle' of the war came to coincide with the first as the people of Sedan began to realise that they were going to be trapped at the centre of the conflict.

It seems clear that Yves Congar's perception of events on the western front had become steadily clearer from the end of 1917 onwards. From this point onwards, the boy had gained a knowledge of what was happening which, though succinct and incomplete, was quite different from the situation at the beginning of the war. But what about his knowledge of the other fronts which constituted the 'third circle' of his geography of the war? Curiously enough, this was more complete that one might have imagined, as we see from his description of the events leading up to the war in the summer of 1914 at the beginning of his Diary when he was not much more than ten years of age. Throughout the conflict he recorded the entry into the war of the various countries, and even the internal events (whether exaggerated or inaccurate is irrelevant) in some of them. Information reached him concerning the introduction of military service in Great Britain, for example, the political changes in France, Germany, Austria, Russia and even in Turkey, though he denied the truth of some of these news items when they did not match his view of the world. Similarly, he was fairly accurately informed concerning the Holy See's appeals for peace in 1915 and again in 1917, as well as of the German peace proposals towards the end of the year 1916. He was equally aware of the events taking place in Asia and in the Middle East, as well as on the Balkan and Italian fronts. Finally, due almost certainly to the occupying forces' preoccupation with events in the east, the Russian front featured fairly frequently in his diary even though his description of events there was rather more fuzzy than elsewhere. There, as elsewhere, his chronology of events in this third circle appears to gain in accuracy as the war came to an end.

Basically, it is not so much the fact of not knowing about events as such that gave Yves a frequently distorted view of the conflict. It was rather his own partiality as a died-in-the-wool patriot, his own personal interpretation of the information at his disposal which pushed him to view everything in a rigid teleology of an allied victory. It was his patriotic faith that prevented him, in spite of all obstacles, from having a more realistic view of the war.

For Yves Congar, in fact, the war was never something that was far off, disembodied, unreal. Several times, the brutality of the conflict touched him directly, justifying his conviction that he was 'making war' and later that of 'having fought it' when he wrote about it afterwards during the 1920's.

The first break, in a sense the 'first blood', was the entry of the Germans into Sedan on 25th August 1914. Yves Congar drew a double black line across the page, thereby definitively separating two epochs. And he wrote: 'Here begins a tragic story; it is a sad and sombre tale written by a child who has ever in his heart love and respect for his country and a great and righteous hatred for a cruel and unjust people.' This text is of paramount importance in the logic of Yves Congar's bearing of testimony, not so much on account of its content as such, which denotes the readiness of a ten-year-old child to remain, in spite of the invasion, faithful to his country and to hatred of the invader, but rather the actual layout of the page, drawing a definitive frontier between a 'before' and an 'after', a 'before' and 'after' the war, a 'before' and 'after' the occupation. So much is this so that this passage is the one which Père Congar, sixty-four years later, copied from his diary in order to insert it into a brief account of his childhood in Sedan[30]. Of course, by 1978, Yves Congar, as he himself explained, had long ago given up his 1914 hatred of a 'cruel and unjust people'. But he had not forgotten the underlying aspect of this first day of the presence of the enemy, a memory which, moreover, was closely linked with the spectacle of the first corpses[31].

The 'second blood' came with the 'general impressions' which, on 15th October 1914, break into the even flow of Yves' exercise book and enable him for the first time to embark at greater length (and a second time at even greater length on 22nd February 1915) on the German atrocities committed at the time of their invasion of Belgium and the North and East of France. At this point he denounced the barbaric and fire-loving 'race' which he at once compared with the Huns: 'Never again in my life, surely, will I see anything so horrible', he wrote in 'this page written in order to state something of the truth.'

The 'third blood' consisted in the putting to death of the family dog decided on by his parents in order not to have to pay the Germans the relevant tax which became compulsory in April 1915. The poison was injected on 15th May: 'Gloomy day, sad day. My dog was put to death'. For the first time since the invasion, the presence of the enemy was expressed in a death very close to him, a death which was nothing other, in Yves' eyes, than a death caused by war. His emotion was such that he wrote no less than five poems on the subject, and these were added to the description of the death itself. In spite of a slight hint of reproach of the dog's masters ['My spirit was wholly shrouded in black/And before you, sombre and sad victim, I did not raise my eyes, for fear of seeing you/Judge of our action alongside your crime'), the dog's death is nonetheless transfigured into the sacrifice of a hero of the fatherland, into a death on the field of honour: the 'bleeding war hero' is emphatically a 'hero of France', making legitimate the laying of a tricolour flag on the tomb two weeks later. Moreover, this 'martyr' of the Fatherland has a soul, the soul of a patriot which will lead it to join this 'divine nation' which, in the little boy's eyes, is represented by non-occupied France. He states this in his last farewell which is worth quoting in full:

> Toto, my dog who is now dead, go to the fatherland
> for which you gave so willingly your poor life.
> make for this Standard, make for the dark red madder.
> make for your country, make for France
> head for the capital admired throughout Europe.
> go quickly, run, trot, gallop,
> jump. Go towards the Gauls, towards the Latin race,
> go towards this nation, this divine nation,
> you well deserve it, hero of our Ardennes
> flee this horde here, this German horde,
> die so that your soul may go to its place

30. *Le Pays sedanais,* 1978, n° 5, pp 27-30. Text published as an annex to the diary [cf Document n° 4 above]. Until this Diary came to light and was published, these few lines were the only ones, of all those written by Yves Congar between 1914 and 1918, to have been published. They were also the only ones quoted by their author who, moreover, made only allusive references to his diary (according to his nephew Dominique Congar).
31. It was in fact concerning this presence of about thirty German wounded and dead men in front of the bridge leading to the station that Yves Congar referred to once more in his 1975 account (*Une vie pour la vérité, op cit,* p 11).

die in peace and be worthy of the race
elder daughter of the Church, daughter of Science
And this race I speak of, 'this race is France'.

A further rupture occurred with the massive fine of July 1915 imposed on the occupied towns as a reprisal for an act of sabotage on the railway. The diarist expressed his protest in large letters, and he even mentioned the possibility of the assassination of two officers of the *Kommendantur*, for it is in reality a question of death and not merely of money, since it seems to him to go without saying that this French ransom would 'be used in killing their brothers'. The drama is thus only seemingly a question of money.

The death of men is even more directly present with the execution on 13th July of the manager of the gas works for communicating with non-occupied France by carrier pigeon. Yves rejects the true reason for this execution and sees in it nothing more than a simple pretext for German vengeance. M Busson immediately becomes a Christian martyr (had he not died a 'very Christian' death?) and a saint of the Fatherland, crying out 'Long live France' as he fell dead and, moreover, executed on the eve of 14th July! Such a patriotic coincidence was certainly not lost on young Congar: 'To celebrate our 14th July, we have something which comes from the fatherland: *an example . . .* ', he wrote on the national feast day.

But on January 2nd 1917, an event of quite a different order took place with the passing through the town of a convoy of Romanian prisoners. Sixth shedding of blood. In Yves' diary, this turning point is equal in importance to the shock of the entry of the Germans into Sedan in 1914. The passing through of such a convoy was linked to the military collapse of the Romanians at the end of the year 1916; the treatment meted out to the prisoners, in turn, is the result of the Germans' ethnic contempt for their enemies on the eastern and southern fronts: Slavs above all, but also Romanians and, at the end of 1917, Italians. Yves' description of the cruelty inflicted on the Romanian soldiers on 2nd January 1917 has, moreover, been corroborated by other witnesses. Yves describes at length the malnutrition deliberately inflicted on those men who were literally dying of hunger, the wearisome march which was forced on them, the blows with a rifle butt that rained down on their backs or even faces, the kicks in the stomach, the blood that poured out and stained the pavement when the cortège had passed by, the collapse and death there in the road of some who could go no further. The pleasure which the Germans took in this spectacle did not escape this Sedanese youngster: the empty cigarette packages thrown in derision, the laughter, the insults... The lad was stunned by this encounter with the brutality of war, in particular that of the Balkan fronts which he perceived here on the rebound. He expressed the immense shock of this discovery – for discovery it was – in terms of deliberate solemnity: 'Romanians! men! Prisoners! The wounded . . . have been massacred. For days and days on end, the boches have been dragging prisoners in the mud of their towns. These men have fought, these men have given themselves up, and the boches have dragged them, dying of hunger and exhaustion for weeks on end, they threw them into a station for 18 days [32] without food . . . They have driven them on with rifle butts, the wounded were falling, and those who fell died! . . . Today is the day on which these corpses who had been soldiers arrived in Sedan.' And this spectacle struck the twelve year old boy so forcibly that he drew a further line of demarcation –less marked than the one he drew on 25th August 1914 but equally expressive – between a before and an after. The first few lines of his testimony, written entirely in a rhetoric designed to emphasise the gravity of his account, and to stress the indignation of the witness, clearly indicate the importance of this new break: 'Barbarity! Shame! Vengeance! Hatred! . . . When in Germany a woman, an old man, a child pleads for mercy from the conquering French, you will reply: 'January 2nd, and you will kill.'

The last major break before the final liberation was the moment when the war, this time, directly affects Yves' own family in the person of his father. He had in fact been selected as a hostage by the occupying forces at the beginning of January 1918, and was forcibly deported to the Mylegani Camp in Lithuania, where living conditions proved to be extremely harsh, as can be seen from the high mortality rate among the hostages after only a few weeks of captivity. Having learnt on 4th January of the

32. This figure was altered to 14 at a later date.

forthcoming departure, the young diarist's hand froze: 'My pen almost refuses to write the following pages (. . .)', he confessed. The first entries for the month of January are devoted to this clearly highly important event of the father's departure: the family's last day together on 5th January; the regrouping of the hostages and farewells to the children on the 6th, making it possible for George Congar to assure them that he was convinced he would return (Yves himself tries to convince himself that the hostages will be treated well) and also to utter some last wishes. The little fellow, deprived of his father, wrote one of the longest entries in the entire diary about these last moments of separation, a fact for which he felt it necessary to apologise to his future readers. But he had no real appreciation of the fact that from this point onwards civilians were regarded as an increasingly maltreated bargaining chip in the confrontation between nations.

With the approach of the front in October 1918, the young diarist who, by now, was fourteen and a half years of age, began preparing himself for one last encounter with the violence of war. By this time, in fact, all the Sedanese realised that the town would become a combat zone. For Congar, the joy of the forthcoming victory was mixed up with the thought of his own death and, for the first time since the beginning of the conflict, he resolved to look this squarely in the face. At the beginning of November, when the Sedanese as a whole rejected any idea of evacuating the town, and his own family took refuge underground as protection from the bombardments, he declared: 'But we will stay put, firm and unshakeable in our duty and if we are to die, we shall die.' On 7th November, he once again envisaged the death of members of his family, noting the sadness of perhaps embracing his relatives 'for the last time'. One last entry, that for 8th November. Then Yves stopped writing. The remainder of his account was not written up until the war was over, in 1923.

Hence it would be a mistake to think of his diary as an uninterrupted whole by allowing oneself to be deceived by the apparent continuity, this discreet monotony conveyed by the day-by-day description of events. On the contrary, circumstances imposed on the boy's diary a series of decisive turning points, eight at least, from the moment when the Germans entered Sedan in August 1914 up to his preparation for the supreme sacrifice in November 1918. These turning points were also phases, thresholds after which his view of the war –and perhaps he himself – was transformed. Seen from this angle, Yves Congar's diary is an introductory text, a transcription of the discovery of a new form of war which served as a model for the rest of the century. We shall see further on what profit the adult Congar drew from it.

The meaning of the war

For Yves as for so many of his contemporaries this war had a meaning. This is true for him at the age of ten, and even more so at the age of fourteen. And this meaning will be clear at once from the young fellow's relationship with the members of the occupying forces.

These, in fact, never ceased in any circumstances to be the *enemy*. Clearly, as is so often the case in the testimonies of the time, whether these come from grown-ups or from children, from men or women, from soldiers or civilians, from those in the occupied territories or in 'free' France, there is at times a dissociation between the adversary when seen at a distance and the actual occupying forces with whom direct contact is established. Where these latter are concerned [and they are clearly part of the picture since the Sedanese were obliged to provide accommodation for the Germans, which must have proved a heavy burden in view of the number of troops constantly passing through], Yves proved to be quite discreet. He had very little to say about the officers who were accommodated in his own home or in that of his grandparents, and it seems clear that he was not particularly interested in the matter. For all that, one of them at least, who lodged with the Congars in May 1916, evoked praise of a sort from him: 'Our boche is really very funny, he is a roisterer and a libertine but he is not wicked'.

Exceptional leniency! Since in fact it concerns a member of the occupying forces, Yves almost never freed himself from a deep repulsion which never noticeably lessened between 1914 and 1918. The constancy of this childish hatred undoubtedly reflects that of the adults around him. It is expressed in writing but also in drawing and caricatures in many places throughout the diary. It is also conveyed in the form of insults, as in the passage concerning the passing through of prisoners in August 1914, where words such as 'you peaked-cap-you' and 'you coward'. But the hatred is not only verbal: it was also expressed openly in very significant gestures such as the moment when Yves, though unprovoked, gratuitously spat at a soldier who was coming towards him on the street on 12th March 1915.

The impression of the invaders conveyed by Yves was very quickly modified by the atrocities which they committed against civilians, and which he described on 22nd-23rd August 1914. At once, the Germans who were already responsible for the war were termed 'nameless barbarians', 'wretches', 'thieves', 'assassins' and 'arsonists', 'nags' and even 'dustbins' in a poem written in December 1914. Yves would never deviate from this until the end of the war. From the start, in his eyes the war was that of Civilisation against Barbarianism, a war of absolute Good against absolute Evil. A trite enough vision perhaps, but this was the view of the majority of the French in his day.

From that time onwards, the countless and tiny acts of 'resistance' to the occupying forces in which Yves took part would not be sufficient to staunch his hatred. The malignity of this 'cursed race', which he sees as in partnership with the Devil, legitimised his recurrent desire for exemplary vengeance, vengeance which justified an appeal from the present to the future, compensation at some future date for present-day humiliation. 'Oh! In 10 years time !!!!?' he exclaimed on 8th November 1914. In fact he reverted several times to this ten year deadline for inflicting punishment. In December 1914 he clarified his idea by expressing the wish that 'in the next war our young people will go to Germany and starve them'. On January 1st 1916, he refers to his 'clenched teeth' due to his rage on account of a night-time gun battle and, at Christmas in this same year, he imagines himself one day in Germany with this motto as his watchword: 'No mercy, no quarter'. After the Romanian prisoners had passed through the town at the beginning of 1917, what he wrote became even harsher, and he calls for the killing of old men, women and children when they plead for mercy from the conquerors of Germany. Six months later, we find him looking forward to the day when Germany will be 'erased from the map of Europe'. 'The boches, this race that I hate, but with a fierce and deep hatred' are the words Yves used in October 1917 concerning the requisition of church bells, which he sees as a supreme profanation; a month later he repeated: 'I hate this race from the bottom of my heart'. All this being so, it is not at all surprising that the news of great hunger in Germany which he records in December evokes from him just one comment: 'My word, let them all die!'.

Thanks to this series of quotations, it is not difficult to perceive the [steadily increasing] radicalisation of this young Sedanese's hatred that accompanied the prolongation of the occupation, the multiplication of the suffering endured and the addition of the atrocious scenes with which he was confronted. What he wrote is quite difficult to understand – or even to accept? – today, and their author himself later rejected them. For it to be understood, it has to be put back into its context. The 1914-18 War, whether one likes it or not, was a collective aggression deeply charged with hatred in all the belligerent societies and, in this regard, what Yves Congar expressed was fully in tune with the deepest sentiments of the adult society around him. Clearly, the people in the occupied territories, especially in the towns, were in the front line of anti-German hostility, but a great many of the people in unoccupied France would easily have recognised themselves in what young Yves wrote. As for the children, they in no way constituted a separate world during the 1914-1918 war, quite the contrary. They were fully and deeply integrated into the 'war culture'; they shared the thought patterns and the sensibilities of the societies at war even if this amounted at times to internalising its most radical aspects[33]. Yves fits perfectly into this picture and, we repeat, the phenomenon was commonplace in 1914-1918, at the heart of the way in which the French of his own day were depicted.

The same is true of his expression of patriotism. In his eyes, as in the eyes of the great majority of the French at war, there was no questioning one's patriotism. It called for total dedication, every sacrifice including, of course, those of children like himself. 'They will let us die of hunger – too bad – after all we are French and if we have to die we shall die, but France will be

33. Stephane Audoin-Rouzeau, *La Guerre des enfants (1914-1918), op cit.*

victorious', he declared to be undeniable as early as November 1914. He repeated this several times, particularly in one of his patriotic poems at the beginning of 1915:

'Oh France! You Queen of the earth,
You leave your children enduring brutal force
Succumbing to need! You see what they have suffered
And what they are still suffering under hands of metal.
All are suffering for you and for your flag
All are ready to die so that you can win;
And all will do so, if they need to, loving mother.
All will do so, of course, because they yearn for your glory.'

This sacrificial patriotism inspired in Yves even more lyrical texts, such as those he reproduced in February 1915 on 'The End of the Flag' or 'The death of a hero'. The diarist lives in depth in an imaginary world of heroes: we have already pointed out how, throughout the diary that he wrote day after day, he dreamt of himself as a child hero. On 14th July 1915, he was the chief actor in a military review put on by the other children which inspired in him the following verses:

'Oh, France, on this day of glory
You say to us: March then! Old men and children
And, starting from your presence inspiring victory
We marched out with our heads held high with our triumphal songs.'

From then onwards, he forbade himself anything which in his own eyes might be seen as a lack of confidence in the fatherland. Thus, there was no question of placing the least trust in the announcement of the military successes of a Germany which is depicted from beginning to end of the diary as being reduced to the last extremities. Systematically, he denies the very existence of German military victories even when the adult population around him seems to acknowledge the reality of them. Accordingly, he refuses to believe in the failure of the French offensive in Champagne in September 1915 and, equally, in the initial success of the enemy offensive in Verdun in February 1916. During the last two years of the war, he refused to believe in the immense German victories in the East, in the Russian collapse, in the Italian defeat in October 1917 ('It's all a joke!), in the bombardment of Paris by long-range cannon and in the undeniable success of the March 1918 offensive ('For myself, I do not believe it and I am perfectly happy not to believe it'). Even after the event, he never admits to having been mistaken in his denials, such was the extent to which the unshakeable certainties of this young Sedanese boy were part of a range of beliefs, beliefs in the Fatherland. His patriotism is a faith, which bursts forth in the cry 'Long live France' several times repeated in the last pages of the diary which were written in November 1918.

A patriotic faith which at times is one and the same as the Christian faith, through a characteristic syncretism in time of war between the cult of the 'eldest daughter of the Church' and that of the 'daughter of Science'[34]: Does not Yves, towards the end of 1917 and the beginning of 1918, identify himself with the longing for the return of France to God in his appeal for rigorous

34. Cf Annette Becker, *La Guerre et la Foi. De la mort à la mémoire (1914-1930), op cit.*

measures, such as those imposed in 1793[35], in order to preserve the Republic? The contradiction is only apparent in the cultural context of the 1914-1918 war. Thus, at the time of the procession in honour of the Sacred Heart in June 1917, the link between the two devotions is stated quite clearly: 'Once again this year, the procession of the Sacred Heart will be in our place, all of us, burning with zeal, will be setting to work, because our work will not only be for our own benefit, but also for France, our fatherland, which we want to be great and victorious.' Yves once again reverted even more specifically to this idea on the occasion of the procession in the following year: 'O Lord, how many prayers are being offered to You, how many petitions concerning relatives, friends, special intentions for our France, or rather for Your France! Hear us, O my God! Hear the people of France, the people of the Sacred Heart, and do not let it fall under the yoke of the sacrilegious barbarians, O ever-living God, good God, just God!'

But the Providence so often appealed to would not grant the victory without suffering, without the collective willingness to suffer 'for the greatness of France.' It was in this sense that he declared, in the summer of 1918, that the war was 'a difficult but important school.' This central idea of sacrifice for the sake of the fatherland, for the redemption of the fatherland through the suffering of all its children, Yves Congar expressed once again, six years later, in the 'postface' he wrote at the age of nineteen. Undoubtedly the way he expressed himself in this text was very different from what he had written as a child. But basically, the young man did not say in 1923 anything other than what he had written in his diary of the war at the age of thirteen.

The impact of the war

One cannot but tackle the question of the impact of the war, both intellectually and spiritually, on the future career of Yves Congar after the end of the First World War, even though one would very much like to avoid doing so for a number of reasons. To begin with, owing to a lack of competence in this matter [36], and also because the risks of 'biographical illusion' [37] are here all too evident: are we to look for the Dominican Yves Congar in his childhood diary? Can one detect the future theologian in what he wrote between the ages of ten and fourteen?

And yet, it is he himself who leads us to this point, and in so deliberate a way that one cannot easily refuse to follow the path that he points out. Here is what he wrote about the impact made on him by the Great War in his testimony written in 1918: 'The years 1914 – 1918 marked me deeply. I know very well that no-one is particularly interested in me, but if anyone **is** interested, they should know that they cannot understand me if they do not take into account what I experienced during those years.' It is worth following up this indication, all the more so since many other texts by Yves Congar written at other times and in different circumstances, serve to corroborate it. Thus, to a question put to him by Jean Puyo about the war years in an interview that he gave in 1975 ('It must have been a difficult time for the child that you were?'), Fr Congar replied at once: 'Very difficult, and I was marked by it[38].' In fact, it is striking to realise that the Sedanese boy become a grown man never lost sight of his childhood diary, to the extent of taking the time to complete it in 1923, to add a postface in the following year, and to refer to it again at the end of his life, during the extended period that he spent in the Invalides. Clearly, in the case of this diary of the war years, one can say that Yves Congar 'developed the habit of taking notes of events for his own use and that of others, and then of carefully keeping a record[39]. The birth of a method. Birth of a personal style?

35. Cf Entry for 4th March 1918.
36. We refer the reader to Étienne Fouilloux's article, 'Frère Yves, Cardinal Congar, dominicain. Itinéraire d'un théologien', *Revue des sciences philosophiques et théologiques*, vol 79, nº 3, July 1995, pp 379-404.
37. *Ibid*, p 381.
38. *Une vie pour la vérité, op cit*, p 10.
39. Étienne Fouilloux, 'Témoin de l'Église de son temps, 1930-1940', as yet unpublished article. I sincerely thank Étienne Fouilloux for his assistance in completing this essay, and in particular for making available to me the texts of lectures or articles which have not yet been published.

Let us now reflect on his religious vocation, as expressed in his own words: 'My conscience and attitudes owe something to the somewhat Jansenistic outlook in Sedan during my childhood. All those from whom I received the seeds, in my parish and my family, still live in my faith and my prayer.' Was it not this faith and this prayer that grew in fervour between 1914 and 1918, thanks to those war years? 'Parish life was intense during those anguished years', Frère Congar wrote in his 1918 testimony. Three years earlier, he had already commented on the extent to which life had been 'centred' on the parish throughout that period. 'It was', he wrote, 'the only place of freedom where it was possible to express the life of the community and the sense of celebration (. . .) the parish offered an intense religious life[40]. His memories did not betray him on this point as is clear from a careful reading of his childhood diary: one has only to see the place occupied in it by the principal religious ceremonies, beginning with the procession organised each summer in the grounds of the Congar property for the feast of the Sacred Heart, a devotion which was so characteristic of the fervour of the Great War. It was, moreover, in the course of his description of this procession in 1916 that for the first and last time in his childhood he mentioned what we can perhaps venture to call his 'vocation'. 'This procession made such an impression on me that I have described it here, the fervour with which one prayed for France, the attitude of recollection, the enthusiasm with which the altars of repose had been made, the single thought that united the spirit of all these people made me think of France, of the country that had been invaded, of *revenge;* it made me dream of new horizons, a future, a mad dream, crazy, then a puff of smoke and that's all ---.' At its roots, this childhood vocation (if that is in fact what it is), the vocation partially glimpsed, would seem to have been inseparably linked with the war and the nation, with liberation and victory, with hope for the punishment of the aggressor.

Curiously enough, in the 1970's Frère Congar does not refer to this first call in 1916. On the contrary, in 1975 he spoke at length on the 'uncertainty', the 'very painful life' that he had experienced at the beginning of the year 1918, and even perhaps towards the end of 1917, whereas his childhood diary bears no trace of this. His retrospective testimony referred mostly to the memory of trials undergone: his own, those of his family and of the people of Sedan, thoroughly fed up with the multiple restrictions, the repression, the various requisitions, the shortage of food: the sufferings of the prisoners too, above all and in particular the Romanians, concerning whom he wrote at length. Retrospectively, it is in the hardships of the occupation, 'in this immense misery in which we were all engulfed' that he sees the origin of his vocation as a preacher. With particular stress on the fate of the prisoners: 'The sight of this material and spiritual distress played a role in the beginning of my vocation', he explained before adding: 'I wanted to preach conversion to all. I wanted to convert France[41]'.

All his memories of the war are gathered together in one word: *suffering*[42] On this point, at any rate, he remained faithful to the exercise books of his childhood, even though these had given way to less gloomy thoughts. He remained faithful, above all, to the lesson that Yves Congar, then aged twenty (he had entered the seminary in 1919) derived from the experience of war and of occupation. That was all indeed suffering, he wrote in an amazing text, but suffering that was voluntary, redemptive, a suffering willingly undergone for France and its victory. This text needs to be quoted at length here:

'I did nothing extraordinary; but with all the French who had been invaded, I suffered; we all suffered and endured to the end: that was how we fought the war; that is also how we won the war; because war is a question of suffering and sacrifice: 'to fight is no longer a question of beating oneself, it is to wear a hair shirt; it is to brace one's soul against one's body, to force oneself to seek, in weariness, being stripped naked, the distress of the flesh['].

40. Une vie pour la vérité, op cit, *p 14.*

41. *Ibid*, pp 15-16.

42. It is striking to note that it was this theme of suffering which accompanied Yves Congar in so many moments in his life, a suffering that is 'transformed into communion, into love' (p 3), that the then Master of the Order, Fr Timothy Radcliffe, made the centre of his homily for the funeral of Cardinal Yves Congar on 26th June 1995 (*Homily given by Fr Timothy Radcliffe, the Message of the Metropolitan Jérémie and the speech by General Schmitt pronounced during the funeral Mass of Cardinal Yves Congar, OP in the Cathedral of Notre Dame de Paris on 26th June 1995, undated, 35 pages.* (Document kindly lent by Dominique Congar).

Yes, indeed! Later on, when we are asked what this war was like, we will reply that it was the battle that takes the monk to the depth of his withdrawal. It was a war of sacrifice, a campaign of renunciation, a battle between two sorrows and two self-denials: and the one who managed to endure the longest will be the one who conquered.

Thus we too have fought the war by enduring; we too have won the victory by our suffering: 'Victory belongs to the one who can suffer for a quarter of an hour longer than anyone else' was what was taught to our soldiers – 'those who suffer well always conquer'!

This document is extremely important from the point of view of the very far-reaching and very grim impact of the experience of war on the intellectual, moral and spiritual formation of Yves Congar. The war certainly reinforced his Catholicism, the austere and sacrificial character of which must have already been in place prior to 1914, as was the case for very many practising families in the early years of the [20th] century. The suffering of the war years was therefore willingly accepted: it was a sacrifice, an offering. In 1923-1924, to quote Frère Martial Leken and Ernest Psichari, it was transformed into an *imitatio Christi:*

'By uniting our sufferings with the sacrifice of our soldiers, we have done better than fight and win; with them we have redeemed!' 'It really seems that our mission is to save the world by the mere force of suffering' – 'If we believe in the power of the blood shed on Calvary, how can we not believe, analogically, in the power of the blood shed for one's country? The power of this blood is as certain, in the natural order, as the power of the other is in the supernatural order. Yes, we know that the blood of the hosts offered for the fatherland purifies us. We know that it purifies France, that all power comes from it, that its power is infinite – that every fatherland only lives due to its power.'

Sine sanguine non fit remissio.[43]. But there is no need to have recourse to the Bible. We ourselves know well that our mission on this earth is to redeem France by means of blood[44]'

Yves Congar was quite right. One cannot hope to understand him, and to understand his intellectual and spiritual journey, without reference to the years 1914 to 1918. This applies to his second experience of war in 1939-1945, his captivity in Germany (which he lived as insupportable, as is clear from the number of times that he tried to escape and his accounts of captivity) and of his precocious anti-Nazi attitudes which he openly expressed in the various prison camps. Can such an attitude be understood except as being linked with his memories of the German occupation in 1914-1918 which for him had been the fundamental experience in terms of resistance to oppression? 'My anti-Nazi militancy, my eighteen months in Colditz and my two years of 'Sonderlager' are in line with my mini-resistance as a child in Sedan', Yves Congar wrote in 1978, fully aware that, had it not been for the intensity of the patriotic and anti-German attitudes that he acquired during his childhood, his reactions later in life might well have been different. 'I have always been interested in Germany [45], he said in 1975, adding lucidly: 'My anti-Nazi reflex was essentially patriotic[46].'

We have already said that the anti-German hatred rooted in his experience as a child was later rejected[47]. But not his patriotism, as is clear from his deep longing for the sacred Unity of the years 1914-1918: 'The moral unanimity of the nation

---

43. Without blood there can be no remission [of sin] (Trans).

44. We should note the very different interpretation of this yearning for sacrifice expressed in 1975: 'Life as an offering, as sacrifice – not in the sense of mutilation, of doing to death; on the contrary, it is to the degree that one is living and active that one makes an offering of one's life.' (*Une vie pour la vérité, op cit* p 166). In the meantime, the theologian Yves Congar had changed the interpretation: less pessimistic, from this time on he thought that his life, his work could contribute to the spread of the faith.

45. *Ibid.*, p 58.

46. *Ibid.*, p 92.

47. As a grown man, Yves Congar drew a distinction between two Germanys: the evil one which he encountered in his childhood and during the 1930's, and the good one, the religious Germany, all branches taken together. Mention needs to be made here of Congar's admiration for Luther, apart from any dogmatic concession, and of his considerable debt to the Tübingen school in the first half of the 19th century. (I owe this point, together with that at the end of note 44 above, to Étienne Fouilloux, to whom I express my thanks once again).

was complete. It has never been recovered since except perhaps in the summer of 1944. Must there be war for the people to dance to the same tune?'

On one point however, Yves Congar's retrospective view of his own destiny calls for closer examination. In speaking of the ecumenism with which his name is closely connected, here too he perceived a link between his vocation as an adult with his experience as a child. 'I belonged', he recalled in 1978, 'to the Fond de Givonne parish where, with my sister, I had made my first fervent Communion on 24th May, 1914. Three months later, our church had been burnt down by the Uhlans who had also taken the parish priest [abbé] Tonnel to the cemetery and threatened to shoot him. For several weeks, our celebrations were held in the chapel of the Brothers' school at the bottom of Avenue Philippoteaux. Then, Pastor Cosson offered Father Tonnel the little chapel next door to the protestant Orphanage, which has since been pulled down This was our chapel for six years. I am convinced that this detail is not unconnected with the ecumenical vocation that I became aware of in 1928.' However, on this point there is quite a gap in relation to his boyhood diary, which mentions the making available of this chapel in a few lines, on 9th December 1914, without, however, attributing to the gesture the deeper meaning that Yves Congar attached to it sixty-four years later[48]: 'Mr Cosson, the protestant pastor, is lending the little orphanage chapel to M le Curé.' That's all he wrote and not very much later on, except for a comment on the smallness of the chapel, but adding: 'we will be happy with it'. Clearly, it was only later that the Protestant pastor's generosity assumed its full importance and its true significance to be seen in Yves Congar's eyes. Everything points to the fact that, on this point, if he did not quite embroider a memory, at the very least he came to understand the true importance, at the time, of the December 1914 gesture[49]. It is a known fact that one's memory reorganises and 'doctors' memories in a series of complex processes.

But, far from weakening the demonstration of the fundamental importance of the 1914-1918 war for Yves Congar, this comment surely emphasises it. On looking back over his life, the theologian unhesitatingly chose to see the origin of his ecumenical vocation in the soil of the experiences and emotions during the war, which clearly also contributed to the formation of his character. However, when all is said and done, it is of little importance for us, here and now, whether this interpretation of his own 'destiny' was correct or not, in accordance with what he had written in his diary or not. His personal conviction does no more than further emphasise the extent to which the Great War represented, in his eyes, a formative period and this is what is important for us now. That period was a crucible, the crucible in which were forged the great choices of his very long life.

Stéphane AUDOIN-ROUZEAU
Université de Picardie-Jules-Verne

48. This significance is even more marked in a letter dated 27th March 1994 written just over a year before his death and addressed to Annette Becker, who granted me permission to publish it: 'I was ten years old in 1914 and I was an immediate witness of what I am about to tell you: The Germans, the mounted Uhlans, Prussians and protestants, hated the Catholic church. In our church, they piled up the benches near the altar, poured paraffin over them and burnt it all down. So we no longer had a church. At first we used a large room in the Brothers' school and then the admirable Pastor Cosson offered us a little used chapel close to my parents' property. A carpenter constructed a kind of covered annex. We opened the windows that looked onto the chapel and that, in effect, doubled the number of places available. Much later a Vilgrain hut was installed in a field. Pastor Cosson, whose son, Christian, was one of my classmates, was also the first to go with a large cart to collect the many German wounded, and some dead, lying in front of the bridge leading to the station that had been blown up. I thought that these two details which I myself witnessed might be of interest to you.'

49. In fact, and this point is stressed by Étienne Fouilloux, Pastor Cosson's gesture was less a point of departure than the result of an 'atmosphere of calm religious peace' between Catholics, Protestants and Jews which was emphasised also by Yves Congar in 1978, and which he never forgot (Étienne Fouilloux, 'Frère Yves, Cardinal Congar, dominicain, Itinéraire d'un théologien', *op cit* p 382*)*. On this point it is equally striking to note that the handwritten text of Yves Congar's 'Mon Témoignage', dated 28th April 1946, with a preface added on 22nd September 1949, and found in the archives of the Saint-Jacques priory by André Duval in March 1997, does not mention the incident of the protestant chapel. In the handwritten account of his 'ecclesiastical and ecumenical vocation' (p 2), he dates it in the years 1929 and 1930, even though the document contains several references to his religious experience during the war years.

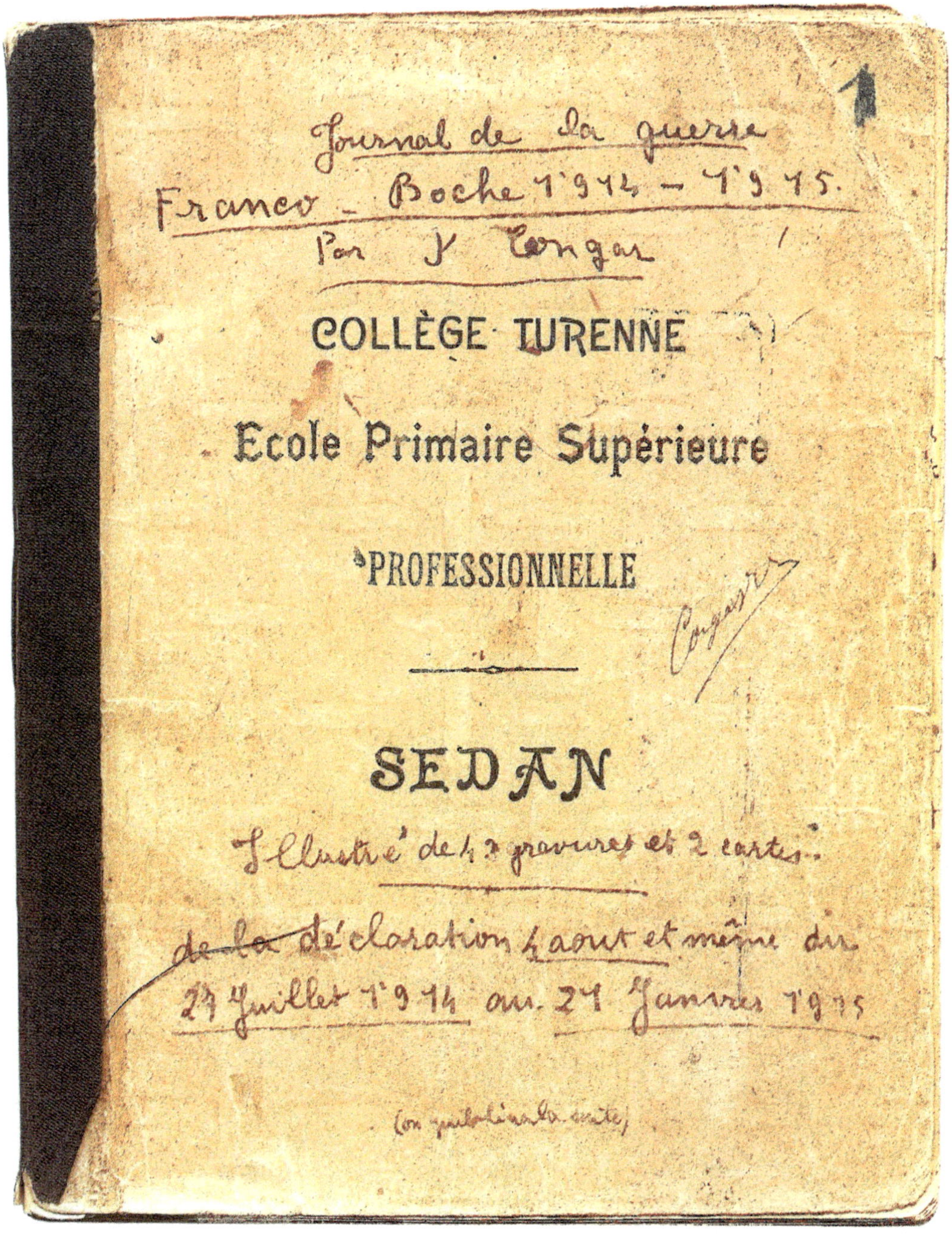

1

Journal de la guerre
Franco-Boche 1914-1915.
Par Y Congar

COLLÈGE TURENNE

Ecole Primaire Supérieure

PROFESSIONNELLE

Congar

SEDAN

Illustré de 42 gravures et 2 cartes.

~~de la~~ déclaration 2 aout et même du
27 Juillet 1914 au 27 Janvier 1915

(on publiera la suite)

sur nous, nous causons à 4 personnes, le gar de
pont avertie d'avance tira sur un attroupement
elle voyait au loin _ les grands et papa prépare
une cave pour ranger nos
pommes de terre et que les
boches ne les prennent pas.
Tere se lève encore un aero
plane a échappé aux mains
des Boches.

L'officier et le solda

Mercredi 27 rien de neuf, on fait toujours
la cave, il y a de grosses pierres à en enlever

Jeudi 28 Il n'y a plus que 2 coiffeur,
un en ville et un au Fond alors
nous allons chez Mr Briand _
Il est passé vers 6 heures du ma
tin 2 aeros au dessus de la Mar
fée _ Un sergent major aurait
affirmé qu'ils avaient quitté
Verdun

Allons Michel il s'agit d
ils s'y connaissent pour

Un combat en Ar gonne _

ndredi 28 : Horreur Catherine avait pu garder son poulain et ses 2 vaches, aujourd'hui ils viennent et lui enlève le poulain, lui donnant pour tout payement un bon de réquisition valable après la guerre. pierre a mal à la tête

La prise du poulain

amedi 30 rien de neuf pierre a toujours mal à la tête

Dimanche 31 On va porter les bécanes : elles sont plus laides l'unes plus laides l'autres.

Lundi 31 Mère vient et dit qu'on dit que nous aurions écrasé le 9e corps d'armée en Alsace, fait 300 canons et 3 étendards prisonniers, que nous aurions eu à Liçonne un beau succès, que guillaume aurait ordonné la retraite du nord d'Ypres. qu'à châlons ils auraient été battus que les officiers allemands ne reçevraient plus que demi-solde et chose sûre, les soldats allemands 30 par 30 ont été dans l'église de Sedan jurer fidélité à l'empereur.

Nous jurons fidélité à l'empereur

(Samedi) mardi 13
Cere se lève. rien

(Dimanche)
Mercredi 16
On entend le canon très loin

Avant la guerre

Après l'invasion.

français aurait fait une démarche au Vatican pour que
pape influe pour nous sur la paix

ndi 8 Le roi de Saxe en colère que Guillaume fasse marcher
hommes au feu au lieu des prussiens, ils se seraient dis
et Guillaume de rage aurait jeté son sabre dans u
glace et l'aurait brisé
Les combats continuent
dans les Flandre et en
Pologne - On prétant
qu'en Alsace nous
sommes à Sarrebourg.

Mardi 9 On entend le canon - Il
pleut - D'après les boches Poincaré aurait prononcé u
discours disant que la guerre ne terminerait tant que
ce prononcerait pas l'anéantissement militaire de l'
magne - à quoi ils ont répondu : Alors, jamais ?! - Mr Cos
pasteur protestant prête à Mr le curé la petite chappell
l'orphelinat - On n'a pas une mie de pain.

ercredi 10 Oh les cochons, il est passé ce matin des convois infinis de bal
de laines volées chez Mr Ringaud - le jeune homme - Ringaud ét
resté seul : quand les prussiens sont venu sans bon de réquisitio
sans rien prendre la laine, il leur répondit : il me faut un
vous devez en avoir un, qu'est-ce que papa va dire quand il ren

Jeudi 11 on va chez elle : les grands changent les bécanes de place, elles ét au grenier parcequ'ils vont bientôt perquisitionner on entend bien le canon x

…edi 12 … Chez Mère X. –

Guillaume empereur d'allemagne ou empereur des Boche ou des Huns | Le Kromprinz (jeune)

–

On doit ramoner sous peine d'amande les cheminées malgré qu'il n'y a pas de ramoneur –

…di 12 On prétend, on dit qu'à Hirson et Rethel sont repris, mais on nous raconte des nouvelles les plus briscornues – Ce n'est pas vrai probablement mais nous avons avancé car l'affiche suivante a été placardée : « il est maintenant défendu sous peine d'amande de 1200 marchs ou 1500 francs, d'aller chercher des proviisons de bouches et autres provisions en Belgique. Ah il veulent nous affamer et bien je les la jeunesse à la prochaine guerre ira en allemagne et l'affamera, ils verront ils se tournent les Français contre eux, tant mieux j'amais je ne les ai tant détesté + Le est augmenté à 7 sous 1/2

di 28 On n'entend encore pas le canon rien. La v
juin s'affolle on croit qu'ils vont prendre les gr
les et autres fruits. !.

ardi 29 } rien de neuf on n'entend encore p
ercredi 30 } juin le canon etonne sais si l'on vit.

udi 1er } juillet } rien de neuf pas canon on va chez m
dredi 2 } dit qu'il est passé 14 wagons de prisonnier

medi 3 } rien de neuf on est toujours sans n
anche 4 } velles et c'est détestable, on entend
ndi 5 } juillet } le canon un peu même assez fort
ardie 6 } le lendemain sans pouvoir se l'exp
credie 7 } on n'entend plus rien.

udi 8 La bonne de madame Benoist est arrêtée e
sommée de 37f,50 pour avoir été chercher a
manger de lapin sur la digue. C'est honte
mais ce n'est rien quand on le lis mais qu
on le vois, c'est un supplice.

dredi 9 rien de neuf comme hier.

s autorités | Alexander | Muller

[L]undi 10 juillet

C'est honteux !!. la ville est sommée de 1'000'000 de marcks !, Lille 3'000'000 et Mézières de 900'000'. Lille dit qu'elle n'a plus rien. Mézières refuse net et Sedan se plie encore une fois et demande de l'argent à ses commerçants. Honteux des Français donner de l'argent pour faire tuer leurs frères !–!. Oh oh. ! ...... attention le vase s'empli ! ...... non seulement cela mais je donnerais 5'000 à celui qui me trouverais 1 litre de lait à Sedan excepté chez les maisons occupées bochardement ! .. attention Muller, Alexandre attention il y a des révolvers chargés à Sedan ! ... et.... !

[D]imanche 14 Rien on attend ce que le maire fera.

[L]undi 17 juillet pour le million on attend et on essaye de savoir ce que Charleville fera. les boches resserrent le cercle de fer qui nous entoure. On fait notre lécie, décidément il faut que ce

NOËL : 25 décembre 1916. sans neige. triste
triste jour, le noël dernier, j'avais l'espérance
que le noël prochain se passerait avec les
Français, cette fois-ci, j'en ai la conviction.
Je n'ai rien à dire d'autre.... ce serait
du superflu ! tout ce que je puis dire, je l'ai
déjà dit, tout ce que je dirais est inutile.
sachez seulement ceci : quand je serai en
Allemagne : voici mon mot d'ordre :
« pas de grâce, pas de quartier ».

Fin de l'année 1916.

Pour le reste du journal, voyez le
cahier n° 10.

CPSIA information can be obtained
at www.ICGtesting.com
Printed in the USA
BVOW07s0532280616
453403BV00020B/20/P

9 781925 309041